Financiers and Railroads
1869-1889

Financiers and Railroads

1869-1889

A Study of Morton, Bliss & Company

Dolores Greenberg

Newark
University of Delaware Press
London and Toronto: Associated University Presses, Inc.

© 1980 by Associated University Presses, Inc.
4 Cornwall Drive
East Brunswick, New Jersey 08816

Associated University Presses
69 Fleet Street
London EC4Y 1EU, England

Associated University Presses
Toronto M5E 1A7, Canada

Library of Congress Cataloging in Publication Data

Greenberg, Dolores.
  Financiers and railroads, 1869-1889.

  Bibliography: p.
  Includes index.
  1.   Railroads—United States—Finance-History.
  2.   Morton, Bliss & Company—History.   I. Title.
HE2236.G73   385'.1   78-66830
ISBN 0-87413-148-0

PRINTED IN THE UNITED STATES OF AMERCIA

To Bob, Roger, Ivan, and Michael

Contents

List of Maps

9

List of Tables

Preface

This study focuses on the functional relationship of private bankers to the single most important industry for capital employment in the postbellum era, the railroads. More than two decades ago, Alfred D. Chandler's seminal work firmly established the significant role of these financial intermediaries in the patterns of early railroad finance. In detailing the techniques employed for mobilizing the enormous sums needed for stretching the infant rail system from the Eastern seaboard to the Mississippi, Chandler revealed the quickening dependence of railroad builders on specialized capital suppliers. Since then a number of studies pivoting on the magnitude of railroad building costs have probed promoters' tactics for attracting high-risk funds, examined the efficiency of the capital markets, and explored a range of investor response. These analyses of the investment process have refined considerably our understanding of the mobilization and flow of funds in the developing nation, without, however, having given sufficient weight to the critical, many-faceted activities of private bankers in shaping the network's rapid expansion during the railroad decades of the 1870s and 1880s.

By 1873 most prominent Eastern private bankers had become executives and directors, and their firms acted as fiscal and transfer agents for corporations whose track comprised a minimum of twenty-five percent of the total network. Banking houses that dated back to the 1850s had retained many of their prewar affiliations and made new and more varied commitments. Also, relatively young firms opened during and after the war, went heavily into railroads, and quickly took their place in the industry's decision-making hierarchy. The list includes Drexel, Morgan & Company; Duncan, Sherman & Company; John J. Cisco & Sons; Henry Clews & Company; Clark, Dodge & Company; Jay Cooke & Company; Fisk & Hatch; Louis Von Hoffman & Company; August Belmont; M. K. Jesup & Company; Adrien

Iselin & Company; Kidder, Peabody & Company; J. S. Kennedy & Company; Kountz Brothers; J. & W. Seligman & Company; Winslow, Lanier & Company; and Morton, Bliss & Company.

The role of these financiers as railroad policy-makers and capital suppliers raises many questions that have still to be assessed. Were these bankers functioning in their institutional capacity representing specialized agencies, or did they think and act as general entrepreneurs? What of their motives for alliances with speculator-promoters, and did they, in fact, exercise a restraining influence to curb competition or curtail excess profits? Indeed, what were their criteria for accepting business; when and to what extent were bankers involved in direct financing; and how important was their managerial role in system-building enterprise? How, for example, did the sharp swings in the business cycle affect their relations to the industry? And when railroads with which they affiliated faced financial difficulty, what were the various tactics bankers adopted, and did they lose or recoup profits? Why and at what point did bankers advocate combination? Finally, we might ask what impact the railroads had on the emergence of modern investment banking and how the instability bankers encountered in the railroad sector shaped their attitudes toward legal and political institutions.

This treatment of the wide-ranging railroad business of Morton, Bliss & Company considers these questions as part of a larger appraisal of banker behavior and influence during the industry's development stage. Contemporaries designated this house as one of the most important of the late nineteenth century—as the acknowledged leader in the federal government's refunding operations and as a foremost dealer in foreign exchange. It is symptomatic of the more general neglect of bankers' railroad activities during the building sprees of the 1870s and early 1880s that the firm's railroad affiliations received little attention. Significantly, even though the partners in this banking house were drawn during the first postwar boom by myriad possibilities for profits as direct investors and capital middlemen, and by the early 1870s were serving as policy-making figures for corporations operating some ten percent of the total network, they deliberately obscured their railroad operations.

The history of their activities reveals financiers who eagerly tracked all railroad opportunities for profits, formulated and implemented system-building strategies, and established themselves as key figures in the railroad sector. Recognition of their role in the industry sharpens our understanding of the broader postwar pattern and places in perspective the later period of acknowledged banker influence of the 1890s.

This study grew out of a discussion with Morton Rothstein, to whom I owe many thanks for his generosity. As a scholar, teacher, and friend, Paul W. Gates offered candid criticism, matched always by constant encouragement. The manuscript has benefited especially from the careful reading and counsel of Vincent Carosso and Alfred D. Chandler, Jr; and I am indebted to Henry Cohen, Heywood Fleisig, Ralph Hidy, and Richard Polenberg for their invaluable suggestions. Arthur Breton of the New York Historical Society was particularly helpful in locating materials; Carl White facilitated use of the Seligman Archives; and the staffs of the New York Historical Society and the manuscript room of the New York Public Library offered many courtesies. Part of my research was supported by a Hunter College grant, the George N. Shuster Faculty Fellowship.

My deepest gratitude is to Robert Greenberg for his keen judgment and many suggestions offered graciously and unstintingly at every stage in the preparation of this study.

Portions of chapters 1, 7, and 10 have appeared in somewhat different form in *Business History* and the *Canadian Historical Review,* and I wish to thank the editors for permission to use this material.

PART I

Bankers and The Postwar Boom

Introduction to Part I

The evolution of private banking houses into modern investment institutions can be traced through a study of the transportation sector and the efforts, during much of the nineteenth century, to develop distant markets. The heavy capital demands of canal building to penetrate the Appalachian barrier initiated a pattern that gained in significance in the decades ahead. From the 1820s and well into the 1880s, private banking matured in tandem with the transportation network as these financial intermediaries increased their investments and influence in projects designed to integrate eastern commercial centers with the rest of the nation.

The canal frenzy of the 1820s to develop the trade of the new West spurred the first sustained attempts to mobilize extraordinary sums of widely scattered surplus capital for internal improvements. When New York led the way in financing high-risk canal enterprise with long-term credits, it created a model that other states quickly emulated in the hope of linking the eastern seaboard with the Ohio-Mississippi River network. Of the $137 million that state and local governments supplied before the Civil War, for almost 4,300 miles of canal, ninety percent was borrowed, raised by state bond issues that were sold to English and American investors eager for government guaranteed interest of five and six percent.[1]

Capital transfers of this dimension in the transatlantic money market opened a profitable new field of activity for a variety of financial intermediaries and provided a special stimulus to private banking operations. What is considered the earliest "large, genuine" private banking house in the country, Prime, Ward & King of New York, was formed in 1826 especially to take advantage of the flourishing canal bond business.[2] The firm found that it could make substantial profit from buying public improvement bonds (individually or in syndicates) directly from state agencies, and then reselling them at home to individual or institutional investors. The firm also bought issues for consignment with Anglo-American houses such as the Barings, or used the bonds as collateral to secure credit lines to finance foreign trade. In addition to Prime, Ward & King, New York private bankers Rathborne & Lord also achieved rapid prominence as purchasers and distributors of Ohio and New York canal loans.[3]

Such houses, although recognizing the potential of securities transactions, probably handled only a limited volume of business in this early period. Domestically they operated in a most imperfect money market, where capital scarcity was compounded by inadequate communication and where a mix of state regulatory constraints, such as usury laws, inhibited interstate transfers of funds. Moreover, they had to compete for their share of canal loans with dominant mercantile interests and with a variety of banking and brokerage institutions, possessing larger capital assets, or extensive overseas connections, or both. The allocation of Ohio canal obligations suggests their still subordinate position. Rathborne & Lord, for example, received $180,000 of the 1826 issue, while John Jacob Astor walked off with the lion's share of $800,000. Of the $4.5 million Ohio bonds, issued between 1825 and 1832, eastern private bankers took $1.4 million in competition with private capitalists, commercial bankers, and one of the first development banks in the United States, the Bank for Savings of New York.[4]

Not until the burst of railroad activity in the 1850s did private bankers develop the services, the techniques, and the magnitude of business that would mark their emergence as modern investment institutions. And not until the 1860s did they create the organizational structure that allowed them to readily import funds for extensive interregional projects. Early rail ventures had offered few opportunities. State overcommitments for canal building, followed by default in the late 1830s, dammed up possibilities for government support of new, high-cost transportation.[5] Foreigners, alarmed by state refusal to redeem long-term debt obligations, vowed never to invest in the United States. Well into the 1840s, moreover, this unproven, competitive carrier generated suspicion and sometimes outright legislative opposition at home. By 1848 only some 6,000 miles of track in rudimentary, unconnected lines serviced passengers and small amounts of freight. Eastern building had been financed almost wholly through sales of corporate shares to keep down the fixed costs of interest on loan capital and to insure stockholder control. In the Midwest, an area of scanty savings, such exclusive financial techniques created a dilemma. Initial construction costs—readying roadbeds, purchasing rails and equipment, compensating for cost overruns—quickly exhausted funds for continued building. After disastrous experiments with barter arrangements, allowing stock subscriptions to be paid for in land and labor, railway managers resorted to borrowing to bring in impersonal, dispersed portfolio funds, but here too bonds were issued in limited amounts for limited construction until the late 1840s.[6]

After two decades of indecision, enthusiasm for fast, cheap, regular rail service suddenly accelerated and rapidly outweighed conservative constraints. In a dramatic shift that produced the nation's first railroad boom, railroad facilities expanded from 5,996 miles at the end of 1848 to 31,283 miles by the Civil War. In less than a dozen years new track connected all of the eastern states, linked the East coast to the Mississippi River system, and permitted traffic to move from the Great Lakes to the South. This five-fold growth in mileage could not have occurred without profound modifications of existing relationships. And, as Alfred Chandler has emphasized, the extension of the rail system, coinciding as it did with increased reliance on oceangoing steamships and the telegraph, created "new patterns of economic and business action and new institutional forms."[7]

The quickly mounting bonded indebtedness of railway corporations reveals the reappraisal of this method of financing and reflects the flexibility of investor behavior that continued to characterize allocations of surplus capital in the worldwide search for investment opportunities in the late nineteenth century. By 1855 long-term rail credits had already climbed to nearly forty percent of recorded investment in the network, or $3 million. By 1872 the bonded debt of $1.5 billion represented forty-eight percent of total capitalization.[8] Both railway managers and the public had revised their investment criteria. Revelations of stock frauds in the early 1850s, frequent delays in stock dividends, and continued calls for assessments convinced capitalists that long-term obligations (with a prior claim on interest and a claim against property to secure debts) offered a safer place for savings. And like stocks, bonds were negotiable and could be traded. Foreigners, in particular, preferred bonds as the most reliable, efficient form of debt instrument in international transactions. The generally higher yields on American issues supplied sufficient incentives to revive capital flows from London, particularly after the federal government favored private enterprise and introduced a land grant policy in 1850. So long as railroad borrowing did not exceed half of capitalization, investors at home and abroad came to consider these corporate loans as a safe and profitable field for capital employment.[9]

Investor eagerness for transportation securities catalyzed important organizational and procedural changes in the mobilization of funds. Once again, as in the canal era, direct purchases of new bonds for resales offered handsome returns to private bankers and stimulated the organization of new firms, such as Duncan, Sherman & Company; Winslow, Lanier & Company; and M. K. Jesup & Company. By the mid-1850s, with the growing market for bonds, private bankers were negotiating rail issues as a major part of their operations, intruding on the business of mercantile houses, and capturing a sizable share of the rising loan volume. Nevertheless, the *American Railroad Journal* had still to convince investors that purchases of new rail bonds would best be made through banking houses, "we mean, of course, those of the highest respectability. . . .A person residing in New York, and competent to conduct a banking business, can hardly make a mistake as to the character of a project before the public."[10] Despite a gradual shift of investment activity, as Vincent Carosso has observed, "The variety of individuals and firms engaged in the business of buying and selling securities was almost as great in 1860 as it had been a half century earlier."[11] To meet the competition, private bankers had begun, in addition to merchandising, to differentiate themselves by offering such special services as publicizing issues, transferring and registering securities, and paying interest and dividends. In this competitive milieu, the more specialized also took an active interest in railroad policy as a means of boosting their reputations and their business. To protect bondholder-clients they became trustees for corporate issues and joined corporate management to oversee general financial planning. When the country slumped into depression after the panic of 1857, they took further steps to protect bondholder interests and gained their first experience in the intricacies of railroad bankruptcy, receivership, and reorganization.[12]

In the 1850s, the impact of rising capital requirements, reliance on portfolio funds, and expanding investment services rapidly sealed the interdependence of railroad corporations and private houses. By the late 1860s, however, the scope and risk of projected interregional programs to develop the vast reaches from the

Mississippi to the Far West gave still further definition to the role bankers would play in the industry. Neither individuals nor groups of private capitalists could continue to meet the extraordinary needs of planned expansion. Reliance on institutional sources for share capital and policy planning became increasingly imperative. As Poor's *Manual* noted, "An extent of line and investment is often reached which is utterly beyond the capacity of one man, or set of men to properly conduct."[13] The early stock subscription lists of the Union Pacific set beside its management rosters foretold the growing postwar trend. The U.P. directorate of 1864 included a heavy weighting of the most distinguished private bankers of the period: partners from Winslow, Lanier & Company; Duncan, Sherman & Company; August Kountze & Company; Clark, Dodge & Company; and August Belmont, while John J. Cisco served as the corporation's first treasurer.[14] More and more, railroad promoters were turning to such firms for substantial direct investment of venture funds, for short-term operating credits, and for internal financial expertise to supplement their contributions as capital mobilizers. Jay Cooke was wooed by the Northern Pacific group, so anxious were they for his participation. Collis P. Huntington, despite his California connections, allied with Fisk & Hatch; Morton, Bliss & Company; Louis Von Hoffman; and the Speyers for managerial and financial aid. Similarly, system builders of the early seventies such as Tom Scott joined with Winslow, Lanier & Company; M. K. Jesup & Company; and the Drexels; while Jay Gould to accomplish his grandiose plans called on the support of the Seligmans and Morton's firm.

Besides the postwar urgency for more capital and expertise, which deepened dependence on bankers' decision-making role, the burgeoning of American partner firms in London and on the Continent served as yet another factor to strengthen their influence. Although methods for marshalling overseas capital had been numerous since the 1820s, the marketing of American securities had necessitated the cooperation of foreign firms. Following the route of state canal commissioners, many railroad representatives had crossed the Atlantic during the 1850s to convince the Rothschilds, the Barings, or lesser houses to sell their offerings. As an alternative, railroads placed issues with import-export merchants for overseas delivery. Private bankers had similarly to act as correspondents for bankers in London or on the Continent who sold American securities.[15]

Transatlantic partnerships, the most important organizational innovation of the 1860s, placed the initiative in American hands, improved services for corporations and investors, and stimulated an incoming flow of funds. Fewer railroad representatives went abroad to negotiate securities. Leading promoters such as Russell Sage, Jay Gould, and William Osborn realized the advantages of relying on Americans with overseas partner firms that could register securities and make coupon payments on two continents; arrange sales in New York or abroad in keeping with the conditions of the money markets; see to intermarket stock trading; and form transatlantic syndicates. Besides mobilizing long-term loan capital they could also be called on, and were, to supply equity and short-term funds. As a group, they were less conservative than established European houses, which did not need, or especially want, the business of roads that were either still unbuilt or extending into areas that were still unsettled.

Jay Cooke, for example, when he tried to place Northern Pacific bonds in 1869, found that his contacts with the Rothschilds ended in "utter failure" since they "never engaged in anything that required risk or trouble in management." When the Franco-Prussian War the following year, which caused only a mild tightening of the money market, disrupted negotiations with a fifth-rate house, Budge & Schiff, he regretted his earlier refusal to form a foreign partnership.[16] In keeping with the trend Cooke, McCulloch & Company was established in London in 1870 to add to American copartnerships, which included Morton, Rose & Company; Seligman Brothers; Clews, Habicht & Company; and J. S. Morgan & Company. American Bankers in Paris included the newer firms of Bowles, Drevet & Company; James Tucker & Company; Drexel, Harjes & Company; Norton & Company; Seligman Frères; and L'Herbete, Kane & Company.[17]

By the late 1860s the mixture of renewed railroad fever, postwar designs for a truly integrated interregional system, and the specialized services and capital assets provided by private bankers insured their expanding managerial role during the nation's second railroad boom.

1
Barter to Banking

The saying went in the 1860s that "to be a banker all one needed was to dress like one."[1] So it may well have seemed, since a small group of New York City bankers and brokers numbering 167 in 1864 suddenly increased to some 1,800 by 1870. Certainly, too, the banking business must have appealed to many who had little theoretical expertise, for as Robert Sharkey has observed, in the great postwar debates over the money question "bankers had almost as many panaceas as there were bankers."[2] Unincorporated, unchartered private banking partnerships, exempt from government inspection, could be quite easily organized with a meager amount of capital, and like brokerage firms they proliferated after Union victory set off a sudden demand for U. S. government securities and the railroad boom offered equal, if not greater, opportunity for profit than prospective federal government refunding operations.

Nevertheless, sustained success in the select array of leading eastern private banking firms during the volatile decades of the 1870s and 1880s did demand prerequisites. New bankers who rose to prominence such as Levi Morton, Abraham Kuhn, Walter Burns, Henry Clews, Solomon Loeb, and Joseph Seligman all shared pertinent qualifications—capital, experience with international credits, and specialized knowledge of foreign exchange transactions.

Levi Parsons Morton, founder of Morton, Bliss & Company in New York and Morton, Rose & Company in London, had acquired these assets by following what proved to be a conventional path among the late-nineteenth-century banking elite. Beginning in rural retailing in the 1840s, he turned to opportunities in the wholesale import-export trade and then, during the Civil War, to transatlantic private banking operations.[3] His active career spanned some six decades of rapid national expansion and economic growth when the commercial spirit possessed more than one minister's son, who was admonished, as Levi was, that his primary concern should be to work diligently, loving and serving God.[4]

While Morton's success hardly attests to the popular rags-to-riches saga, it illustrates the possibilities middle-class young men could make much of as economic institutions matured. Coming from a well-known family of New England Congregational ministers, Morton could claim the social connections that offered, as his brother emphasized, "so many advantages for entering business."[5] However, like Junius Morgan, Henry Clews, George Bliss, the Goldmans, and the Lehmans, his lack of capital and experience induced him to begin his career in small-scale retailing. In 1842, at the age of eighteen, he decided against college and became a clerk in a dry-goods commission store in Concord, New Hampshire. "You can educate yourself, and a self-taught man is worth two of your college boys," his lawyer brother had counselled, while urging him to save from his salary of $200 a year.[6] His employer soon sent him to open a branch store in Hanover, New Hampshire, where he bought country produce—eggs, butter, potatoes—in exchange for cloth, tea, molasses, and coffee. The transactions were largely barter, and when the goods arrived at Concord, Morton received a commission on their sale.[7] These initial business encounters, like the early peddler activities of Jewish bankers, serve to highlight the informality of retail operations before the growth of more sophisticated modes of distribution.

The improvisation of flexible retail forms reflects the vigor characteristic of the period, but during this era of rapid economic change failure occurred as a common phenomenon. So it happened that just as the business of the country began to revive after the extended depression of the late 1830s, Morton's employer failed. One of the principal creditors, an important Boston merchant-capitalist, James Beebe, decided to continue the business under Morton's supervision. Although Hanover was a small college community, the surrounding countryside had been well settled by farmers, and the town served as the relay station for the coaches that ran up the Connecticut River Valley from Boston to Montreal. Morton prospered, soon bought Beebe out, and while still in his twenties became the proprietor—his newfound success illustrating, too, how in an economic milieu that was both expansionary and open-ended, general instability could be transformed into possibilities for personal advancement.

In 1849 Morton was invited to join, as a junior partner, the wholesale firm of James M. Beebe & Company. Here was the perfect opportunity for an ambitious young man. America's merchants for well over a century had been perfecting techniques for collecting and distributing goods. The completion of the canal system by the 1840s and the introduction of the clipper ships had rejuvenated America's languishing overseas trade and given added stimulus to internal commerce. Beebe, a middleman on a grand scale, facilitated the transatlantic flow and distribution of raw materials and finished goods. He bought cotton in the American South and shipped it to England for resale, where he purchased manufactured goods for resale in the United States. This import-jobbing house ranked, it was said, as the largest in New England, second largest in the United States. Morton entered the wholesale trade in 1850 investing $12,000 in cash, the assets of his Hanover store. Another New Englander, Junius Morgan, became a partner the following year and the firm reorganized as Beebe, Morgan & Company.[8]

Levi Morton and Junius Morgan acquired their formative knowledge of international trade and finance while partners in Beebe's importing firm. Beebe, like other importers, financed foreign trade with credits advanced by English bankers. The mechanism, in the concise summary of Margaret Myers, operated as follows: "The merchant. . .applied to the English bank agent in New York for a letter of credit; upon investigation it was granted and the British banking house notified. The English manufacturer from whom the goods were purchased then drew documents (invoices and bills of lading) to the bank in America, where they were held as security for the payment by the importer."[9] Beebe's financial agent in London was George Peabody, a New Englander who as the correspondent of many American firms had established himself as a specialist in foreign-exchange operations in the London financial district.

Besides the specific know-how acquired at Beebe's, Morton enlarged his frame of reference, shedding the provincialism of a local businessman. In 1852 Beebe sent him to London to "become initiated in foreign affairs."[10] During these years, too, he became acquainted with mobile New Englanders who later figured in his career in banking and politics. Here he first met George Boutwell, subsequently Grant's Secretary of the Treasury, who in 1870 would offer Morton's banking house the government's first refunding contract. Cornelius Bliss, later Chairman of the Republican

State Committee, was also a member of Beebe's firm.[11] With Junius Morgan, Morton formed an especially close friendship which shaped his subsequent career.

In 1854, Junius Morgan accepted a partnership in the House of Peabody, sold his Boston church pew to Morton, enrolled Pierpont in school in Switzerland, and moved his family abroad.[12] Morton decided soon after to move on to New York, which by then had outstripped Boston as a commercial and financial center. At age thirty-one, in 1855, he achieved the goal that soon became the stuff of Horatio Alger dreams: he became the senior partner of a wholesale dry-goods commission firm, Morton, Grinnell & Company. Located on Broad Street in lower Manhattan, the business stood just a few blocks away from Seligman and Stettheimer, the dry-goods importer, and from the soft-goods store of Solomon Kuhn. Described in 1856 as a "prosperous young merchant in New York,"[13] Morton belonged to the Chamber of Commerce, cast his vote for the Republican presidential candidate—as he was to do ever after—and married. The partners did a good business in the boom years from 1855 to 1857. By the 1850s, the cotton mills of New England were manufacturing goods that could compete with British textiles and domestically mass-produced white sheeting was especially useful in the agricultural South. The firm built a large interregional trade selling cotton to the New England mills and delivering their products south.

The panic of 1857 left the wholesalers unharmed, but scarcely had the Civil War begun than bankruptcy threatened. More commercial failures had in fact resulted from the repudiation of Southern mercantile paper (inevitable once it became illegal for Southern merchants to pay debts to Northern creditors) than had occurred in the 1857 panic.[14] Morton made the rounds of creditors with a packet of promissory notes and then immediately reorganized. He chose as his partner his employee, Walter Burns, a Harvard graduate of a well-established mercantile family. But faced with the embargo on cotton and the halt in the Southern trade, the partners decided to turn to what appeared a more promising business. In 1863, L. P. Morton & Company, Merchants, became L. P. Morton & Company, Bankers.

Thus far Morton had traveled the familiar route from a country store, to a partnership in a wholesale importing and jobbing house in Boston, and from there to his own commission firm in New York. Whatever his immediate difficulties resulting from the war, his decision to relinquish commerce for finance proved typical, in keeping with a general trend that dates back to the 1840s, when merchants in the foreign trade increasingly gave up the wholesale import-export aspects of their business to concentrate on banking.[15]

Having abandoned one line of business because of the war, Morton capitalized on the new possibilities. For the second time failure would again be the prelude to success, for within the decade both he and Burns became known as international financiers. The new banking house advertised its specialty as dealers in commercial paper and as drawers of foreign bills. Announcements in bold print gave notice that L. P. Morton & Company would "draw Sterling Bills of Exchange, at sight or sixty days, on the Union Bank of London, in sums to suit the purchasers; and also issue Circular Letters of Credit, on this Bank for Travellers' use." In the first few years, in an attempt to attract business, the firm offered to buy and sell government securities; to take orders for stocks and bonds (both at home and abroad); to trade in gold; and to take collection of dividends, drafts, etc. To complete this range of general banking services, and hoping to attract country bankers' balances, the house promised to pay interest on demand deposits—"Interest allowed on Deposits, subject to cheques at sight."[16]

In the early 1860s private bankers took over the foreign-exchange transactions previously handled almost exclusively by mercantile firms.[17] For the principal contingent of the new private banking group, former merchants adept at international credits, this business in remittances held special attractions. The profits of exchange had risen continuously since the outbreak of war as the need for overseas payments increased. Quantities of war supplies ordered abroad, as well as imports of luxuries and goods of all sorts, had added up to larger foreign outlays at a time when the gold premium was rising. In addition to this outflow, $200 million of American securities had been returned from abroad between 1860 and 1863 for conversion into gold or exchange on Europe. This demand for foreign-exchange bills to be used in actual payments effectively pushed prices up, while at the same time purchases by speculators who were investing in exchange at unprecedented rates further inflated the market.[18]

The flourishing business in exchange in the early 1860s, certainly one of the incentives to the proliferation of new private banking firms, also constituted the single most pervasive factor contributing to the creation of American overseas private banking partnerships until the end-of-decade opportunities in railroads and refunding.

Morton extended his operations to the center of the world money market almost immediately after establishing the New York house. In the winter of 1863, Walter Burns opened a London office and remained there as the resident partner. In part, the milieu of the early 1860s had encouraged the move. The speculative fever in Wall Street rivaled a virtual mania for credit and banking enterprises in the London money market. A burgeoning of finance companies, discount firms, and banks revealed not only the eagerness for investing, but also the ingenious techniques freshly devised to attract new capital. The year Morton set up in the City, the English version of the Crédit Mobilier, an investment-promotional bank, first appeared and Junius Morgan became a director of the newly formed International Financial Society.[19]

The partners' sights fixed on what promised to be the sustained growth in exchange transactions which accompanied the boom in the London financial district. By 1863, English trade had again expanded, having recovered quickly from the dislocations prompted by the American Civil War. Since the currency of international commerce was the bill of exchange drawn on shipments of merchandise, this business appeared flourishing and safe: or so claimed the British and American Exchange Banking Corporation formed in London in 1863:

> Transactions in exchange are of magnitude, and they will have a large margin of profit if arranged with prudence, and it is not too much to say that the field is one which can be immediately developed.[20]

The practice of attaching bills of lading to bills of exchange as collateral security worked to make exchange operations comparatively safe, and the shipment of gold involved "scarcely any risk whatsoever." However, as Walter Bagehot noted, most English bankers would "as soon think of turning silk merchants" as engage in large-scale remittance operations. Foreigners, on the other hand, believed the "exchange business—that is, the buying and selling of bills on foreign countries—a main part of banking."[21]

In establishing a London firm in 1863, Morton, like the Browns, anticipated a grander future. As Leland Jenks has observed, "To astute dealers in progress and poverty one centre of operations had proved too circumscribed,"[22] which explains why most of the outstanding banking houses in London after the mid-1860s were of American or European origin. The new firm quickly gained publicity from the aid it gave to Robert Walker, Treasury Secretary Chase's special agent sent to negotiate a loan in London and gain sympathy for the Northern cause. Perhaps the bankers had extended the government a line of credit, or took some of the issue Walker failed to place with the Barings.[23] While the business could not have amounted to very much, it later earned Morton, Burns & Company the reputation of supporting the Union when other European and American financiers remained reluctant. To some observers, the entrance of the ambitious "new international banking house," as "challengers" in a field dominated by the Barings and the Rothschilds, seemed somewhat "presumptuous."[24] Nevertheless, the newcomers, aided by a connection to the House of Peabody, did a good business, particularly as exchange dealers. When the war ended, these profits continued—"With exchanges after the Civil War, and great cotton shipments to be covered, the profits continued handsome."[25]

Joined to the potentialities of exchange, the postwar bond boom contributed another incentive to transatlantic partnerships. Union victory had sparked a sudden demand in foreign money markets for U. S. government securities. Speculation pushed the amount of U. S. bonds held abroad to $350 million in 1866 and to $1 billion by 1869. Although numerous American bankers opened in London to trade in twenty-year U. S. issues paying five percent, Morton's house became the leader in the field.[26]

As the sphere, as well as the magnitude, of operations enlarged during the later 1860s, the Morton firm moved toward greater specialization. It dropped general banking services in 1867 so that greater attention could be given exchange and securities transactions. That same year Morton took his first step toward involvement in railroads. He became a director in the Dubuque & Sioux City, of which New York banker M. K. Jesup was president. That year, too, the firm announced that it was receiving subscriptions for the securities of the International Ocean Telegraph Company, planning to land cables on the shores of Florida, Cuba, and Puerto Rico. The $1.5 million issue was bolstered by the privileges the company had received from Florida, Santo Domingo, and Spain for the enterprise.[27]

These expanding opportunities of the late 1860s stimulated frequent reorganizations as men moved from firm to firm in the proliferating private banking community. How crucial such shifts of personnel could become in prompting fresh appraisals for new alliances is illustrated by the departure of Walter Burns, whose marriage in 1867 to Mary Morgan, the daughter of Junius Morgan, opened other possibilities. While the break did not follow immediately, within the year Morton began seeking new partners.[28] Compelled to reassess, he formed an organization which differed in structure and size from its predecessor and in the process he increased both the capital and the connections that contributed to the firm's success.

In preparation for the U.S. government's anticipated refunding transactions and for new possibilities in railroads, what had been a simple transatlantic partnership became an overlapping copartnership joining two separate organizations. The creation of Morton, Bliss & Company in New York and Morton, Rose & Company in London in 1869 provided for separate legal entities each with its own members and capital. This structuring offered special advantages. Although the senior partners insisted on close scrutiny of all investments, decisions regarding exchange operations could be made quickly. Each firm, moreover, remained responsible for obtaining its own business and for managing its own capital accounts. At the same time, accounts of profit and loss could be transferred from the books of one firm to the other when the occasion demanded. Of overriding importance was the fact that liabilities were legally limited to the assets of each partnership. And not least among the benefits was the enhanced reputation gained by having the individual firm directly responsible to its clients. In other words, the advantages of branch banking were supplemented without incurring the problems of ownership.[29]

Morton had especially distinguished his house when the Canadian Minister of Finance, John Rose, resigned in 1869 and became the senior partner in London. After a year-long invitation, Rose agreed to replace Walter Burns. At the time he joined the banking house, he had been negotiating disputes between the United States and Great Britain arising from the *Alabama Claims,* and as Minister of Finance for the Dominion had been pressing Washington for more liberal trade relations between Canada and the United States. As a private banker in London, he maintained close connections with the Confederation, though in other forms. He became a member of the London Committee of the Bank of Montreal, and his close friend, the Prime Minister, Sir John Macdonald, named him to a specially created post as unofficial high commissioner for Canada. Macdonald counted on Rose to serve the Dominion in London as both lobbyist and diplomatic troubleshooter.[30] Rose's reputation as a statesman of wide experience, with government connections in Ottawa, London, and Washington, considerably strengthened the standing and business opportunities of the Morton House. One of the New York Cookes, furious at the preference shown this new rival by Treasury Secretary Boutwell when arranging the govenment's first refunding contract, inaccurately charged, "The Morton firms don't know any more about Bonds than Hottentots. They have always been a Stock House—They are stock Brokers, through Sir John just fledging [sic] into Bankers & selling Govt. Loans."[31]

Morton's new senior partner in New York, George Bliss, a former Connecticut dry-goods merchant, brought with him experience in international credits, an interest in railroads, and substantial capital.[32] Like Morton, he shared a Puritan New England background, had begun his career as a clerk in a retail store, and by his twenties had become a partner. Bliss married the boss's daughter and in 1844, when he was twenty-seven, moved to New York to join the newly opened import-jobbing house of Simeon B. Chittenden and John Jay Phelps. Phelps, Chittenden, and Bliss, 12 Wall Street, prospered in the late 1840s. It was rumored that during one year their purchases in Europe netted a clear profit of $100,000. Encouraged by success, Bliss started his own wholesale dry-goods business in 1853 and during the panic of 1857 enlisted Phelps as a partner. In this instance, the merchants reportedly profited from the effects of the Civil War. Anticipating a price rise, they had extended their purchases and then just before the war's end had sold heavily. By then Bliss's interest had already moved to railroads; he figured among the star-studded list of subscribers to the New York Metropolitan Railroad Company, proposing in 1864 to build the city's first underground.[33] He also held considerable investments in New York City real estate, whose appreciation contributed to his wealth. When in 1869 he entered the final phase of his career, private banking, it was estimated that he brought anywhere from $900,000 to $2.5 million to the Morton firm, while Morton's own share totaled only an estimated $100,000.[34]

The junior partners in New York comprised a group with interesting affiliations. Walter Watson, a Canadian, had been with the British Bank of North America in New York, an agency which specialized in buying and selling exchange. In the mid-1870s, when Watson left to open the local office of the Merchants Bank of

Canada, the senior partner's son, George Bliss, Jr., replaced him.[35] George Bowdoin, a young stockbroker fresh from three years at Harvard, became a junior partner in 1871. The son-in-law of Moses Grinnell, he was a close friend of Pierpont Morgan. When the "ambitious and young" Bowdoin accepted a proposition to join Drexel, Morgan & Company in 1883, both Bliss and Morton, who believed they were nearing the end of their careers, approved the move to "the young and active firm" as understandable and appropriate.[36] Another junior partner in the 1870s, Stuyvesant Fish, the son of Grant's Secretary of State, had started in the financial offices of the Illinois Central. He held an appointment with the railroad while a junior partner of the banking house from 1872 to 1877, when he resumed his full-time tie to the Illinois Central.[37] R.J. Cross also worked closely with Bliss on railroad matters and stayed with the house until its reorganization as the Morton Trust Company following the death of George Bliss in 1896.[38]

Toward the end of January 1871, Delmonico's was the scene of a gala ball in honor of the Prince of Wales. A group of New York bankers so monopolized the royal visit and were so visibly represented at the festivities that the press headlined the event an evening for "The Prince and Bankers." Prominent among the "metropolitan magnates" were Moses Taylor, president of the City Bank; August Belmont, agent for the Rothschilds; and private bankers William B. Duncan, Adrien Iselin, Louis Von Hoffman, George Bliss, and Levi Morton. As the Prince had dined with Morton and made his appearance at Delmonico's in his carriage, the "Street," putting a monetary value on events of all sorts, computed "this honor to the new firm at from fifty to over a hundred thousand dollars (lawful money) which perhaps is not setting it too high."[39]

No comparable estimate indicated the value to the house when the Queen conferred the title of Baronet on John Rose in the summer of 1872 for his special services in connection with the *Alabama* treaty and the settlement of indirect claims.[40] It came as no surprise, however, when the English government chose Morton, Bliss & Company; Drexel, Morgan & Company; and Jay Cooke to handle the transmission of the $15.5 million awarded to the United States by the Court of Arbitration.[41] Also, the following year the United States government named Morton, Rose & Company the

Fiscal Agent in London for the Navy and State Departments, agencies they held until the Democrats captured the presidency in 1884.[42] Whatever the profits of such business, they were considerably compounded by the accruing prestige.

Morton meanwhile had become known in Washington society as a good friend of President Grant and Secretary Boutwell. In 1873 his four-year-old firm won the management of the government's second refunding contract, having declined the first because of its part at the time in the *Alabama* negotiations.[43] Rumors abounded that Morton, designated the "representative of Wall Street in the Republican Party," would be the next Secretary of the Treasury.[44] By 1873, moreover, the partners had joined the directorates of such well-established railroad companies as the Illinois Central and the Delaware, Lackawanna & Western, and had also become major stockholders and board members of such relatively new roads as the Missouri, Kansas & Texas; the Milwaukee & St. Paul; the Indianapolis, Cincinnati & Lafayette; the New Orleans, Mobile & Texas; and the Union Pacific. Because of their heavy railroad investments, when he returned from a trip abroad in October, shortly after the failure of Jay Cooke & Company, the press observed that he could "have the satisfaction of finding the standing of his house here improved by the manner in which it has withstood the shock of the recent panic."[45] Even before Morton became a member of Congress in 1878 and then Minister to France in 1881, his banking house had the business, the political influence, and the international connections to be ranked among the foremost financial firms of the era.

2
Railroads: "The Big Plum"

Descriptions of bankers' relations to the railroad industry in the 1870s and early 1880s have rested on certain assumptions: first, that they functioned primarily as capital middlemen; secondly, that they preferred cautiously to restrict their rail affiliations to established Eastern roads; and thirdly, that there is little, if any, evidence of their control in the industry.[1] None of these assumptions is sustained by the record of Morton, Bliss & Company. When Morton's firm turned to railroads during the postwar boom, it did not restrict its affiliations to established Eastern railways. Rather, it provided capital to extensive new and even competing roads in the South and West. Moreover, these financiers were considerably more than advisors to railroad executives or investor clients—they became influential participants in the decision-making process, determining the goals of railroad policy. For in addition to their role as mobilizers of portfolio funds, the bankers directly financed risky and long-term projects. They eagerly sponsored the creation of interregional through ties and drew their profits from construction finance and stock trading. Characteristically, they cooperated with other private bankers in both facilitating and fostering the expansion of the early 1870s. Their investment criteria and behavior will receive sharper definition when the firm's business is examined in subsequent chapters. That their responses were by no means atypical, but fit a well-defined pattern, is suggested by the parallel involvements of other prominent private banking firms examined in this chapter.

In the immediate postwar years of 1865 and 1866 trading in United States government bonds had dominated the investment market. For as long as these securities offered a high rate of return and provided private bankers with a safe, lucrative business, they

Railroad Investment: 1867-1874

Stock, Mortgage Bonds, Equipment, Obligations, Etc.
(In millions of dollars)

Year	Total	% change from Preceding Year	Capital Stock	% change from Preceding Year	Bonded Debt	% change from Preceding Year
1867	1,172	—	756	—	416	—
1868	1,869	+ 59.5	*	—	*	—
1869	2,041	+ 9.2	*	—	*	—
1870	2,476	+ 21.3	*	—	*	—
1871	2,664	+ 7.6	1,481	—	*	—
1872	3,159	+ 18.6	1,647	+ 11.2	1,511	—
1873	3,784	+ 19.8	1,947	+ 18.2	1,836	+ 21.5
1874	4,221	+ 11.5	1,990	+ 2.2	2,230	+ 21.5
%Change 1867-1874		+ 260.2		+ 163.2		+ 436.1

SOURCE: Adapted from U.S. Bureau of the Census, *Historical Statistics of the United States, Colonial Times to 1970* (Washington, D.C.: Government Printing Office, 1975), part 2, p. 734.
*Not available

looked askance at the risks entailed by large-scale railbuilding ventures. "We cannot afford to build R R's and neglect our manipulations of Govt Securities. They are good enough," Jay Cooke was advised in 1866, the same year his firm refused to participate in financing the projected 500 mile Northern Pacific.[2] A year later Jay Cooke & Company declined to act as special agents for the nation's still incomplete transcontinental, the Union Pacific. While government issues paid as high as six percent, Cooke, whose great success derived from wartime Treasury bond sales, continued to believe it would be almost impossible to merchandise railroad loans. Similarly, J. & W. Seligman & Company, busy in the mid-1860s with trading in governments and foreign exchange operations, viewed railroads with suspicion. "I consider this a speculation entirely out of our line," Joseph Seligman warned his brothers. "We can make enough money in a legitimate way without gambling hazard."[3]

The public's attitude toward railroad investment, however, had begun to alter even before the end of 1867. During the summer of that year, when John J. Cisco & Company accepted the Union Pacific business Cooke rejected, the firm sold $10 million worth of these securities in less than six months.[4] Within the next two years, public enthusiasm for new construction spread like contagion to the Pacific, making railroads the "big plum" for investment bankers.[5] Not only did the completion of the first transcontinental buoy investor confidence, but heavy purchases of governments by national banks in 1869 sent their prices up and their yields down, so that rail issues became especially attractive. Newspapers filled with advertisements for bonds paying seven to twelve percent, and into 1872 high interest rates made rail securities the "most popular form of investment of a personal nature open to the people of the United States." Moreover, the prevailing, "almost unlimited confidence" masked potential risk. Such was the faith in railroad enterprise that investors willingly purchased legally unsecured bonds, for unbuilt track, of new companies which had never paid a dividend.[6] Even foreign issues were subscribed to by 1870 with surprising success. Exported American loan capital helped build the Honduras Oceanic Railway, the Southern of Buenos Aires, and the Peruvian Railway. The money in the Panama Railroad was exclusively American.[7]

These had been halcyon years for railroad construction. The laying of iron or, better still, steel track seemed to promise the certain route to economic development and continuing prosperity. And it was believed that the South too could pin its hopes for economic reconstruction to the expansion of its railroad network. For business analysts, the railroad answered as the certain catalyst for progress: "As railroads have made the western states populous and prosperous, so railroads connecting the great agricultural regions of the south-west, with their natural markets and shipping ports, are to be the main agency increasing the wealth of the South, and in turn roads will find large profit in the traffic following their opening."[8]

Unprecedented amounts of funds were mobilized to build 31, 218 miles of track in only six years from 1867 to 1873. While in 1866 bonded indebtedness had totaled $410 million, by 1872 the figure had risen to $1.5 billion; in the same period the nominal value of capital stock increased from $750 million to $1.6 billion. Total rail investment, which came to $3.2 billion in 1872, rose during 1873 by $625 million, bringing the figure to some $3.8 billion.[9] From 1867 through 1874 total capital stock plus bonded debt increased 260 percent. Even allowing for the inaccuracy of the data and the fact that recorded figures on capitalization represented book value, the amounts and increases are impressive. So great was the cresting demand for construction funds that it exceeded

		Railroad Mileage and Investment: 1867-1874		
	Mileage		Investment (millions of dollars)	
Year	Road Operated (Dec. 31)	%Change from Preceding Year	Capital Stock and Bonded Debt	%Change from Preceding Year
1867	39,050	—	1,172	—
1868	42,229	+ 8.1	1,869	+59.5
1869	46,844	+10.9	2,041	+ 9.2
1870	52,922	+13.0	2,476	+21.3
1871	60,301	+13.9	2,664	+ 7.6
1872	66,171	+ 9.7	3,159	+18.6
1873	70,268	+ 6.2	3,784	+19.8
1874	72,385	+ 3.0	4,221	+11.5
%Change 1867-1874		+85.4		+260.2

SOURCE: Adapted from U.S. Bureau of the Census, *Historical Statistics of the United States, Colonial Times to 1970* (Washington, D.C.: Government Printing Office, 1975), part 2, pp. 731, 734.

even the increasing supplies. Already by the fall of 1871 intense competition for rail capital prompted promoters such as Collis Huntington to complain bitterly that funds were hard to come by,[10] when in absolute terms rail investment continued to grow.

Reportedly, there was "no difficulty obtaining money in Europe for American railroads."[11] However, a larger share of foreign funds might have been available for American issues if the rail craze had been less universal. The English mania of the early 1860s for railway construction quickly swept five continents, and by the late 1860s the demand for rail transportation reached from Bavaria and Rumania to Egypt and Turkey. At the same time, roads were being built with English and European funds in India, Japan, Russia, and South America. English, Dutch, and German investors, who had a choice of government-guaranteed loans from virtually all over the world, worried about the bulk of American rail issues which lacked federal assurances. Adverse publicity questioning the financial integrity of American roads may have further inhibited the flow of funds.

Whatever the constraints, what is more significant is that the nation's rail bonds were absorbed in this highly competitive market. Indeed, in 1872 the *Commercial and Financial Chronicle* criticized foreigners for responding too eagerly and for pursuing an indiscriminate, rather "reckless investment policy."[12] Jay Cooke's well-known difficulties, when he tried unsuccessfully to merchandise a Northern Pacific loan in 1869, were anything but typical. New York financiers such as James Lanier marketed "dozens of new issues" in Amsterdam and Frankfurt from 1868 to 1870, peak years in those centers for United States rails. And then, after 1870, a mounting supply of loan capital became available in London.[13]

According to the lowest estimates, foreign holdings of U.S. rail bonds rose from $50 million in 1866 to $243 million by 1869, while by 1876, probably the worst year of the depression of that decade, the figure stood at a minimum of $375 million.[14] Sales of American rail bonds had continued active in London up to the news of the failure of Jay Cooke & Company and then were only temporarily halted. Even after the panic began in September 1873—though *new* issues of *new roads* were seriously checked and prices of older issues depressed—the general traffic from the West helped maintain confidence in a majority of established lines. Foreign capital was reported "abundant"; with "adequate guarantees," funds for rail investment were "waiting to come in." By the year's end, "the class of railroad bonds placed in the foreign market was better than those placed in any previous year."[15] Taking a longer view, certainly the most notable feature of the 1860s and 1870s was the widening market for U.S. rails marked by the flotation of high-interest-bearing securities at discounts which brought a steady appreciation to the holdings of domestic as well as foreign investors.[16]

However, overseas investors, unnerved by rumors and scandal, looked to American-connected bankers for firsthand knowledge of U.S. railroad properties. By 1873, the growing demand for American investments, especially those promising safety, had led to the formation of a number of foreign trust companies. The American Trust Company in London, created specifically to appeal to small investors lacking access to dependable information, promised, as its name implied, to "rely on leading American financiers."[17] For the substantial investor, transatlantic banking houses served more effectively to solve this problem, so frequently commented on abroad. American-connected houses with offices in London listing United States railway issues for public sale on the London Exchange in the early 1870s included Speyer Brothers; Morton, Rose & Company; Cooke, McCulloch & Company; Clews, Habicht & Company; Brown, Shipley & Company; and

J.S. Morgan & Company. Besides the bonds sold publicly, and therefore identifiable, these firms placed millions more privately in London and on the Continent.

Although the foreign contribution to American building reached its peak during the first postwar boom, outside capital accounted for a fraction of the monies invested in the growing network. Granting the inflation of railroad capitalization, and granting that the foreign contribution to the actual dollar costs of building probably figured higher than the percentages reveal, still imported funds constituted no more than a small share of the total. In 1869 the proportion of foreign investment came to an estimated nine percent; by 1876 the foreign proportion of total capitalization had dipped to eight percent.[18]

The bulk of capital requirements could, by the 1860s, be met at home with private monies accounting for the largest contribution to the expansion of the railway system. Like the foreign share, direct public aid constituted a small portion of total investment. Most of the government's funds were supplied before 1873, and for the entire period from 1861 to 1890 direct federal outlays added to state and local commitments came to, at most, $350 million.[19] Government land grants, as Lloyd Mercer has shown, allowed significant subsidies for the Texas Pacific, for the predecessor to the Great Northern, and for the Northern Pacific systems, but did not in any case "come close to paying for investment" even for these beneficiaries.[20] However, in serving as collateral, land did lure investors, and, similarly, other forms of government support (cash donations, stock and loan subscriptions, guarantees) attracted investors, loosening the influx of private capital that could make the difference between success and failure.

Together, the availability of foreign funds and government support created a bouyancy that proved critical in encouraging promoters' plans for continued building and supplied the crucial marginal capital for such projects. Whatever the source of funds, however, public or private, individual or institutional, foreign or domestic, private banking firms acted as key intermediaries for channeling increased flows to the expanding system.

In contrast to the prebellum period, when firms such as Winslow, Lanier & Company often sold securities on a commission basis, in the postwar period private bankers purchased blocks of securities outright, individually or in syndicates, and thereby relieved railroad corporations of both the delays and the risks of merchandising. Then after private placement, with special clients and friends, with individuals and institutions, they saw to stock exchange listings to make securities available to a broad investing public. They handled interest payment on bonds, saw to registration or transfer of ownership, and disseminated difficult-to-obtain investment information.

In addition to these services, as financial intermediaries, mobilizing other people's money, they enacted other indispensible functions. Approached constantly with new schemes affording multiple alternatives for the lucrative use of funds, they purchased senior securities for their own account; invested vitally needed, but hard-to-come-by, venture funds in new construction; furnished monies for new acquisitions; supplied short-term operating credits; and acted as trustees for mortgages. As a result of these many-faceted activities, they not only entered but at times dominated management and on occasion completely took over railroad operation.

To inform the public of these close ties to rail enterprise, and of course to emphasize their particular expertise, some private bankers began advertising themselves as "railroad specialty houses." The designation was a certain indication of such firms' participation in policy making, direct investment, and capital mobilization.

M. K. Jesup & Company, for example, a railroad specialty house dating back to the 1850s, concentrated on Western and Southern roads. From 1865 through 1873, Jesup was both president and a director of the Dubuque & Sioux City, an Iowa road leased to the Illinois Central in 1867. In this period he also served on the boards of the Dubuque & Southern, the Southern Minnesota, the California Pacific, and the Orange & Newark. His firm became the Fiscal Agent for the Detroit & Milwaukee while Jesup acted as a manager of the parent road, the Western of Canada. The banking house had close ties to the Chicago & Alton and functioned as Transfer Agent for two of their leased lines, the Chicago & Joliet and the Louisiana & Missouri River. In the South, Jesup was elected a director for the Macon & Western, the Macon & Brunswick, the Northern (S.C.) Railroad, the Charlotte, Columbia & Augusta, and the Southern Railway Security Company.[21]

The Dubuque & Sioux City, of which Jesup was president, relied on his banking firm to provide short-term funds, to float loans, and to pay coupons on its bonded debt. As his firm also imported iron and steel rails, it provisioned the road as well.[22] The practice, not uncommon, occasioned stockholder charges that Jesup & Company had received unjustified profits selling supplies to the railroad. Jesup furthermore determined the general financial policy of the road, albeit in such a way that Platt Smith, the vice-president, acting as local operating manager, became frequently piqued at both the banker and the board in New York for making decisions without consulting Smith.[23]

In what are early examples of informal interlocking directorates and community-of-interest arrangements, Jesup often cooperated with other private bankers in handling railroad matters. Charles Dabney, J.P. Morgan's partner in Dabney, Morgan & Company, joined Jesup in the management of the Macon & Western and the Macon & Brunswick in 1870 and 1871. At the same time, Morgan and his brother-in-law, Walter Burns, became directors in Jesup's Dubuque & Sioux City, while in 1872 Morgan joined the board of the Illinois Central, which leased the Dubuque & Sioux City.[24]

Like other financiers, Jesup worked closely with railroad executives in furthering strategies for consolidation. When Tom Scott undertook an expansion program to create a north-south route for the Pennsylvania, he decided to assume control of the Charlotte, Columbia & Augusta. A majority of the share capital was acquired through his Southern Railway Security Company, the first American holding company. W.T. Walters and B.F. Newcomer, holding company directors, were elected to the board of the Charlotte line and an interlocking directorate resulted when Jesup, one of the original railroad directors, simultaneously became a member of the holding company board. Besides Jesup, R.T. Wilson of the East-Tennessee, Virginia & Georgia, another New York banker, sat on the board of the Southern Railway Security Company, which by 1872 had gained control through stock purchases and lease arrangements of a consolidated system of over 2,000 miles.[25]

John S. Kennedy emerged as a particularly important railroad specialist, well known as a financier of Western roads and as one of the government's commissioners for the Union Pacific. A Scot, he had come to the United States in the 1850s as a representative of a British iron and coal company. When Jesup went into banking in 1857, Kennedy became his partner, but a decade later opened his own firm, which, in addition to negotiating loans, bought and sold railway equipment, and acted as commission agents for the Bowling Iron Company, the West Cumberland Hematite Iron Company, and the Cambria Iron Company. In the late 1860s and early 1870s, Kennedy and Jesup dominated the management of the Dubuque & Southwestern and the Orange & Newark, while Kennedy also belonged to the board of the Cedar Falls & Minnesota, a road leased to Jesup's Dubuque & Sioux City. His other management positions included the Oil Creek & Allegheny, the International Railway, and the Washington & Ohio.[26] As a director of the Indianapolis, Cincinnati & Lafayette, he was one of a banker group that forced that road into receivership in 1870 and controlled its management throughout the decade. His firm, acting for foreign bondholders, forced the St. Paul & Pacific into receivership in 1873 and retained operating control until the negotiations which led to the road's reorganization in 1879 as the St. Paul, Minneapolis & Manitoba.[27] Kennedy obtained a one-fifth interest in the reorganization, continued in the management for another decade, becoming vice-president in 1884, and was elected to the board again in the 1890s. This Canadian connection also brought the banking firm into the direct financing of the Canadian Pacific in the early 1880s.[28]

Like Kennedy and Jesup, Duncan, Sherman & Company first moved into railroad finance in the 1850s, though originally as agents for the London house of George Peabody. On joint account they floated portions of issues of the Ohio & Pennsylvania, the North Western Virginia, and the Belvedere railroads. Initially hesitant to go it alone, in 1853 they became bankers to the Ohio & Mississippi. In the 1860s, the firm became Transfer Agents for the Hannibal & St. Joseph, a Missouri road which attracted considerable Eastern capital. They retained this agency into the 1870s, when they acted as Transfer Agents also for the New York Central. Isaac Sherman was a director of the Milwaukee & St. Paul from 1870 to 1872, while William Duncan, who joined the management of the Erie and the New York Viaduct in 1871, was in the 1870s also a director of the Cleveland, Columbus, Cincinnati & Indianapolis and the Mobile & Ohio. He became the president and the receiver of the latter company when it faced financial difficulty in 1874 and held both these positions until 1883.[29]

A similar diversity of roles characterizes the business of Winslow, Lanier & Company, one of the first merchandisers of Western securities in the 1850s. Having helped reorganize the Pittsburgh, Fort Wayne & Chicago in 1859, they kept their place in the management and served as the road's Transfer Agent. When in

1869 the Pennsylvania arranged to take control through a 999-year lease, J.F.D. Lanier remained on the board and his firm continued as Transfer Agents. Charles Lanier now became a director in another Pennsylvania road, the Cleveland & Charleston, and the banking firm became Transfer Agents for the Memphis & Charleston, absorbed by Scott's holding company.[30]

These reputable banking houses, then, whose experience with railroads dated back to the 1850s, did not, as has been assumed, shy away from new projects, or from lines to be built in the South and West. If as claimed "private bankers saw better places for their investment funds back East, where there were some people,"[31] there is ample evidence that they financed construction and played significant roles in the management of new roads and old lines extending or projected from the Atlantic and Gulf coasts to every point in the interior.

Relatively young firms, such as J. & W. Seligman, also sought out railroad business. Joseph Seligman was working behind the scenes for the notorious Jay Gould and Daniel Drew in the Erie War of 1868, doing a profitable business in Erie stock manipulation. By 1869, his firm had invested heavily in developmental building in the South and West. What was to be the Seligmans' dominant role in the affairs of the St. Louis-San Francisco Transcontinental resulted from direct investment and policy determination dating back to 1870 in two Missouri roads, the Atlantic & Pacific and the Missouri Pacific. Also in 1870, Joseph Seligman joined Levi Morton and Louis Von Hoffman in the syndicate which took over the management and financing of the New Orleans, Mobile & Texas to build an interregional route connecting the South and Southwest to properties they were financing to the north and east. In the same period, Seligman, Morton, August Belmont, and George Clark directed the expanding Missouri, Kansas & Texas, and as in the New Orleans corporation, the bankers were major stockholders.[32]

Joseph Seligman may have been, as H. Craig Miner concludes, "one of the first practitioners of finance capitalism,"[33] but if so he was one among many. The Seligmans' railroad business is marked, moreover, by the promotional and speculative tenor so typical of the early 1870s and their behavior bears little resemblance to the long-accepted portrayal of cautious investment bankers striving to restrain the competitive projects of speculator-promoters. The Missouri, Kansas & Texas, for example, was the most formidable rival of the Atlantic & Pacific, and the latter was a competitor of the Missouri Pacific going west. However, profits from the construction of new and competing lines became a source of the Seligmans' fortune in the early 1870s. According to Joseph Seligman, their railroad returns outweighed the rewards of foreign exchange, government bonds, or general banking services. He reminded his brothers in 1872 that "we have made a fortune, these past six years & made it principally out of *new* R. Roads."[34]

Whether supporting expansion of new or established companies, a distinguishing feature of bankers' behavior during the postwar decade is that they welcomed alliances which would keep open all possible sources of funds. No American firm yet had the stature or the capital of the great European houses, and rather than the joint stock companies English private bankers had formed in the 1860s to handle enlarged transactions, American financiers informally formed loose clusters and intertwining groups in order to share, and thereby limit, risk. Consequently, the absence of exclusive ties between railroad corporations and individual private banking firms does not, as Cochran has argued, provide evidence of railroad autonomy in the 1870s and early 1880s.[35] Cooke's insistence on exclusivity was so unusual that it had led, as his partner Harris Fahnestock warned it might, to failure.

> We could not in an emergency make them [Northern Pacific bonds] to any extent available as collateral because everybody knows that their value depends upon one man's ability to make them good. All other important roads have the aggregated responsibility of many good men.[36]

In response to the optimism of the postwar boom, then, bankers diversified their railroad affiliations, invoked both long-term and immediate investment criteria, assumed multiple and significant roles in the industry, and formed capital alliances within the banking community. A highly conservative estimate, based on an inspection of 1873 management rosters, reveals that prominent Eastern firms publicly affiliated with corporations operating some twenty-five percent of the total network.[37] The figure might prove to be considerably higher if we knew more of banker operations. For financiers, reputation counted as a priceless asset and as a consequence they preferred frequently to conceal their railroad business, particularly when they joined with publicly censured promoters. Morton, Bliss & Company carefully guarded the respectability upon which credit ratings rested and as a matter of policy often refused to let their railroad ties be publicly identified. Thus, when Gould entered the management of the Union Pacific in 1873, Morton refused the directorship to which he had been reelected and which he had held since 1871.[38] The resignation, calculated window dressing, earned him considerable praise in the press, as it was meant to, for supposedly his firm had relinquished a most important business as the Financial and Transfer Agent of the Union Pacific. *The Commercial and Financial Chronicle* described the resignation as a "great blow" to the railroad, explaining that the banking house could not afford this degrading affiliation, especially in London, "where Gould is held in such abhorrence."[39] The fact that an unknown junior partner immediately replaced Morton, or that he rejoined the board the following year, received no such publicity.

The "legitimate" image that financiers deliberately conveyed has been too readily perpetuated. Fritz Redlich, in his classic study of investment banking, identified the period from 1865 to 1880 as an "active phase" of railroad-banker relations, serving as preparation for the coming era of Finance Capitalism. Redlich views the era as one of buccaneering business ethics, and his analysis assumes an antagonism between respectable financiers and promoter-managers. He posits that postwar bankers, motivated by "self-defense," sought to protect their interests from the irresponsible decisions of railway executives by increasing their participation in companies whose loans they floated.[40] In a shift of emphasis, Chandler distinguished two types of railroad financier—the speculator-exploiter, on the one hand, and the reorganizer-system builder, on the other. In the first category he identifies those private capitalists who were more concerned with increasing their own immediate profits than with securing returns for the corporation or the investor. In the second, and antithetical, category he places reputable private banking firms described as performing the more "legitimate functions of financial intermediaries."[41] Acknowledging that even these latter cooperated sometimes in construction company and land schemes, he presents them as essentially capital middlemen and advisors to those with surplus funds, who continued a tradition that extended from Winslow, Lanier & Company in the 1850s to J. P. Morgan & Company in the 1890s.

Neither investment criteria nor ethical inhibitions prevented the Seligmans from allying with Jay Gould in the Erie stock dealings of 1868; as we shall see, they did not prevent Morton or Isaac Sherman from designing, with Oakes Ames and Russell Sage, construction company arrangements and stock manipulations; nor did they deter Morton, Bliss & Company from acting for Gould and the Union Pacific until 1877. As the crucial question for investment bankers was "What to do with money?" they followed the opportunities of the investment market, seeking profit where they could find it. If at moments they displayed caution or acted conservatively, the overall pattern of their activities in the early 1870s was both speculative and expansionary.

3
Directing Railroad Expansion

Immediately after the formation of Morton, Bliss & Company in 1869, the partners turned to opportunities in railroad enterprise. These initial affiliations reveal both their early support of inter-regional expansion and their dual role as capital suppliers—characteristics that would continue to mark their participation in the industry. On the one hand, the bankers acted in a relatively limited capacity as capital middlemen, buying railroad securities from corporations and then distributing them to investors at home and abroad. Such transactions brought short-term profits, particularly in the rising security market of the early 1870s. Considerably more important in terms of time, money, and effort were their more inclusive commitments to interregional through routes. In these instances the partners risked their own and the firm's funds, directly financing new lines of new companies projected across the relatively undeveloped sections of the South and West. Major stockholders, they either worked behind the scenes or, more frequently, became directors to determine overall policy. In either case, they found that such ventures necessitated constant attention to a wide variety of corporate concerns and careful monitoring of newly tried techniques devised to facilitate long-range strategies.

What Bliss called a "Young America Spirit" conditioned their investment criteria, encouraging participation in extremely ambitious projects. Both partners had begun their careers during the territorial expansion of the prewar period. They shared the prevailing belief that the nation's extraordinary physical growth was only the prelude to a new era of economic development and that the railroad would be the advance agent fulfilling the nation's manifest destiny. Whatever the inducements or drawbacks of specific schemes, the partners acted from the underlying convic-

51

tion that population and prosperity would follow rail extensions into the hinterland of every port and across the country. Convinced of the developmental benefits of rail building, they envisioned growing urban markets linked to flourishing agricultural centers. At the same time, as very practical men, they counted for the short-run on the profits from construction company financing, stock trading, and bond sales. Supportive government policy and the public mania for rail investments figured heavily in their calculations. Like other bankers they judged by the returns of land sales to the Illinois Central and by the excellent position of the Central Pacific that revenues from federal and state land grants would bring in working capital and together with state guarantees on interest would further insure loan capital for continuing construction.

The massive capital demands of projected strategies posed more of an immediately felt problem than potential risks. Both factors, however, account for the partners' alliances with other bankers, part of a trend that first emerged in the 1860s. To cope with capital accumulation and contingent liability, Morton and Bliss affiliated with partners of J. & W. Seligman; Duncan, Sherman & Company; Louis Von Hoffman; J. S. Kennedy & Company; Drexel, Morgan & Company; and August Belmont. Such group-banker alliances for direct financing of interregional railroad expansion constituted a significant feature of the postwar industry.

It has been argued that in the period before the 1890s when financiers made direct investments in railroad enterprise, they acted as general entrepreneurs continuing a pattern of intertwining business interests already observable by the 1840s. According to this interpretation, banker-stockholders on railroad boards only "indirectly" represented their firms,[1] and their behavior was indistinguishable from the general entrepreneurs'. Certainly general entrepreneurs purchased large quantities of securities directly from railroad corporations; they participated, too, in purchase and retailing syndicates; and they supplied short-term capital to the industry. The similarities should not, however, obscure a crucial distinction for capital transfers. The relationship of individual financiers to the railroad industry—even when their banking firms' services were not involved—derived from their institutional role in the money market. And conversely, the business of private banking firms as capital suppliers rested on the personal investments of the partners.

The matter of personal investments was so "vital" in the 1870s that George Bliss had sharply to criticize Charles Rose, a new partner in London: "I am impressed with the fact that you are not aware fully how important is the manner in which each member of a firm makes personal investments."[2] He quite pointedly explained that the financial position of each partner, as well as that of the house, were subjects of public discussion. Negative rumors could damage credit ratings upon which opportunity rested. Since reputation ranked of utmost importance in attracting business, no member's investments could be allowed adversely to affect either firm's standing. Although the articles of copartnership specified that no one had the right to interfere with the investment funds held by a partner as trustee, or for that matter interfere with decisions affecting personal funds, nevertheless, as small as the amount might be, these latter investments had to be made through the firm "precisely as if an order was received from an outside party."[3] Moreover, all orders for the members' own accounts, for joint accounts, or for trusts had to be made in the name of the firm. For an Anglo-American copartnership, subject to the disadvantages of geographic separation, an added necessity existed for careful scrutiny. Unless there prevailed "the undoubted and entire confidence not only in the integrity but the practices of each member of each firm . . .there [could] be no comfort or propriety in continuing."[4]

In practice, personal investments were governed by both companies' overall investment policy and were subject to the approval of the senior partners of both firms. In this sense, the affiliation of the partners with the railroad industry, even when the services of the banking house were not called for, reflected and was directly tied to the business of the firm. Or put another way, it can be said that the investments of the individual partners defined the risks the house might undertake since, as a general rule, potential liabilities were calculated in terms of the proportion each member could sustain with his personal assets.[5]

Perhaps we need most of all to get beyond the deceptive bookkeeping so typical of the period. The letterbooks of this firm reveal the extent to which stocks and bonds were held in other names, how investments were juggled between the partners' personal accounts, their joint accounts, those of the firm and of the partner firm in London. To disguise profit and loss, there were also joint accounts with railroad executives and with friends. These intricate arrangements, so difficult to pin down because of the covert nature of so many dealings, suggest the inadequacies of statistical analysis in calculating investment returns to insiders and emphasize the value of a detailed examination of banker-operations and criteria for decision-making in gauging their performance in the industry.

Among the early affiliations of Morton, Bliss & Company involving direct financing, that with the Milwaukee & St. Paul illustrates the partners' willingness to back an aggressive young company with grandiose plans for western expansion. From its organization in 1863, the road's promoters, Wisconsin banker Alexander Mitchell and New York businessman Russell Sage, worked to extend this local Wisconsin line into Minnesota, the Dakotas, and Montana.[6] Primarily as a result of purchase and consolidation, by 1868 the company owned 835 miles of line going west from Milwaukee to St. Paul, reaching to Minneapolis, as well as a spur across to Prairie Du Chien on the Mississippi.[7]

The M. & St. P. had become the largest system in the Midwest when Sage announced still more ambitious goals in 1868. But continued growth depended on Eastern capital, which in turn necessitated the education of Eastern stockholders. In calling for authorization of a half-dozen new connections, Sage coaxed stockholders to come west to see for themselves the potential and immediate opportunities. He explained how the McGregor & Sioux City would provide a through route for future agricultural and precious metals traffic from Montana territory; the West Wisconsin going to St. Paul would similarly develop sparsely settled area; the St. Paul & Pacific, projected across the continent, could provide a valuable traffic interchange; the Lake Superior & Mississippi already carried important lumber traffic; while acquisition of the Hastings & Dakota and "one of the best land grants ever made" was crucial for financial reasons.[8] Plans as expensive and as complex as these also necessitated new institutional alliances. Within the next two years both Levi Morton and Isaac Sherman of Duncan, Sherman & Company had been named directors.[9]

Not all of the connections Sage announced to the stockholders materialized, but rapid growth characterized the early 1870s. The company boasted nine divisions by 1874; the length of line owned and operated had increased to 1,399 miles of main track and the company had purchased a controlling interest in Western Union.[10] Expansion both east and west had resulted from leasing agreements, purchase of share control, outright acquisition, and from significant amounts of new construction financed by construction company techniques.

Morton and Sherman, working with Sage and the other directors, including Oakes Ames, soon to be a central figure in the Crédit Mobilier scandal, favored the "inside" construction company for financing new mileage. Despite the name, such companies had nothing at all to do with actual building, but rather served as financial intermediaries between building contractors and railroad corporations. Formed almost always by the directors of the parent railroad, the subsidiary company, operating as a separate corporate entity, took financial responsibility for construction, issued its own stock, and when track was completed resold it to the parent line, sometimes for exorbitant sums greatly exceeding actual building costs. Arrangements varied to meet specific situations, but the techniques adopted for extending the Hastings & Dakota were fairly common.

The procedures are worth following, step by step, for the model reveals why bankers favored the device. When the M. & St. P. obtained share control of the H. & D. in 1870 the railroad had built only thirty miles of its line, chartered to extend two hundred miles to the territorial boundary. In order to obtain lands assigned under its legislative grant, thirty-five additional miles had to be constructed by July 1872.[11] Before going ahead, seven M. & St. P. directors took seats on the nine-member H. & D. board to guarantee managerial control. Secondly, to raise immediate building capital, the H. & D. new board issued 15,000 shares of preferred stock, at an undisclosed price, to be purchased by the directors. As a third step, to raise monies for continued construction, the directors authorized an issue of $700,000 H. & D. seven percent bonds, priced at ninety, secured by a mortgage on the still unbuilt line as far west as the Dakota border. Then, after seventy-five miles of track reached Glencoe in June 1872, Russell Sage, president of the H. & D. (who was also the M. & St. P. vice-president), sold the whole stretch to the M. & St. P. for $1.8 million, exclusive of the land grant. And finally, to pay for the acquisition, the M. & St. P. floated a loan of $1,350,000 in seven percent bonds, and issued 7,500 shares of common stock for private distribution to the director-shareholders.[12]

Similar arrangements were widely used in these years and did not become subject to legal or public censure until 1873 when the Crédit Mobilier became the symbol for railroad fraud, corruption,

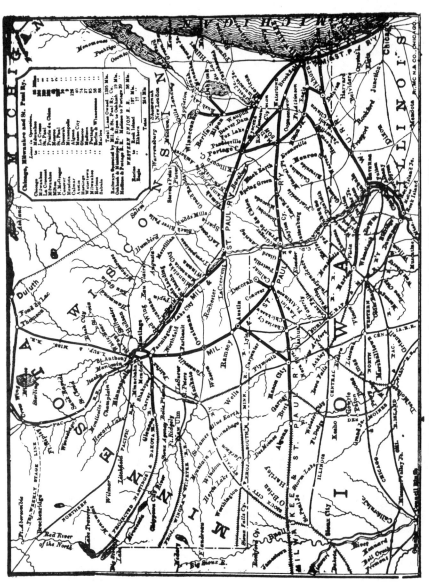

The Chicago, Milwaukee & St. Paul Railway, 1874. Stuart Collection, Rare Book Division. The New York Public Library, Astor, Lenox and Tilden Foundations.

and chicanery. Since Robert Fogel's study of the Union Pacific as *A Case in Premature Enterprise,* historians have tended to emphasize the practical difficulties promoters encountered in attracting venture funds. As Carl Degler puts it, "devices that now appear unscrupulous were often employed to compensate for high risk."[13] The point to be added is that construction-company methods, so indelibly associated by contemporaries with "buccaneer promoters" were shaped and relied on by investment bankers as the most satisfactory instrument to increase their share holdings, wield control in interlocking corporate structures, and further their business as financial intermediaries dealing in long-term credits. As railroad executives recognized in construction company financing a malleable technique, adaptable to varied legal and economic circumstance, so bankers could count on a series of steps which inevitably climaxed in the mobilization of loan capital for acquiring new line.

For the second large project of this period, the river division from St. Paul to La Crescent on the Mississippi, a very complex version of the construction company had to be devised. Russell Sage became president of the specially created Minnesota Railway Construction Company and again the M. & St. P. directors became stockholder-directors of the construction company.[14] Yet another subsidiary, the St. Paul & Chicago Railway, chartered in Minnesota, received a state land grant to build the line. It subsequently contracted with the Minnesota Construction Company to complete the road and turned over the land grant in exchange for securities. The members of the Minnesota Construction Company retained ownership of the state land grant, ownership of the bonds granted by the cities along the route, and ownership of the construction company stock, and only they knew the amounts received from these sources. After 103 miles of projected track reached Winona, the M. & St. P. agreed to buy the whole road from Sage's construction company for $4 million.[15]

To pay for the acquisition, Morton's banking house handled the next phase—the flotation of a $4 million loan. The many advantages of allying with transatlantic bankers are apparent in the sudden modification of the purchase agreement to meet an unexpected tightening in the domestic money market. According to the alteration, payment for the bonds would be in pounds sterling allowing the loan to be brought out abroad. In London, Morton, Rose & Company announced subscriptions (as of May 1871) for a £600,000 loan to the M. & St. P. so the company could purchase additional track for its river division. Another £200,000 in bonds were delivered for sales through the Rotterdamshe Bank in Holland, and to attract Dutch investors, F. A. Mueller of Rotterdam was named a M. & St. P. director.[16] Sales advanced rapidly for bonds issued on the completed road to Winona, with $3 million worth quickly disposed of. When it became clear that foreigners would not subscribe for bonds on the unbuilt portion, Morton decided to bring these out at home. In December, the New York firm opened subscriptions for $1 million of gold bonds bearing seven percent interest and invited U. S. investors to furnish funds for the completion of thirty miles of road from La Crescent to Winona. As insurance, the railroad issued securities only as sections of track were finished, and as added security Morton and Sage acted as trustees for the bondholders until the whole line was completed.[17]

Banker presence did not inhibit construction company finance; nor did it restrain what has traditionally been thought of as promoter-induced competition. For again when Morton and Sherman were shaping policy, the board called on investors to loan money to build eighty-five miles of line between Chicago and Milwaukee, running parallel to the track of the Chicago & Northwestern. The new connection, which the directors declared "manifest and pressing,"[18] only increased competition for eastbound traffic from Minnesota, Wisconsin, and northern Texas. "It would have been more economical for both companies," as the *Railroad Gazette* noted critically, "if they had agreed upon terms by which the Milwaukee & St. Paul might have the use of the Northwestern's line from Chicago to Milwaukee either at a fixed rental or in exchange for parts of its line which the Northwestern would like to use."[19]

The maneuvering that had in fact preceded the decision to build unnecessary track reveals the conflicts engendered by early attempts at consolidated system-building in the West and suggests why promoters turned to New York bankers. Sage and Mitchell had both been elected to the C. & N. board in 1868. In the same month Henry Keep, the road's New York president, joined the M. & St. P. board. Then the following year Mitchell replaced Keep as president of the C. & N. after seven members of the ten-man board had also been replaced in this putative transfer of control. With Mitchell as president of both roads, totaling 2,300 miles of line, rivalry decreased considerably.[20] Yet his group's attempts to gain share control failed for lack of ready cash and Mitchell, Sage, and

Keep were quickly ousted from the C. & N. By 1870, New York banker Isaac Sherman had joined Morton on the M. & St. P. board to broaden the corporation's capital base. The banking house of Adrien Iselin had entered the C. & N. management, which had been almost totally reconstituted,[21] and heavily weighted with new New York members.

Despite the subsequent M. & St. P. justification that building a Chicago connection had been dictated by traffic needs, the new track neither assured strategic control nor could it bring desired returns. Indeed, with the parallel track complete, competition between the roads became keener and more bitter than ever before. Vying for traffic proved so injurious that in 1873 the controlling owners agreed to pool earnings as a solution to sustain share value.[22]

With the completion of its building program by 1873, the M. & St. P. laid claim to the shortest and "best possible line of railroad from Chicago to St. Paul" but its financing had become increasingly complex. As a result of expansion total indebtedness came to $26,225,500 in a variety of different issues. With the board's consent, Morton prepared a circular explaining the need for shareholder approval of a $35 million consolidated mortgage for the road, now renamed the Chicago, Milwaukee & St. Paul. According to the plan, Morton, Rose & Company would float the issue abroad.[23] The brisk business in railroad bonds in London, especially with older issues favored, encouraged the move. Notwithstanding the September panic, new loans introduced in the first quarter of 1874 were being promptly marketed, with Morton, Rose & Company particularly successful, having obtained twice the announced amount for an Illinois Central loan.[24] Little difficulty was expected when Morton and Sage were named trustees for the $35 million consolidated mortgage in February 1874.

But in the months that followed, problems of another sort emerged. Alex Mitchell decided to take control. The maneuvering led to a bitter contest, publicized as a struggle between Wall Street and the Northwest, with Mitchell avowedly defending the company from the suspect stock schemes of Sage and Morton. Mitchell, the key political figure in Wisconsin and the unchallenged leader of the business community, had for years held tight control of both economic and political power in the state. He had successfully quelled considerable antimonopoly sentiment until a burst of reform activity in 1874 attracted the support of Milwaukee businessmen. Their rebellion against his own monopoly of banking, railroad, and grain-elevator operations added impetus to swelling farmer demands for railroad rate-law reform and helped crystallize legislation for statutory rate control. It is suggestive that Mitchell's attack on Eastern control came a year after passage of the Potter Law and a year before its repeal, during the interim when Mitchell was actively repairing his old alliance with Milwaukee and state business interests. It certainly could not have hurt him at home when he invoked the self-defense principle against eastern financial manipulators and informed shareholders that "among other contemplated reforms, it is intended that the office in New York shall be used exclusively for the business of this Company and be under management that will have no interest in the stock market inconsistent with that of the shareholders."[25]

The local press, focusing on the sectional aspect of local vs. Eastern control in its appeal to anti-urban, anti-Eastern prejudices, reported that the conflict was over "whether the policy of the Company shall be dictated by Russell Sage and his friends, as representing the interests of New York, or by Mitchell and his friends, as representing the interests of Milwaukee and the Northwest."[26] The antagonism to Wall Street was real enough, but such a simplistic rendering obscures Western antagonism to Mitchell, who continued to be attacked in the Granger press for policies declared detrimental to community and agrarian needs. The rhetoric of East-West hostility, indiscriminately invoked in the 1870s, frequently masked, as in this case, the complexity of local interests and the similar economic ethos shared by Eastern and Western commercial capitalists. If anything, shared economic values merely intensified the struggle for control.

At the beginning of June 1875, a new mortgage presented to the board named the Farmers' Loan and Trust Company of New York as trustee. Then as a result of an election that same month, "several of the persons who had acted as . . .[directors] from the commencement of the road were left out of the Board and new men elected in their places."[27] The unidentified members "left out" were, of course, Sage and Morton. New York banker Julius Wadsworth succeeded Sage as vice-president and the new board now approved the new consolidated sinking-fund mortgage instead of that prepared by Morton. Though Morton's managerial participation came to an end, his relationship to the road was not entirely severed. He and Bliss still had an account in H. & D. securities and were called upon to directly finance new construction by the end of the decade. Also, during the market upsurge of

1879, Mitchell and Wadsworth unhesitatingly called on the banking house to purchase and place millions more of C. M. & St. P. bonds.

Reviewing the building of the early 1870s, Henry Varnum Poor entered the following indictment:

> The parties largely chargeable with the excess of line not called for by any business want are the railroad companies themselves. A spirit of rivalry, or advantage to parties connected with these works, has led to the construction of a large extent of unproductive mileage. The greatest offenders in this direction are the Chicago and Northwestern, the Toledo, Wabash and Western, the Michigan Southern, and the Erie. The Toledo, Wabash and Western and the Erie have in consequence been forced into liquidation. The Chicago and Northwestern and the Milwaukee and St. Paul have probably sacrificed the value of their share capital upon wild and visionary schemes.[28]

Morton's firm not only assisted with these "wild and visionary schemes," but had a hand too in stock manipulation. Isaac Sherman resigned from the board in 1872, but his partner, William Duncan, was a director of the ill-famed Erie in this same period. Moreover, these reputable financiers had worked in close alliance with two of the most censured railroad promoters of the era, Russell Sage and Oakes Ames, apparently with little discernible difference in their ethics and mores. Similarly questionable are sectional distinctions contrasting the conservative business morality of Easterners with the more aggressive stance of Westerners.

The profits proffered by interregional construction beckoned bankers South as well as West. The same year, 1870, that Morton joined with Oakes Ames on the board of the Hastings & Dakota, he joined with him also to finance, build, and operate the first all-rail route from New Orleans to Texas. Besides Ames, Morton, and his partner, George Bliss, the banking group financing the project included Louis Von Hoffman and Joseph Seligman. Former New York governor and senator, Edwin D. Morgan, together with the most notorious of all bosses, Tammany William Tweed, as well as John A. Stewart, Sub-Treasurer of the United States during the Civil War, completed the syndicate which agreed to purchase control of the small, but strategic, southern line, the New Orleans, Mobile & Chattanooga. The acquisition attested to Southerners' reports that "nearly all the new lines of railway that are projected in this section, and many of the completed roads that can be used in extending long through lines, are in possession of keen, enterprising and energetic capitalists in the North who seek safe investments."[29]

The new directors took over the road, completed 140 miles from Mobile to New Orleans in October 1870 with the intent of extending the line west of the Mississippi into Texas as far as Houston.[30] Both Bliss and Von Hoffman were also directors of the Illinois Central, and were considering plans for an I.C. north-south tie to New Orleans. Morton and Seligman were directors of the Katy and envisioned an eventual route for this company from Kansas City south to New Orleans. For these bankers the New Orleans road would be the southern base of the triangle, supporting their other ventures.

Promises of government guarantees and liberal aid further enhanced the project as a promising field for capital employment. Louisiana considered the line so important that the state made an outright donation of $3 million in eight percent bonds; subscribed to $2.5 million of capital stock to be paid for in state bonds drawing eight percent interest; and endorsed the road's second mortgage bonds to the extent of $25,000 per mile. The city of New Orleans granted the company perpetual use of depot grounds said to be worth about $1 million. And by special law, Alabama and Mississippi exempted the company from all taxes. With such liberal state and municipal incentives success seemed assured.[31]

Reorganized as the New Orleans, Mobile & Texas, the 475-mile route, touted as a great trunk line, would connect New Orleans and Mobile in the East, and would offer the only rail connection between New Orleans and Texas in the West. The railway, designed to traverse four states—Alabama, Mississippi, Louisiana, and Texas—was billed as passing through vast districts with "unlimited possibilities" having "enormous productive resources" for cotton, sugar, molasses, rice, wheat, and corn.[32]

Construction, financed by the directors, began immediately. By the summer of 1871 track reached sixty miles west of New Orleans to Donaldsonville. On its completion, the board announced first and second mortgage bonds to the amount of $12,500 per mile at ninety with interest of eight percent currency payable in New York, or seven percent gold payable in London. By the fall of 1872, the funded debt of the road stood at $13,950,000; $11,125,000 of first-mortgage bonds and $2,825,000 second-mortgage bonds.[33] Still to be finished was the road to the Sabine. Under the terms of the state land grant, it had to be completed by the summer of 1873, and the remainder of the route to Houston in the six months following.[34]

The project which just two years earlier had begun so auspiciously now encountered opposition from local steamship interests, just when the tightening of the money market increased the difficulty of finding outside funds. Impeded in mobilizing the loan capital urgently needed to finish the stretch west to Houston, the directors charged that Charles Morgan had deliberately created distrust in the securities of the State of Louisiana. Morgan, who operated a steamship line which carried the traffic from Berwick Bay to Galveston, was not about to allow a competitive carrier to take the business, at least not without a struggle, and it was said that he had instigated political efforts to foil the building into Texas. In the Louisiana legislature, the railroad measures, granting the company over $4 million in aid, suddenly became a subject of "violent controversy."[35] Accusations that bribery had bought their passage were matched by allegations that competing shipping interests had tried, with payoffs, to thwart their adoption. The charges and countercharges which resounded somewhat belatedly in the legislature injured the company's reputation. Equally damning was a widely distributed circular signed by 300 prominent citizens of New Orleans claiming that the state would repudiate "certain state bonds should they be negotiated."[36] In question were the $2.5 million state bonds in payment for the subscription of stock intended to facilitate building into Texas.

Hoping to calm the situation, the railroad mobilized a group calling itself the Railroad Committee of Fifty of New Orleans. It circulated a counter-declaration insisting that the state had no intention to repudiate any portion of the bonds issued to this company, provided the company complete its road to the Sabine and the branch to Shreveport. The group pledged to "assist the company in every way in its power."[37] Meanwhile, a New York syndicate consisting of the company's directors, and a New Orleans syndicate headed by the local State National Bank, agreed to finance construction from Donaldsonville to Houston. An issue was made of $3.5 million income bonds, secured by $7,419,000 state bonds, to be distributed pro rata among subscribers. The state securities were placed with the banking firm of J. & W. Seligman and the new bonds were to be taken from the Seligmans and paid for at fifty cents on the dollar as the road progressed in ten-mile sections. As the work was done and until the sections were completed, the money would be paid by the syndicates to the contracting company, Messrs. Bushnell & Company. The Seligmans headed the subscription, taking $1 million worth of bonds for half the face value. The New Orleans group, it was expected, would take another million, leaving a million and a half for other parties.[38]

Building did begin, but little of the road to the Sabine was completed, when in May 1873 foreclosure and sale of the road was announced. Officially, suit had been brought by the first mortgage bondholders, of $4 million worth of securities, who had not received interest in six months. Actually, the proceedings had been initiated by the directors who were both stockholders and creditors of the corporation. When the road came up for sale in New Orleans on June 7, 1873, they purchased it in four separate sections through their trustee representatives. Even after the sale, the directors still hoped for an agreement with the state legislature to continue support. When they appeared in New Orleans in December, they tried to convince the legislature to guarantee the sums already granted. They sought, too, the withdrawal of the injunction against the road for defaulting on bonded interest payments. Frank Ames, who succeeded Oliver Ames and Edwin Morgan as trustee for the line west of the Mississippi, claimed the right to an issue of subsidy bonds as soon as the road was completed west to Vermillionville. If Ames's demand had been admitted by Governor Kellog, he would have invalidated all of the state's claims against the old company. Instead, the state refused to enter into any arrangement and the Superior Court issued a Writ of Sequestration resulting in seizure of the property until 1874.[39]

What we have, then, is the story of private bankers joining with private capitalists to purchase the stock of a small but strategic Southern road. Richly supported by government guarantees and looking to interregional traffic ties, they willingly risked financing construction of a major through route in the Southwest. When local rivalry and politics hampered bond sales in 1872 in an already stringent money market, the backers added further funds for continued construction, but still could not find the necessary market capital to complete the extension. Default and bankruptcy were in fact decided on by the directors themselves, who thought it better to have the road brought up for resale and reorganization so they could retain the land grant; that is, have it reassigned by the court to newly formed companies they controlled. The panic in

September, followed by a long and severe depression, further altered their plans. Complicated negotiations persisted until 1881 before the different sections were taken out of the hands of the trustees. The settlements intertwined with the plans of Charles Morgan and the North Louisiana & Texas; with Collis P. Huntington's designs in the Southwest; and with the growth of the Louisville & Nashville. During these years, as we shall subsequently see, the matter of sustaining the different companies and their disposition was determined by bankers George Bliss, Louis Von Hoffman, and Joseph Seligman. The failure of the project did not automatically mean that the "insiders" lost their investment; the financial difficulties did, however, insure the bankers' engagement over a considerable period in deciding the fate of the property to recoup their investments.

Promotion of this New Orleans to Texas connection must be placed in the context of the bankers' other railroad affiliations. In 1870, George Bliss was the director of the Illinois Central when that company made plans for a north-south acquisition. He and Von Hoffman, also a director of the I.C., could thus look forward to a Chicago connection for their New Orleans project.[40] That same year, Morton and Seligman had joined the management of the Union Pacific Southern Branch as it began its expansion program. If plans went well, the line would reach New Orleans from Kansas City via the Arkansas and Red Rivers.[41] And if a connection materialized, as planned, for this road to meet the Missouri Pacific, in which Seligman had an interest, yet another link would be forged to contribute to the pattern of overlapping interregional through ties. The formation of capital alliances within the banking community was an inevitable by-product of such business since the magnitude of these ventures and the liability involved were simply too large for one firm to cover.

The appeal of direct financing of interregional schemes and the banker alliances which resulted are again well illustrated in the case of the Katy. In 1868, a group of Eastern financiers headed by Levi Parsons, president of the Land Grant Railway & Trust Company, obtained share control of the Union Pacific Southern Branch. "Our object," Parsons imperiously announced to the local board, "is to build your road and we come sufficiently endorsed to meet no opposition."[42] Having been immediately empowered to name the executive officers, he designated J. B. Dickinson, president of the Tenth National Bank of New York, president, and George C. Clark, of the private banking firm Clark, Dodge & Company, secretary. An executive committee was specifically created to act for the board that consisted of directors Parsons, Dickinson, and Thad Walker—"and thereafter the business of the railroad was transacted largely in the offices of the Land Grant Railway & Trust Company."[43]

A year later, Morton's associates in the M. & St. P., Russell Sage and M. A. Cowdry, were brought in as trustees for a $4.3 million first mortgage placed on 170 miles of track and a Congressional land grant of 1.3 million acres. Soon after Seligman, Morton, and August Belmont joined the board. As of May 1870, Parsons' Land Grant Company held over 10,000 of the road's shares; J. & W. Seligman & Company, 1,900 shares; August Belmont, 1,501 shares; Morton, Bliss & Company, 1,472 shares; George Clark, 200 shares.[44] Since those involved may have had joint accounts listed in the name of other shareholders—a frequent practice—these figures do not necessarily reflect actual holdings, but even in revealing minimum estimates they indicate group banker control.

The plan of the financier-directors, which Parsons announced to the local managers, was to reach the southern boundary of Kansas before James Joy, president of the Chicago, Burlington & Quincy, in order to build through Indian Territory and claim the three-million-acre land grant promised by Congress. Their aim to integrate specialized production centers with distant markets had been explicitly formulated. They would build east to join the Missouri Pacific at Sedalia, and build and buy roads offering an outlet to Kansas City and St. Louis to connect the cattle regions of Texas with the markets of the North and East. Such a route would "be instrumental in largely developing eastern Kansas and western Missouri, which are justly considered the finest agricultural sections of the West, and will form a connecting link between the great cattle-raising regions of Texas and the cattle-consuming sections of the North, the value of which can scarcely be estimated."[45] Underlying these developmental plans was the anticipated market value of securities which were expected to appreciate: at first, simply by the announcement of the project, and in the long-run through increased traffic returns. In keeping with these goals, the name of the company was changed in March 1870 to the Missouri, Kansas & Texas, popularly called the Katy.

From all accounts, the future looked promising for the Katy,

The Missouri, Kansas & Texas Railway, 1873.
Courtesy of The New-York Historical Society, New York City.

which in 1870 ran through 180 miles of the choicest parts of Kansas, "thickly settled" by immigrants from the North and East. The *Railroad Gazette* concluded that "there is at the present time nowhere in the United States so remarkable an increase in population and such an extension of civilization into the wilderness as in the country southwest of Chicago and chiefly in Kansas. Texas might possibly dispute the claim, but we will settle the dispute by including Texas with Kansas."[46] The project kindled by the optimism of the boom and sustained by Eastern bankers seemed certain. Besides the potential traffic loomed the possibility of the coveted land grant, and in addition Texas had become a "Canaan" for railroad builders with its assurances of state subsidies.[47]

In 1871, just as the Katy succeeded in reaching Indian Territory, disturbing reports reached the directors that the Atlantic & Pacific was trying to take control of the Missouri Pacific in an effort to corner the traffic of the Southwest by cutting the Katy off from the Sedalia interchange. In the ensuing struggle, the A. & P. did get control, intending to ruin the Katy and then acquire it through foreclosure. At this point, Seligman, a director of the M. P., withdrew from the Katy board and was quickly replaced by J. P. Morgan.[48]

The next two years held difficulties, but building continued at a rapid pace. The main line had been constructed from Hannibal, Missouri, to Dennison, Texas—577 miles. With branch lines the system totaled 787 miles. While millions for continuing construction had been obtained in London, Amsterdam, and Frankfurt, after 1872 the company failed to find loan capital either at home or abroad for continued building to the Southwest. Although gross earnings continued to increase (even into 1874), the company was compelled to issue floating obligations and dipped into current earnings in 1872.[49] When the money-market tightness culminated in the panic of September 1873, the company did not meet or renew these obligations. With the failure of the Union Trust Company, trustees of a Katy mortgage, default followed.

Morton and Morgan took over at once as the new trustees of the mortgage. Parsons was dispatched to Europe to pacify disgruntled bondholders and gain their approval for deferring interest payments. Holders of temporary obligations were similarly asked to defer claims. Meanwhile, Morton and Morgan, representing bondholders' committees in the major money markets, attempted to reorganize,[50] only to encounter internecine maneuvering.

It appears that Sage and his group had sold out to Gould and his representative, William Bond. Exactly what the issues were and who stood where are not clear. The road's biographer assumes that the honest bankers stood opposed to Sage, Gould, and the forces of greed. Yet whatever the immediate source of contention, Sage and Morton were working hand in hand at the time in the M. & St. P. and Morton was also the financial agent for Gould in the Union Pacific. According to V. V. Masterson, "On October 22, [1873] Jay Gould surreptitiously entered the Katy. Through his henchman, the crafty moneylender Russell Sage, who held the mortgage covering the Katy's Union Pacific Southern Branch bond issue, Gould had placed on the Board one of his own men, William Bond, president of the Denver Road." But perhaps the entry of Gould was not so surreptitious after all. At any rate, when the bankers, as trustees, requested that Bond, who was president protem in Parsons' absence, step down in favor of Parsons, their demand was denied. "The two tycoons in high dudgeon immediately threw the company into bankruptcy."[51]

There is no question that default and bankruptcy injured the reputation of the investment bankers, particularly in Europe. But for at least two years they had successfully sold bonds, received the profits of a rising security market, and benefited from the construction company financing of the new track. And in 1872 the possibility of profits tempted J. P. Morgan to join the company when Seligman resigned. According to Masterson, the bankers "withdrew their interests in the company" in 1876 when the Gould faction effected a reorganization.[52] But at the close of 1877, Bliss was still negotiating with the Land Grant Railway & Trust Co. In January 1878, he wrote that not a day passed that he did not press for settlement for the M. K. & T.[53] In 1879, Gould gained complete control of the Katy after arranging with the Dutch bondholders and making heavy purchases of the common stock.[54] For the bankers, whose mode was to hold out, Gould's takeover and the rising securities prices of 1878 and 1879 probably allowed them to recoup losses suffered during the intervening years. At the close of 1879, after Gould had taken control, Morton, Rose & Company came to a settlement with the Land Grant Railway & Trust Company which left the London house "a considerable sum."[55]

If the profits to be made in financing new companies entailed risk, the expansion projects of stable, well-established roads seemed

safer. When called on to place the loans of finished and paying
roads, private bankers anticipated little difficulty in 1869 and
1870. Investors both at home and abroad were seeking choice
securities. Those of the Illinois Central, which had paid dividends
of ten percent each year from 1865 to 1870, were absolutely gilt-
edged. So when the I.C. turned its attention to acquiring a new
connection for southern traffic, it had no problem in enlisting the
cooperation of the financial community.

Expansion had begun cautiously in 1867 when, looking west, the
I.C. took a first step to extend beyond its original north-south
charter line and fulfill long-term plans sketched in the 1850s. To
obtain an east-west link between Chicago and the Missouri River,
the company leased the Dubuque & Sioux City and assumed the
sublease for the Cedar Falls & Minnesota. This procedure, essentially a traffic agreement, required the I.C. to pay the leasee thirty-
five percent of gross traffic revenues.[56] Then in 1869, the year
George Bliss became a director, the company completed, at a cost
of $1 million, a bridge across the Mississippi from Dunleith to
Dubuque. Four hundred miles of road in Iowa were thereby added
to the seven hundred in Illinois to create a system extending north
to Minnesota and from Chicago west (via Dubuque) to Sioux
City.[57]

The entrance of private bankers into the I.C. management is
usually identified with the financial troubles of the later 1870s: "A
coalition of old and highly respectable New York financiers and
bankers such as the Astors, Belmonts, and Morton, Bliss and
Company . . . had gradually, between 1877 and 1885, interested
themselves in the Illinois Central."[58] However, it was in 1870 that
George Bliss was joined on the board by Louis Von Hoffman and
J. P. Morgan, the latter a director of the leased Dubuque & Sioux
City. Their support proved of special importance to William
Osborn, former president of the company, who had hopes of
perfecting a Southern tie to offset Eastern trunkline competition.
With long-haul grain traffic seriously jeopardized by the extension
of the Pennsylvania and New York Central systems west, Osborn
believed a direct I.C. connection from Chicago south to the Gulf
would divert some of the grain freight to New Orleans and Mobile.
While the directors "approached the subject with great
hesitation," the damage to the grain freight, coupled to the
threatened local lumber and coal traffic, convinced the more conservative to comply with Osborn's urgings for new strategies.[59]

The consolidation plan worked out in 1872 later became a com-

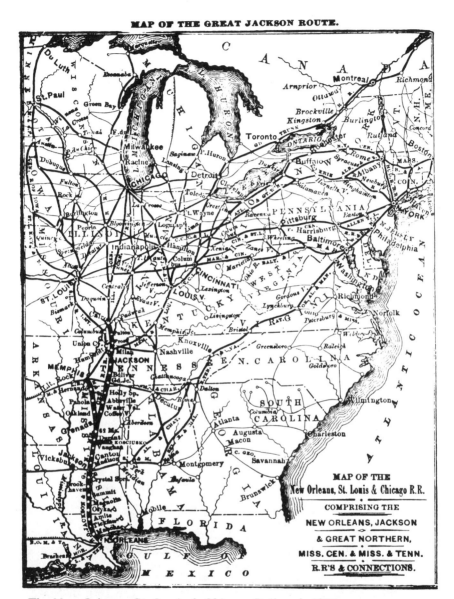

The New Orleans, St. Louis & Chicago Railroad, 1874.
Stuart Collection, Rare Book Division, The New York Public Library,
Astor, Lenox and Tilden Foundations.

mon model for such agreements. The I.C. contracted with the Mississippi Central and the New Orleans, Jackson & Great Northern—two roads operated under joint management as a single trunk line—for direct rail communication from the Gulf to almost the mouth of the Ohio at Jackson, Tennessee. The contract resembled a simple traffic agreement, with the stipulation that the Southern lines would issue new consolidated mortgages bearing an I.C. recommendation to bolster sales of the lesser-known companies' securities, particularly among English investors. Part of the funds would go to build the Mississippi Central 108 miles to East Cairo for a traffic exchange with the I.C.; part would be used to improve the New Orleans, Jackson & Great Northern. Originally, the I.C. agreed to invest one-eighth of its annual earnings from the traffic interchange in the consolidated bonds, but then to assure more monies the board decided to purchase up to $6 million at par, outright, at the rate of $200,000 a year.[60]

The next step was to take control, and again the technique employed later became common. After the completed 1,650-mile route opened in December 1873, the I.C. advanced $5 million in exchange for the Southern lines' seven percent bonds. Then to replenish the treasury, it floated a loan of $5 million in discounted I.C. five percent bonds, secured by the consolidated mortgage issue. Interest from the $5 million seven percent Southern bonds was placed in a fund to meet the interest and pay the principal for their own issue. The two percent gained by the exchange served as a sinking fund to retire all the I.C. bonds before maturity, leaving $5 million in the treasury free of cost.

The bankers on the board had such confidence in the I.C.'s standing abroad that in London, five months after Cooke's failure, Morton, Rose & Company announced the opening of subscriptions to the $5 million sterling issue:

The Illinois Central Railroad Company, through Messrs. Morton, Rose & Co., are inviting applications to an issue of £1,000,000 in five percent sterling sinking fund bonds of £200 each at the price of 84 percent, or £168 per £200 bond; 10 percent is payable on allotment, 40 percent on the 16th of March, and 34 percent on the 15th of April. The loan is raised for the purchase of an equal amount of the 7 percent consolidated gold bonds of the New Orleans, Jackson & Great Northern and Mississippi Central Railroads, with which roads the Illinois Company has made arrangements for direct through communication between Chicago and New Orleans over a conjoined mileage of 1,650 miles. The Illinois Company covenants that this issue shall be included in any future mortgage which hereafter shall be created, and that such mortgage shall be made to secure no more than $15,000,000, which shall include all prior liens on the mortgaged property, and without preference.[61]

The loan proved an immediate success. In New York, Morton, Bliss & Company announced to the press that subscriptions in London, with bonds selling at eighty-four, had netted $10.5 million—over twice the amount called for. The prestige of the banking house coupled to the road's reputation attracted investors. Sterling issues with interest payable in London enjoyed a particularly distinguished position and, moreover, the bonds had been offered at substantial discount besides being favored by a sinking fund provision.[62]

The I.C. had been exceptionally prosperous in the 1860s. In the early 1870s after the bankers had entered the management, traffic returns, though threatened by competition, were still high enough so that the company's earnings allowed a dividend of ten percent in 1873 and eight percent in 1874. Declines in revenue from public land sales had only just begun to show up,[63] but here too, as in the case of less established companies, by mid-decade private bankers were charged with resolving unexpected difficulties.

Like other private bankers, George Bliss and Levi Morton had readily invested their own and clients' funds in long-range plans for new construction to tie together the North, South, East, and West. They looked ahead to an integrated system, with overlapping triangular trade routes, extending east and west from Chicago and reaching south to points along the Gulf. Grodinsky contends that when it came to Western roads "even seasoned, hard bitten capitalists hesitated to commit their funds." As for the South, Stover maintains that "Northern capitalists were still reluctant to invest any large sums in Southern ventures in the early 1870s."[64] If anything, these bankers had shared in the naive optimism which characterized decision-making during the early 1870s and the difficulties that resulted derived specifically from the scope and size of projects they advocated. In directing different enterprises stretching over vast areas, they were continually confronted with internal as well as external problems, ranging from the maneuvering of on-the-scene personnel for domination of corporate policy, to the competing plans of local and Eastern capitalists seeking to extend control over the traffic of the South and West. Unexpected changes in government policy and the stringency of the money markets added further to these difficulties. By mid-decade, the capital needs of heavily funded, large-scale projects brought default, insolvency, receivership, foreclosure, and reorganization to almost all of the roads they had affiliated with.

PART II

Resolving Railroad Tie-Ups

Introduction to Part II

For the first time in eight years the construction figures for 1874 presaged a brake on railroad expansion. Only 2,117 miles of road were built that year compared to 4,026 in 1873, 5,870 in 1872, and 7,379 in 1871. The check to the "railroad interest" appeared "inevitable," since much of the construction of the preceding period exceeded the nation's needs.[1] But as for long-term investment, the forecast remained favorable for several reasons. Although competition had generally reduced rates, costs of labor and materials had also declined substantially. These economies of operation had meanwhile been accompanied by actual increases in tonnage, pushing earnings in 1874 to considerably higher levels than those of 1873. Lower rates might continue, still Poor's *Manual* unhesitatingly predicted that the ratio of net returns to gross would continue to increase. Quick recovery in overall business conditions was expected so that despite the defaults and difficulties, opinion generally regarding investment opportunities stayed sanguine.[2] M. E. Ingalls, president of the Indianapolis, Cincinnati & Lafayette, expressed a widely held view when he assured the directors in June 1874 that "the effects of the panic are fast wearing away and general business will soon be as good as before the 19th of last September."[3] Improved traffic from the West sustained confidence well into 1875 when the combination of reduced rates, traffic, and new construction touched off a marked shift from railroad securities.[4]

In 1873, foreigners were not, as Rendigs Fels suggests, "shunning new issues of railroad securities"; nor after the panic was "the shortage of capital accentuated because foreign investors stopped buying American securities."[5] Like domestic investors, they had indeed become suspicious, but, as the *Chronicle* emphasized, of *issues of new companies*. By contrast, the demand for new bonds of established companies on completed road continued strong. London would take them if "offered by the right parties" and J. S. Morgan "placed several loans at good prices" in the first half of 1874.[6] Early in 1874, the bonds of the Illinois Central were oversubscribed in London for twice the call of $5 million, and the Speyers intended to place a large block of Southern Pacific land-grant bonds.[7] The demand in London for first-class bonds also prompted the $35 million consolidated mortgage issued by the board of the Chicago, Milwaukee & St. Paul in March 1874, while the month of June brought cable dispatches reporting negotiations in England of bonds of $2 million for the Eastern Railroad of Massachusetts and similar sales for the Northern Central and the Wyoming Coal & Iron railroads. At the same time, the Penn-sylvania successfully merchandised its consolidated issue abroad.[8]

Even in 1875 a Dutch financial writer still looked to the bright side. Noting that forty-eight percent of the bonds held in Holland paid no interest and four and a half percent paid less than half, he observed that all issues made or guaranteed by old companies paid in full. In spite of the lamentable experience with new companies which unfortunately had created distrust—the sound roads could still be relied on.[9] However, if first-rate investment houses could still find foreign buyers for long-term credits of established dividend-paying corporations, one consequence of the panic which did affect capital imports, as the Pennsylvania discovered, was that the low exchange rate of the dollar reduced anticipated receipts from foreign bond sales.[10]

A business revival still seemed just on the horizon in the early part of 1875. As the *Railroad Gazette* pointed out, "the effects of the panic, it was thought, would begin to pass away."[11] Net earn-ings, a key economic indicator, had been larger in 1874 than in 1873. The new figures on receivership, which more often than not were taken as advertisements of economic malady, also allayed suspicions. In January 1874, only three percent of total track, 2,329 miles, belonging to seventeen companies had been assigned to receivers, while the nine percent reported in January 1875 did not as yet signal trouble.[12]

Gradually, however, the full severity of repeated blows to the in-dustry became apparent. Rail rates dipped to the lowest levels "ever known" during 1875 and at the same time the volume of leading staple traffic declined precipitously over the year. An-thracite coal shipments registered losses of thirty-seven percent;

Northwestern grain traffic was off by thirty-five percent, and the volume of Southern cotton by twenty-seven percent. Since these declines had not been offset by further reductions in working expenses, the large funded debts of old as well as new companies could not be met.[13] By January 1876, the number of miles in receivership had reached seventeen percent.[14]

Granger legislation put the final onus on railroad credit abroad. "Throughout Europe the opinion prevailed that capital invested in American railroads—in Northwestern railroads especially—was at the mercy of a reckless and unprincipled democracy. The result was not only a total cessation of new investments in such railroads, but a withdrawal of the old ones."[15] George Bliss wrote repeatedly during 1876 of unsatisfactory conditions both North and South. By the spring he feared that the uneasiness in London, reflected in stock prices, would reach panic proportions, though he hoped that the Centennial Exhibition in Philadelphia celebrating industrial growth might make the public "think less of the skeletons among their own assets."[16] When railroad rates continued to slide through the summer, William Osborn, of the Illinois Central, also sensed fears of panic.[17] There was "little money loaning on time except for mortgages for long periods, nor by banks, and the latter, if they accept low rates, generally confine themselves to demand or very short term loans."[18] The winter saw no improvement in traffic returns owing to diminished business aggravated by severe competition. The number of miles in receivership climbed to an alarming peak of eighteen percent and the lessening value of railway securities created "universal distrust."[19] It became difficult for railways to borrow short-term funds, except on the best collateral, and few investors, either private or institutional, would put money into new companies. Railroad capitalization dipped to a trough in 1876.[20]

Not until the third quarter of 1877 did good crops in the Northwest and South hold out promise of recovery. With the economies of operation introduced since 1873, improved business, it was expected, would tell rapidly in net earnings. Such hopes and those for even better times after the election sent securities up in the fall of 1877. The advance proved temporary, with rate wars, strikes, and Granger regulation continuing to cloud investment prospects until 1879.[21]

Since the role of railroad financiers had not yet been fixed in what was still a pioneer industry, the financial strains proved crucial. The depression, calculated as the longest and, in monetary

	Mileage		Investment (in millions of dollars)	
Year	Road Operated (Dec. 31)	%Change from Preceding Year	Capital Stock & Bonded Debt	%Change from Preceding Year
1874	72,385	+ 3.0	4,221	+11.5
1875	74,096	+ 2.4	4,658	+10.4
1876	76,808	+ 3.7	4,468	- 4.1
1877	79,082	+ 3.0	4,806	+ 7.6
1878	81,747	+ 3.4	4,772	- .7
%Change 1874-1878		+12.9		+ 13.1

Railroad Mileage and Investment: 1874-1878

SOURCE: Adapted from U.S. Bureau of the Census, *Historical Statistics of the United States, Colonial Times to 1970* (Washington, D.C.: Government Printing Office, 1975), part 2, pp. 731, 734.

terms, one of the most severe on record,[22] altered earlier commitments and expanded banker-influence. That depressions would intensify dependence on bankers' services became apparent as early as the panic of 1857, but in the mid-1870s bankers emerged as major problem solvers for considerably more complicated corporate structures. As stockholder-directors, they were called on to devise methods to rehabilitate vast systems in distress. Their bondholder clients similarly turned to them either to purchase and operate defaulted properties, or arrange for lease or sale agreements. Railroad executives sorely in need of operating funds or long-term credits to complete construction projects also became increasingly open to banker initiatives and intervention.

The railroad business of Morton, Bliss & Company in the 1870s illustrates the effects of the pronounced alterations in the business cycle which characterized the decade. How the bankers reacted in this experimental period to salvage their own and clients' investments, their motives and diverse tactics, will be explored in the following chapters. Each is a case study of how they resolved railroad tie-ups initiated or aggravated by the cyclical decline and each points to a dominant principle—they increased their involvement and investments while holding out for recovery.

4
Protecting Share Capital: The Indianapolis, Cincinnati & Lafayette

The history of the Indianapolis, Cincinnati & Lafayette railroad in the 1870s highlights the alternative possibilities of banker behavior in response first to prosperity and then to the protracted business downturn. The management of this company, dominated for the entire decade by financiers George Bliss, John Kennedy, and Thomas Perkins, illustrates many of the modes accompanying group-banker control. Here again we find a pattern in which Eastern bankers became major shareholders, wrested control from local interests, and when confronted soon after with the complications of continuing depression, remained active in the company's direction. Their primary aim had been to recoup their own share capital as well as a variety of securities, or as George Bliss recounted, "to save what we could fairly for ourselves and others. For a time we wholly failed in this and there was no hope of any return for the large sum invested in the Company in Shares, and some of the junior securities were only of a nominal value."[1]

After a decade of financial experiments the bankers realized a profit. Receivership in October 1870, followed by bankruptcy, foreclosure sale, and reorganization in 1871, did not as we might assume reflect loss to the insiders. On the contrary, these devices provided novel legal solutions for alleviating financial difficulties. They insured continuing control so that the property could be scaled down financially and new strategies implemented. When default and receivership were resorted to again in 1876, stock depreciation followed, but the bankers soon began buying low-priced securities to increase their equity in a future reorganization. Returns from heavy inside purchases eventually validated their belief in a self-adjusting market mechanism and what is more conditioned investment decisions during the next decade.

Although banker strategy centered originally on transforming this local road into an east-west through system, plans sketched in the early 1870s for a trade route south emerged as a dominant goal to offset the disastrous effects of Eastern trunkline competition. Not only did the expanded system survive the depression intact, but new building and new combinations were first on the ambitious agenda of 1879.

Morton, Bliss & Company had no direct investments in this corporation and did not perform any service for the railroad until 1880, when it agreed to act as Transfer Agent to handle the exchange of old securities for those of the reorganized road. George Bliss, however, as a major stockholder and creditor, served continuously as a director from 1869. Although the monies he invested were for his own account rather than for his firm's, as observed earlier, personal outlays had to be approved by all the banking copartners and had to be consistent with the firm's investment portfolio.[2] Furthermore, Bliss's behavior derived from his specialized relationship to the money market and reflects concerted action with other investment bankers.

A year after Appomattox, a small local line, the Cincinnati & Indianapolis, consolidated with another local road, the Indianapolis & Lafayette, which served as a connecting link between the Ohio River and Chicago. The merged lines incorporated as the Indianapolis, Cincinnati & Lafayette Railroad and three years later the young company operated 289 miles of track, including two leased branch lines, the Cincinnati & Martinsville and the Whitewater Railroad.[3] To secure funds, Cincinnati promoters brought New York railroad financier John Kennedy and Boston banker Joseph Fay into the management in 1868, and in 1869 George Bliss joined the directorate.

Banker management produced an immediate impact. Within a year the Circuit Court at Indianapolis had appointed a receiver for the road creating nothing short of a "sensation" in business and railroad circles. The court action completely surprised the industry for here was a solvent company and the main line, which ran from Cincinnati to Lafayette, a distance of 179 miles, enjoyed "a better business than ever before."[4]

Receivership was rare in 1870—only three were declared during the whole year—and besides, such action commonly denoted default on bonded interest as preliminary to foreclosure of a mortgage.[5] Nothing of this sort had occurred, though the company reported some loss on its branch lines, the Martinsville and the Whitewater Valley. Possible explanations abounded in the press. One account alleged that the Pennsylvania had secured a controlling interest and adopted this tactic to bring about a change in management. The Pennsylvania could use the road to advantage to complete the main line between Chicago and Cincinnati and as a feeder to Indianapolis. Simultaneous rumors spread of an agreement between the I. C. & L. and the B. & O. for a traffic interchange or some "other close relationship." Possibly the B. & O. had acquired it as a valuable feeder for its Marietta & Cincinnati line and planned a through route to Chicago by building a connecting line from Lafayette to Kankakee.[6]

The speculation missed the mark. Receivership granted atypically in this instance, reflected the complaints of leading stockholders. The plaintiffs, the bankers on the board, had decided to take control and to transform an essentially local operation into an east-west interregional through route.[7] As they saw it, the company suffered from a $7 million debt for the construction of branch lines the bankers believed dead weights. The expense of the branches ran over $100,000 a year, and coupled to rentals, guaranteed by perpetual leases, the cost was exorbitant. Moreover, the road's other liabilities included a floating debt of over $1.2 million plus overdue interest coupons.

Kennedy had accused the president, H. C. Lord, and the Cincinnati directors of questionable purchases of materials in addition to appropriation of securities for personal use, and charged them with general mismanagement. Unless they agreed to an immediate receivership, Kennedy threatened that the bankers would refuse funds for operating costs, for further construction on the branches, and for interest payments on the bonded debt; they would force the road into bankruptcy.[8] Rather than bankruptcy, the bankers much preferred a legal means for effecting policy change swiftly—before the next scheduled election. At their urgings, the court appointed Thomas A. Morris as receiver on October 26, 1870. Morris, a director, stockholder, and creditor of the road also happened to be president of the Indianapolis & St. Louis, a line that figured in the financiers' strategy.[9]

In theory, the receiver, supposed to be a completely

disinterested party appointed by the court during pending litigation, functioned impartially to protect all concerned. However,
the legislation covering receivership dated mainly from the eight-
eenth century, when it was designed for the dissolution of banking
corporations and business partnerships. In the post-Civil War era
the meager existing legislation lacked specific applicability to
railroads. As late as the 1880s virtually no federal legislation per-
tained to railroad receiverships, while the statutes of the states and
territories were likewise few and inappropriate.[10] Without a legal
definition of a disinterested party, or a codification of his specific
powers and duties, the receiver remained, in effect, unrestrained
by the law and subject only to the judgments of the courts. The
courts meanwhile could formulate policy and they did so, frequently with little regard for the existing legislation. Here, the
court, in appointing Morris, had disregarded the single most common restriction in the existing legislation—that no party, attorney,
or person interested in the company's suit be so appointed.

Immediately after Morris' appointment, election of a new board
reenforced the bankers' control. Joseph Fay gave up his seat,
although he remained intimately concerned with the company's
financing. Another Bostonian, Thomas Perkins, of an old-line
mercantile family, became a director in his place and his banking
firm, Head & Perkins, became the road's Transfer Agent. Melville
Ingalls, also of Boston, was brought in as a director and to be
president protem, while William Harris completed the Boston
group. All the New Yorkers—George Bliss, John Kennedy, and
William Booth—were reelected.[11] When the composition of the
board changed during the 1870s, the three financiers, Bliss,
Perkins, and Kennedy retained their seats in every election; and in
1877, when Perkins considered resigning, Bliss forcefully objected,
indicating the importance he assigned to the position.

> I am not prepared to express an opinion in which of the two
> positions you name, you could be most useful to the I.C.L.F.
> Personally I should much regret that a necessity should arise for
> your resignation as Director. I will confer with Mr. Booth, and
> when an opportunity occurs, with Mr. Ingalls on the subject.
> Meantime I hope you will let matters rest as they are.[12]

Before going ahead with refinancing, the bankers had insisted as
"a preliminary condition to their lending money that they . . . be
represented in the receivership"[13] by Melville Ingalls. They held a
substantial share of the equity capital, had already advanced

funds, and planned to mobilize long-term credits. From their perspective it had become imperative to insure an uncontested voice before the court. Notifications to local stockholders politely informed them that more than two-thirds of the stock and the greater part of floating debt were now held in Massachusetts, New York, and Rhode Island, so "for the purpose of obtaining future necessary loans, and the management of the trust . . . these Eastern interests should be in harmony with the receivership."[14]

Outraged Cincinnati backers now looked to the courts for protection. In an application to the Common Pleas Court of Cincinnati they protested that Ingalls and Morris, both stockholders and creditors, hardly acted as disinterested parties; that the law disqualified them to serve as receivers.[15] The court, paying little heed to the appeal, assigned the property as requested; Morris and Ingalls retained joint possession from April 1871 until October 1872 when Morris resigned and Ingalls alone became responsible.

"What this city needs most for her commercial prosperity is first-class railroad talent. . . . Who is the coming man?" the *Cincinnati Gazette* had queried in 1870.[16] Melville Ingalls would be the answer for the next twenty years. Nevertheless, in the early 1870s real power belonged to the banker-dominated board, which worked hand-in-hand with Ingalls to sort out the tangled economic affairs of the road.

No sooner did the bankers take full charge than litigation began with the former president and "a group determined to wreck the Road and annihilate the stock, as well as impair the interests of a portion of its Bondholders and creditors."[17] To avoid a lengthy complicated court battle, the board devised a three-step formula. First, a stockholder group petitioned for bankruptcy—declared in November 1871; following bankruptcy came the sale and repurchase by a majority of the bondholders; in the interim, the property was reorganized by predesignated trustees (William Booth, J.S. Kennedy, Thomas Perkins, and Preserved Smith), so that the creditors would have interests proportionate to their claims. William Booth consented to act as nominal president under Ingalls' receivership and until the road could be formally restored to the directors.[18]

With the Cincinnati people finally ousted, the directors moved quickly. They had to restore the company's credit rating and at the same time build up working capital to improve a road that already had outstanding claims against it of some $2 million. The techniques involved a flexible combination of increasing capital inputs and new short-term loans. First the board assessed each

stockholder $8 a share. Proceeds from this levy were turned over
to Kennedy, appointed stockholder trustee, to purchase the $1.2
million floating debt. Then another half million was obtained by
temporarily deferring interest payments to bondholders.[19] If the
receiver could not pay the remaining claims from anticipated traffic returns, the board considered the possibility of a long-term
loan. In the meantime, Kennedy supplied a short-term advance for
"extraordinary expenditures," to make repairs and purchase additional rolling stock to handle prospective business from newly
negotiated east-west traffic ties.[20]

To put their traffic strategy in effect, the directors relied on
pooling and traffic agreements to create a through route, the Continental Line, which ran east to Baltimore from the west and northwest over the track of the B. & O., the Marietta & Cincinnati,
the Indianapolis, Bloomington & Western, the Chicago, Burlington & Quincy, the Cincinnati, Lafayette & Chicago, and the
Logansport, Crawford & Southwestern. In November 1872,
another traffic tie was arranged with the Indianapolis, Bloomington & Western for a freight route between Cincinnati and the
Northwest, to be named the Queen Line. Negotiations with Morris, president of the Indianapolis & St. Louis, stipulated that cars
go over that line and the I.C. & L. on what would be called the
Cincinnati Road.[21] Together with these new connections, and a tie
to the I.C. line under construction between Lafayette and
Kankakee, the I.C.& L. could claim the most direct route between
Cincinnati and Chicago.[22]

The corporation emerged from bankruptcy in July 1873 and
"entire control of the property reverted to the directors."[23] To
make up for the recent outlays they outlined new financing. A
funded debt bond, paying seven percent secured by an income
mortgage, would repay stockholders for their assessment and also
repay Kennedy for purchasing the $1.2 million floating debt. For
reimbursing trustee advances for plant and equipment, the board
issued $375,000 ten-percent equipment bonds. Subscriptions for
these were restricted to stockholders, with the trustees and directors taking one-third to show confidence. Perkins and Kennedy
received payment for trustee services, collected interest on their
cash advances, and increased their security holdings.[24]

Receivership and bankruptcy between 1870 and 1873 did not
signal distress. The directors improved the property and expanded
through traffic agreements to effect a division of business and
maintenance of rates. The financial condition of the company had

The Indianapolis, Cincinnati & Lafayette Railroad, 1874.
Stuart Collection, Rare Book Division, The New York Public Library,
Astor, Lenox and Tilden Foundations.

similarly been strengthened. They converted the floating debt to a bonded debt and though the bonded debt increased, so had the rolling stock. Gross earnings had risen each year as well, causing the *Financial and Commercial Chronicle* to forecast that the through line had "every prospect of increase for years to come."[25]

The unexpected panic that September ushered in a protracted business depression. As Ingalls, now president, informed the stockholders, "We had but fairly got our affairs settled and in a condition to do business, when the panic came and prostrated every industry of the country, particularly railroad business."[26] Yet as late as the summer of 1874, the outlook for the road remained good. Net and gross earnings reached the highest point in its history. The corporation had consolidated with the Cincinnati, Lafayette & Chicago to create a 253-mile line between Cincinnati and Kankakee (the junction of the Illinois Central) stretching its connecting line to the North and Northwest. It formed the shortest and best route from Cincinnati, the entrepot for merchandise produced in the Ohio Valley, to the grain country of Indiana, Illinois, and the West. Two-way traffic seemed assured by the continued growth of Cincinnati, while in Indianapolis the Board of Trade boasted that the Eastern "money panic" barely affected their manufacturers—all industries were flourishing. Indianapolis would be a great grain center, second to Chicago in pork packing, and "one of the most important iron centers of the country."[27] Not only was greater traffic expected in the West, but anticipation of business between Cincinnati and St. Louis engendered plans for further expansion south, for a tie from Cincinnati connecting with the Chesapeake & Ohio to Huntington, West Virginia.[28]

Continued depression soon dispelled the optimism of 1874. The Boston and New York bankers who had undertaken the road's management in 1870 and resolved repeated complications, when now faced with the need for further financial doctoring, became reluctant to advance new funds. Although the company had maintained rates in 1875, earnings had fallen off when extremely low trunk-line charges had diverted business. In particular, the opening of the Chicago division of the B. & O. had injured the Continental's freight traffic. Having operated at a deficit during 1875, the company could not cover interest payments scheduled to fall due in January 1876 on the funded debt bonds. Rather than advance monies, the directors called instead for conversion of the bonds into preferred stock, warning that default would follow if bondholders declined the exchange. (The funded debt bonds were not to be cancelled but held by Messrs. William Booth and George Bliss as Trustees "to protect the owners.")[29]

The apparent stabilization of net earnings by June 1876 did not reflect the financial trouble of the road, nor did the report of the company's president: "Considering the depressed state of business and the competition that has existed generally with railroads, we may congratulate ourselves that our rates have fallen no lower. Our pool on business between Cincinnati and Chicago still works harmoniously and makes money for all the parties."[30] Ingalls neglected to point out that he had been unable to make a deal for maintaining rates between Cincinnati and Indianapolis with the Cincinnati, Hamilton & Dayton. The real problem, as he well knew, went deeper. Even with rigid economy of operation and reductions in labor costs, a bonded debt of $9 million left the company with no margin. Ideally, in order to extricate itself all of the funded debt bonds had to be converted to preferred stock; holders of C. & I. bonds had to agree to defer interest payments; and in some way the floating debt had to be paid. Instead, when earnings for July 1876 suddenly dropped below what they had been at any point since 1865, the banker-directors refused to put up funds for August interest payments. Once again they resorted to receivership.[31]

From 1876 and on into 1878, bankers generally hesitated to advance short-term operating funds to railway companies except on the very best collateral. In the summer of 1876, the New Jersey Central sought "desperately" to raise $4 million to carry the company into January of the next year; but unable to offer substantial security, it could not obtain new money. Bliss predicted receivership, followed by reorganization and a large reduction of the bonded debt.[32] Similarly, in the fall of 1876 after news that the "Reading clique" were selling bills drawn on McCalmont Brothers and had also drawn large amounts in sight drafts on Kidder Peabody, Bliss anticipated serious trouble for that company. The Reading owed a "fearful amount" on bonded debt, had guarantees to cover, and had besides a large floating debt which was carried chiefly by issuing acceptances. The acceptances would now have to be paid as they matured, for the banks and trust companies "were a little alarmed." Bliss saw no way of relief. "Messrs. McCalmont would doubtless aid if good security could be had. So far as I know this is lacking."[33] Continuing difficulties resulted in banker intervention; the"Banks brought pressure on Gowan [of the N.J.C.] telling him they won't loan him what he needs in January, nor renew loans unless a plan is formed that will advance the price of Coal—maybe it will abate his pretensions."[34]

Conditions proved no better in 1877 and persisted unfavorably until the middle of 1878. Without solid collateral, the monied institutions refused to make short-term funds available to the railroad industry. Referring to the affairs of the Atlantic & Pacific, Bliss again asked, "Where will the money come from, Keene has none to spare, and finds difficulty today to borrow with such collateral as he can offer. [D.R.] Garrison hasn't put in a cent and probably won't. Gould is tied up with his U.P. and wants nothing so much as money."[35] Financiers remained unwilling to make short-term funds available except on the best security and until 1878 neither the public nor financial intermediaries would provide much in the way of long-term funds for new or financially troubled roads; it had "become useless to offer such securities."[36]

In the face of continued distrust both at home and abroad, Bliss had to increase his investment because of his intimate tie to the company. "Very few people," he explained to Ingalls, "have money to put into new companies and I have been forced to put so much money into the I. C. & L. and the C. L. C."[37] But when asked by Perkins to take part of a new issue of equipment bonds in 1877, he refused: "My investments in the concern altogether are as large as I am willing to have them."[38]

When necessary, he did supply a limited amount of short-term credits. These loans extended for six to twelve months and ranged from $10,000 to $20,000, usually at seven-percent interest, plus a commission for cash advances. For a loan of $17,500 in the winter of 1876, he received in addition to seven-percent interest, a $5,000 commission for the cash advance, and $5,000 in stock for connected trustee services.[39]

Further to meet the corporation's capital deficiencies, Bliss interceded with George Coe of the American Exchange Bank to secure credit for the road. Bliss had become a director in 1869 of both the bank and the railroad, and that same year the bank became New York Transfer Agent for the road.[40] Thereafter, Bliss served as liaison between the two boards. As the road's earnings declined, his anxiety over its public standing heightened and he consistently urged Ingalls to maintain the corporation's credit rating at the bank.[41] Severely reproving Ingalls for requesting extensions on notes due, he complained that the American Exchange

Bank had less security for loans than "any other creditor." "Is it not possible to induce a reduction for the amount due the bank as the claims fall due, say to the extent of 10 percent upon each renewal till the aggregate is somewhat reduced? If it cannot be done, perhaps it can be accomplished by making new loans of sums a little smaller than the payments made by the Receiver."[42]

Into 1877, the company's earnings suffered from the competition among the trunk lines, which had begun with the completion of the Chicago branch of the Baltimore & Ohio. "It has been difficult to determine just what to do," Ingalls, again the receiver, reported to the court: "If we charged fair rates, our business left us. If we attempted to do through traffic at current rates, we most certainly would have been ruined."[43] Consequently, as few cars moved east as possible for each one registered a large loss.

While hopes for improved through-traffic earnings depended on the cessation of competition among the trunk lines, pooling agreements prevented competition for local traffic. The earlier division of business and rate stabilization between Chicago and Cincinnati continued in effect, and in May 1877 a similar accord was concluded with the Cincinnati, Hamilton & Dayton. The managers kept expenses to a minimum, reduced labor costs, and asked bondholders for time extensions on their interest until a reorganization settlement.[44]

Another reorganization—to be attempted as soon as market conditions improved—stimulated insiders' purchases of the company's depreciated securities. Still hesitant while awaiting further market declines, by the summer of 1878 Bliss was "inclined to buy at low prices a few bonds to average down some that have cost too much."[45] By the end of the year he instructed Perkins confidentially: "I hold a considerable amount of the blanket bonds of the ICLF and incline to increase the amount with a view of reducing the average, if I could buy at fifteen or thereabouts. See what you can do—I think I should buy as many as 25th$ and perhaps 50th$ could I get them."[46] Perkins & Head, as Boston Transfer Agents, recorded and therefore knew of all changes in ownership. They could in addition arrange for secret transfer of ownership to prevent public knowledge of inside dealings. Since not only Bliss, but Ingalls, Ingalls' Cincinnati friends, and Perkins began accumulating low-priced securities, this information could mean a jump in prices. "Until our earnings increase considerably I see no reason why the public should take a favorable view of our condition or advance the price of the securities. Of course if any of those connected with the Co. are purchasing, it will cause an advance: but there is nothing in the gross traffic returns which should stimulate a demand or increase the prices at present."[47]

William Booth, former president and current secretary, saw his own chance for profits. As secretary, Booth also traded over the counter and he had been buying and then reselling securities to insiders at inflated prices. In making bond purchases through him, Bliss at first affected extreme indifference to convince Booth he was not overanxious to buy. Finally, in great pique, he warned Ingalls of Booth's operations, which had pushed available blanket bonds beyond fifteen, and he himself turned to purchases of preferred stock obtained through Perkins.[48]

In the summer of 1878, at the same time that Bliss and Ingalls worked on settlement terms to present to the bondholders, they continued buying preferred stocks and 1869 bonds, individually, and for a 3/3 account with Thomas Perkins. They intended to increase their interest in the reorganized company with securities obtained at virtually rock-bottom prices—the blanket bonds of 1869 were bought at anywhere from fifteen to twenty-seven cents on the dollar and the preferred stock for as low as five and a half cents.[49]

Bliss had meanwhile convinced Ingalls of the importance of the reorganization plan which should be carefully worked out before presentation to the bondholders. Corporate management, being both major creditors and stockholders, had to mediate between the two groups to facilitate the best possible returns for the respective interests. "As directors we were chosen to represent the Shareholders and see that justice is done to the holders of the various issues of bonds— It is not possible to perform our duties to the former without taking care of the latter."[50] In essence their plan enabled creditors to turn depreciated bonds into stock of the new company, all at par. It allowed holders of the seven percents of 1869 to receive seventy percent of their face value in stocks of the new company; holders of the bonded debt seven percents or the preferred stock would receive forty percent of their face value in stocks of the new company. Bondholders had until the end of December 1879 to join in the reorganization settlement.[51]

At the time of the July announcement, general business recovery appeared imminent. Large crops, at good prices, changed the mood of the country from "hopelessness to expectations of immediate and lasting prosperity."[52] As confidence crested, security prices rose—especially of companies previously showing no returns in dividends or interest. Investors had begun looking to the possibility of profits and dividends in the near future. This optimism and the improvement in the road's business encouraged continued buying for the 3/3 account. In December, ten days before the official time limit for participating in the reorganization plan, Bliss instructed Perkins he would finance any and all purchases to enlarge their holdings in the reorganization.[53] Learning later of Perkins' purchases of $100,000 in rights, he sarcastically inquired if the whole amount or any portion were for sale either for himself personally or for their 3/3 account.[54] Ingalls too busily bought rights, for himself and for their joint account. Among his best deals were the rights obtained on $10,000 1869s for $300 and on $50,000 funded debt bonds for which he paid nothing.[55]

The active demand for stocks made the year 1879 a particularly good one for railroad reorganizations and indeed their increased incidence became its "marked feature." Prospects for traffic, earnings, general business conditions, all favored these newly reconstituted companies. "I really believe those of us who have an interest in the new Company will find it a 'good thing,' " Bliss wrote Perkins.[56]

A connection south had been contemplated in the early 1870s and now during the final stage of reorganization settlements, negotiations began for a link to the Chesapeake & Ohio. Bliss and Ingalls, who had originated the plan, secretly agreed to give Collis P. Huntington, C. & O. president, a major share in the newly reorganized company renamed the Cincinnati, Indianapolis, St. Louis & Chicago.[57] On Huntington's promise that he would build to Cincinnati and make this road his line to the Northwest, Bliss and Ingalls promised in return to provide him with 2,000 shares of the old company at sixty by the middle of April 1880 and soon after to secure another 2,000 at the same price. They would further work the market to buy him a quantity equal to their own holdings and then buy for a 3/3 account.[58] To accommodate Huntington, Bliss persuaded Noah Porter, president of Yale, to sell some 500 shares held by Porter and his associates. He hoped that the Booths would furnish another 500 and that they might convince others to sell. As a last resort, he and Ingalls would sell some of their own holdings to make up the first 2,000 and then pick up some in the market to compensate.[59]

Huntington accepted the terms and the 2,000 shares, "hoping this will be the commencement of many transactions that will be largely to [their] mutual interest."[60] Before agreeing, he had insisted quite specifically that "it should not be known that he is in any way connected with the line for some time to come."[61] A public disclosure of plans to build to Cincinnati would, Huntington claimed, add "a million to the cost of the right of way."[62]

The technique used for secretly transferring the shares is of some interest; it reveals the significant role of Transfer Agents in facilitating inside arrangements. Until the 1850s, and even after, railroad treasurers often served as Transfer Agents. In 1854, because of fraudulent practices by corporation officers, the New York Stock Exchange required that all share certificates be signed by two company officers, then registered by an independent bank or trust company, and countersigned by another independent institution. The corporation became liable for the acts of officers issuing fraudulent or otherwise illegal securities. This system, designed to insure honesty, provided a check of the amount of securities outstanding.

It became common practice for new purchasers personally to bring their recently acquired securities to the Transfer Agent, where they would exchange them for a receipt. This receipt was then presented to the registrar, who kept presigned security certificates ready for distribution. The operation, essentially a bookkeeping function, could on occasion serve other purposes. The Transfer Agent could put to use its authority to receive old certificates and issue receipts for new ones. If, for example, a prospective seller could be persuaded to assign power of attorney to the Transfer Agent to arrange for the sale of his holdings and handle all the ensuing steps, then the identity of the new owner could be kept anonymous. Since such arrangements could be carried out without the knowledge of the board, it could be exploited, as in this case, to concentrate share control.

To meet Huntington's insistence on absolute secrecy, Morton, Bliss & Company became Transfer Agent to exchange the old I. C. & L. shares for those of the reorganized company. In order to insure that only the trio would be privy to the arrangement, they excluded Head & Perkins and the American Exchange Bank from the operation.[63] To protect Huntington's anonymity and assign the 500 shares purchased from Noah Porter and his New Haven friends, Bliss relied on a relatively simple procedure. When these holders agreed to come into the reorganization settlement, they would surrender their old securities to the Purchasing Committee that would buy the road at the foreclosure sale in February 1880.

In return, the parties received Purchasing Committee certificates which they sent to Bliss with an attached memorandum distinguishing the number of old shares each person agreed to sell from the amount he wanted exchanged for new stock. Bliss then prepared one new certificate for the new stock desired by the owner and a second for the balance to go to Huntington. The former owners signed the certificates of new stock to be turned over to Huntington on the back, giving Bliss power of attorney to dispose of them. After delivering these to Huntington, Bliss remitted payment to the original holders.[64]

More complicated exchanges with other parties absorbed so much time in the New York banking office that in May the railroad treasurer came to New York to fill in new certificates, see to their delivery, and obtain endorsed Purchasing Committee receipts where necessary.[65] Getting enough to make up the amount agreed on with Huntington, especially the second share lot, constituted a major difficulty. With only 3,109 shares delivered to him by May, Bliss promised to make it 4,000 as fast as the stock could be acquired. Finally, he reduced his own holdings to just a little more than 4,000 shares to satisfy the terms of the agreement.[66]

The securities of the new company were listed on the exchange in June and attention now focused on stock-market returns. Of the total capital stock, reported at 40,000 shares, Huntington, Bliss, and Ingalls each held ten percent, besides their holdings on joint account. Within days after the announcement of the stock-market listing, Bliss began manipulating the market. According to his plan, the stock, bid up to 63½, would be advanced gradually; the bonds, at 93½, would be advanced to 95. "It would not be well to advance the stock too rapidly and then let it fall unless we want to buy. . . . I suppose Gould's way would be to bid it up—if no stock was offered—to 70, and then offer it at 68 and so on at lower prices with the view of catching weak holders, but we have no motive of this sort."[67] Demand for the stock continued to push prices up during July, so that even at eighty not much more could be picked up. "So much of it has gone to . . . [Cincinnati] to stay that it would be difficult for anyone to execute orders here [New York] unless from small lots." By November, ninety was being openly bid. Huntington was still anxious to buy, but there was none on the market for sale.[68] "His purchases of our shares as a stock manipulation," Bliss exclaimed to Ingalls, "was a good one but where is our reward for selling our own and securing other people's for him."[69]

Huntington's delay in building the promised Cincinnati connection remained a source of annoyance, but all in all matters had worked out well. After two receiverships, a bankruptcy, and two reorganizations the road was in a better position than ever. The bankers reduced the large floating debt of 1870 and canceled expensive branch leases. What had been a local road when they took over in 1869 had emerged a decade later as the Cincinnati, Indianapolis, St. Louis & Chicago Railroad. Plans to move goods east through negotiated traffic alliances were now subordinated to attempts to create a west-south axis. Rate pooling, which had eliminated local competitive problems between Cincinnati and Chicago, would now be supplemented by the construction of new Western connecting links, while the tie to the C. & O. figured in an enlarged building program to enhance Southern traffic opportunities.

The bankers had maintained an active interest in the company's management and put in large additional sums to increase stock and bond holdings. By his own account, Bliss recouped his losses and "realized a large profit" in what had been a "loving term of labor and effort."[70] His congratulatory message to Ingalls, named president of the new company, expressed how closely the two had worked and how satisfactory the outcome for the directors.

> You have given to the service of the Company, ability, perseverance, and earnest devotion, and greater success has resulted from your efforts than anyone of those in the management expected.
>
> I congratulate you, my dear Mr. Ingalls, most heartily.
>
> My connection with the management of the enterprise would not have been endurable but for my personal respect for you and confidence in your skill.[71]

Two years later, in 1882, the same mood of success informed his appraisal. To his early associate, Joseph Fay, he wrote of his "great satisfaction that the efforts on behalf of the parties interested in the I. C. & L. have resulted so favorably. We encountered, as usual in such cases, a good deal of friction and some difficulties but they have, one by one, disappeared and at this time I think favorably of the Co'y. in every respect."[72]

5
The Route To "Business Politics":
The New Orleans, Mobile & Texas

The Indianapolis, Cincinnati & Lafayette had been physically extended, as we have seen, by a series of through-traffic alliances and had survived the depression intact. Purchases of depreciated securities eventually allowed the bankers to recoup their equity. Salvaging investments in abortive large-scale building programs could demand quite different tactics. In the case of the New Orleans, Mobile & Texas, banker strategy had from the outset centered on interregional new construction to join New Orleans to Houston. The financiers for this costly project counted on substantial supplies of portfolio funds to supplement state subsidies and their own sizable direct investments. When politically inspired capital scarcities thwarted building goals as early as 1872, the bankers set out to save a four-state franchise. In order to circumvent forfeiture provisions of state charters, they put the largely incomplete road up for foreclosure sale and then bought it back. Continuing problems during the depression eventually forced the breakup of the planned route and the sale of separate segments to other systems.

Despite the tactical change which brought dissolution, the dramatic business oscillations of the 1870s in no way weakened banker advocacy of interterritorial expansion. Counting from the start on a through route, the first and only tying New Orleans to Texas,[1] Joseph Seligman, Levi Morton, George Bliss, and Louis Von Hoffman, the bankers who in 1870 agreed to finance and manage the extensive system, envisioned still further connections with their other rail properties to integrate the Midwest, South, and Southwest. They anticipated that the vast districts to be

99

covered in the South would offer unlimited traffic possibilities, and they were even more enthused about the prospective business between this area and Chicago.[2] While interterritorial expansion did not generally become the goal of Southern management until the 1880s,[3] the benefits of such a strategy were publicly endorsed as early as 1870.

> People who have settled in Texas have an intense liking and affection for Chicago as a trading point. . . . They say it is the only city in the world. They send there for all manner of articles, including agricultural implements, steam engines, machinery of all kinds, plows, reapers, seed corn of fine class and varieties, and everything that they require. They have been used to dealing with your merchants and are eager to continue their custom, and hence they look forward with great anxiety and hope for the railroad in Texas to be finished to New Orleans, that they may reach Chicago as quickly as possible, either in person or by orders, for the articles they require.[4]

Investment bankers, in particular, counted on handsome returns from developmental building set within the context of an integrated network. What they also figured on and then failed to find was the necessary institutional security promised by state governments. During the enthusiasm of the early boom Southern state "subsidies provided by legislative action had invite[d] the attention and enterprise of operators from every quarter of the country."[5] Yet in a milieu where public policy was shaped by competing private groups such state support proved unreliable. In this instance, financiers found that the guarantees, bond subsidies, and stock subscriptions which Louisiana had enacted successively in 1869, 1870, and 1871 aroused bitter opposition which reached the state legislature. They discovered that they had to contend with political maneuvering generated by interindustry competition and that rumors raising the specter of state repudiation could seriously impede efforts to find loan capital. By the winter of 1872 building west of the Mississippi was jeopardized by bad publicity in an already stringent money market. The final blow came when, after a sharp struggle, the legislature, responding to continued pressure by local shipping interests, halted its financial aid.[6]

It was most often the case with high-cost construction ventures in the postwar boom that commercial risks hinged on government action. Conversely, as Bliss complained to his friend, Boston banker Joseph Fay, the South's disregard for its public obligations had been a drawback to developing business in the area. "You and I, however, are so well acquainted with the cases that have led to this, that we are not inclined to censure so severely as others."[7] Perhaps the bankers did not "censure so severely" because they well understood and accepted the premise that the government was one of men, as well as laws, wherein special-interest groups contended continually for the power of privilege. Despite some occasional reflections about government responsibility, these bankers acted on the assumption that within the existing framework, where government policy served private rather than public ends, political influence and subsequent privilege might, at any moment, pass from one group to a more powerful group. Special interests could be expected to compete, indeed had to compete, strenuously, not only to obtain influence, but to keep it. In short, government dispensations, particularly at the state level, could not be trusted.

Besides distrust, government enactments provoked confusion. With cities, counties, and states issuing charters, taxing property, granting rights-of-way, subscribing to bonds, and guaranteeing interest payments, differing legal stipulations amassed to confound railway administrators. No cadre of corporate lawyers had yet been trained in the 1870s to interpret subsidy or bonded aid provisions or to cope with railroad legislation that differed from state to state.[8] The task of overseeing these matters often fell to banker managers.

Taken together, the instability of government support, the perplexity caused by government enactments, and the embroilment in constant litigation convinced bankers that they should broaden their sphere of interest to encompass the legal dimensions of decision-making. In what they perceived at best as a fragile legislative and legal framework, financiers looked increasingly to the courts to protect railroad properties. With conflicting rulings emanating from state courts, only to be delayed by later resolutions, and then overruled by the further interpretive variances of federal judges, bankers kept a sharp eye on the judicial process. By 1880, after a decade's experience in the South had impressed them with the crucial impact of judicial rulings, Morton and Bliss decided to actively lobby in Washington so the "right man" would be appointed to the Gulf Circuit Court. They became enmeshed in an all-out effort directed at the President, the Congress, and the Judiciary that allows a fascinating insight into the workings of the political economy of the Gilded Age and helps explain the coming transition to stronger central government with its promise of greater legal and political stability for the era of big business.

Having been initially encouraged by a system that inconstantly fostered hopes for economic gain, the disappointed backers of the N.O.M.&T. faced practical questions by the winter of 1873. Should they put in more money to continue the originally planned construction, or sell the road, or "buy it in" and save the four-state franchise? The third alternative, the one they chose, allowed them to circumvent forfeiture provisions of the state charters; they secured court permission to put the largely incomplete road up for foreclosure sale and then bought it back. This decision reflected the syndicate's appraisal that the road be evaluated in terms of its interregional potential; the local portions, it was realized, were by themselves of considerably lesser value. So the property, once touted as a "great trunk line," came up at foreclosure sale in 1873 in four separate parcels. Although the press did not report the detail, the original promoters, in their capacity as bondholders, purchased all four sections (through trustee representatives), formed two new companies, and retained all franchise rights.

As creditors, they bought the completed line, 140 miles from New Orleans east to Mobile, for $400,000 and immediately reorganized it as the New Orleans & Mobile. Seventy miles of track running from the Mississippi to Donaldsonville and the partially finished section stretching to the Sabine River were bought for a combined total of $250,000. The still unbuilt portion from the Sabine to Houston was purchased for $1,500. These three parcels west of the Mississippi were incorporated as the Texas & New Orleans.[9] By 1881 the line of both companies had been disposed of in four separate transactions, and the interim history identifies the problems encountered, the decisions made, and the techniques utilized.

The bankers acted immediately to raise funds to complete the unfinished segments west to the Sabine.[10] Here the syndicate tried to obtain Charles Morgan's cooperation. The terminus of Morgan's L. & T. at Brashear, Louisiana, was 176 miles from the Sabine. An unfulfilled contract signed by Morgan in 1872 bound the two companies to finance, build, and run a common road from Vermillionville west to the Texas boundary. Thirty miles were already graded, and the remaining work was light. However, when Morgan agreed to participate in the venture he hoped to offset any

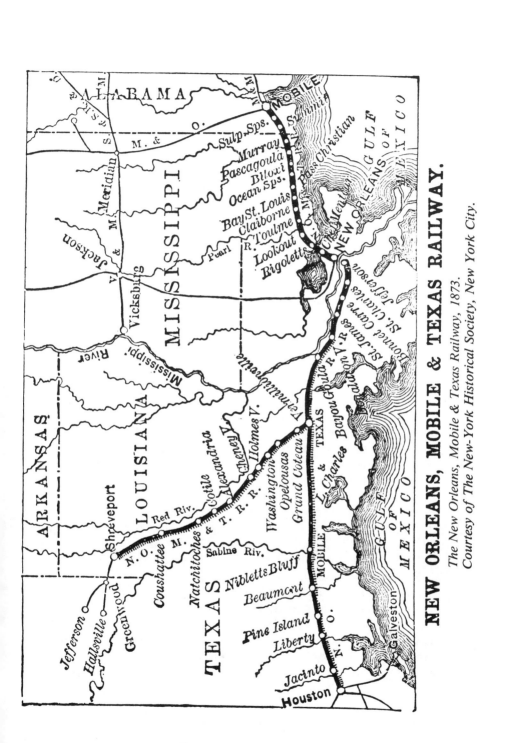

NEW ORLEANS, MOBILE & TEXAS RAILWAY.

The New Orleans, Mobile & Texas Railway, 1873.
Courtesy of The New-York Historical Society, New York City.

potential loss to his steamship traffic. Once the threat of the through route fizzled, Morgan had little reason to continue the work. As late as 1876 he remained quite content with the unrivaled business of his steamer lines from Brashear to the Texas ports, and he continually refused to put up the necessary funds.[11]

As it turned out, a court decision favorable to the New Orleans syndicate moved Morgan to action. Unable to raise inside funds for completing the Sabine link, the syndicate had turned to the Circuit Court asking to buy in the property from Westwego to the river.[12] Their motive in repurchasing a second time was again to keep control of the franchise, which otherwise would have been forfeited because of their inability to fulfill the charter's construction schedule. At the news that the sale would be permitted, Morgan's L. & T. made application for the court to exempt the westernmost end (from Brashear to Vermillionville) from the sale,[13] and since the syndicate could not prove any immediate intent to build, the judge had no grounds to resist Morgan's application.[14] Consequently, on May 31, 1878, the N. O. M. & T. Bondholders' Committee purchased at foreclosure only the completed track from the Mississippi sixty-five miles to Bayou Goula, and the partly graded roadbed from there some sixty miles to Vermillionville, for $350,000.[15]

Shortly before purchase, in a new development, Eastern capitalists offered to furnish $400,000 for completing construction all the way to the Sabine. The bankers were asked to participate and put up prorated proportionate shares to improve its condition from the Mississippi to Bayou Goula. They also decided to assess themselves sufficiently to pay off the nonassenting bondholders.[16] Bliss advised Morton to take their portion "in case others do the same so as to raise the whole sum."[17] If Morton thought it unwise to invest as much as their pro rata proportion for their joint account, he might be willing to take the sum himself; for them to refuse "could somewhat lessen the enthusiasm of others."[18]

Rumors that the syndicate had access to venture funds again moved Morgan to action. Although he had prevented their repurchase of the western end, and the court had granted him the privilege of taking it at an appraisal fixed by the Railroad Commission, he had made no move to acquire it. However, once it appeared that the Sabine route might finally be realized, he immediately proposed to buy the 125 miles just bought by the New Orleans bondholders.[19] From Morgans' perspective, the defensive strategy would deter eventual sale of a continuous link (from which he was excluded) to any other system. The New Orleans group, meanwhile, eager to tie up the business, accepted his offer that they take $300,000 in L. & T. debentures.[20] By October 1879 the sale was completed.[21]

By 1879, then, the promoters of the old N. O. M. & T. remained still in control of the reorganized New Orleans & Mobile, of the property from the Sabine to Houston, and of the western segment to the Sabine exempt from the earlier foreclosure sale of 1878. Of the three parcels, they calculated that the completed road of the New Orleans & Mobile, clearly the most valuable, would be of interest to the aggressive Louisville & Nashville as an asset to its large southern system.

Franchise problems now hindered what was thought would be a relatively smooth negotiation that had been in the making for almost four years. Since 1875 the L. &. N. had cooperated in restoring, repairing, and improving the road. Of the $3 million spent, $2 million came from earnings to match $1 million supplied by the L. & N.[22] In 1879, after the securities market had risen sufficiently to promise a favorable exchange of issues, according to the reorganization settlement, a Purchasing Committee consisting of George Bliss as chairman, Louis Von Hoffman and Oliver Ames, representing a majority of the bondholders, was appointed to work out the consolidation informally agreed to earlier. In bringing bondholders into any plan there were always difficulties. In this case, they were compounded by the L. & N.'s attempts to convince bondholders to sign an agreement which surrendered the charter and right-of-way. To meet the danger that those who had already signed the agreement prepared by the Purchasing Committee might be tempted to dispose of their bonds to the L. & N., Bliss assumed the role of legal advisor. He insisted that the signatories now sign another specially prepared document to prevent any transfers.[23] Oliver Ames in Boston was instructed to "get as many signatures of Boston Bondholders as you can," since it was crucial to save the charter and right-of-way.[24] The bankers carefully distinguished between working control and absolute ownership and headed off the L. & N. maneuver.

If the charter could be saved, there was no reason to "regret the trade" which allowed holders of New Orleans eight-percent first and second mortgage bonds to receive L. & N. six-percent gold bonds, equivalent to the face value of their first mortgage bonds.[25]

I have expressed the opinion that, if we had reorganized ourselves issuing 4 millions of first Mortgage Bonds and two or three million Income or Preferred Stock and then some Common Shares (in the way we discussed) we would have realized six million for the property instead of four. The L. & N. people gave out yesterday that they had purchased this road on such terms that their stock was much more valuable, and it is said to have advanced 10% upon it. I don't however regret the trade.[26]

Bliss remained deeply engaged in the negotiations, which dragged on until late April 1880, when R. J. Cross, a junior partner in Morton, Bliss & Company, went to New Orleans with power of attorney to act for the Purchasing Committee at the auction ordered by Judge Woods of the Gulf Circuit Court.[27] Cross's instructions were to bid a sum not less than the amount of the liens prior to the first mortgage, and then to bid under the instructions of L. & N. agents. He was not to go above the prior liens plus the first mortgage bonds and interest on the coupons, unless the L. & N. people put money in his hands to cover the excess.[28]

When the press reported the sale, it was generally assumed that the L. & N. had taken complete control.[29] Actually, the road had been purchased by the committee representing ninety-eight percent of the N. O. & M. bondholders, so that a reorganization could take place and the property leased with its franchise. As of May 8, 1880, the line was operated by the L. & N. as part of its through tie from Kentucky to New Orleans, but the franchise was safely in the hands of the original group.[30]

By June, there had been as yet "little time to fix a market" for L. & N. six percents. Morton and Bliss decided to wait until they could more profitably move the $500,000 six-percent gold bonds they received for their N. O. & M. first-mortgage bonds.[31] Bliss felt generally pleased with the property transfer. He complained only that the New Orleans court had awarded undue compensation to the N. O. & M. trustees, James Raynor and Governor Edwin Morgan. As chairman of the Purchasing Committee, Bliss claimed to have "devoted more time in the past three months to this business than Governor Morgan did in the 5 or 6 years of his trusteeship." The compensation to Raynor of $25,000 per year and to Morgan as co-trustee of $10,000 per year was, he felt, excessive and he wrote Judge Billings, who made the award, to say so:

> I have had to do with foreclosing and reorganizing several railways and with the selection of suitable persons to take charge of the properties in the Northwest, and have had no difficulty in finding able railwaymen and more thorough experts in management than Mr. Raynor to take charge for a compensa-

tion of Five Thousand a year. In fact in one case, about three years ago, I secured the services of a man who I thought peculiarly qualified, under an arrangement to pay him a higher salary, but the United States District Court refused to sanction a higher compensation than $5,000.[32]

Sale of the segment from Vermillionville to the Sabine had also bogged down over franchise questions. Bondholders' claims that the right-of-way was secure and that the franchise evidenced legal title of a valid property[33] was challenged in court by the Easterners who earlier agreed to finance building. A sympathetic judge counseled settlement, a good thing for all interests. Bliss was plainly tired of the business, complaining to Morton that "no one of the Committee but I have given it attention for a long time. It will be a relief when finished."[34] In January 1881 he notified Frank M. Ames, the trustee, that the Purchasing Committee was finally ready to distribute the proceeds of this sale to the bondholders.

The Texas division, the last unsold remnant of the old N. O. M. & T. involved the competitive plans of Gould and Huntington in the Southwest. Once again Huntington's affiliation with Bliss affected the map of railway development. Huntington had long sought a route to New Orleans for the eastern section of his proposed transcontinental system.[36] Gould, on the other hand, was in the process of completing his system from St. Louis and Kansas City in the North to the Gulf Coast and Rio Grande in the South. Just as Gould was assisted in his railroad acquisitions by the Seligmans, so Huntington's close association with Morton and Bliss now worked to his advantage.

Back in 1876 the original creditors of the N. O. M. & T. had agreed to furnish venture capital for building the Texas division from the Sabine to Houston. Holders of a minimum of $1,250,000 in securities agreed to subscribe to at least $2 million in capital stock and if necessary to as much as $4 million to incorporate as the New Orleans & Texas. A specially created committee consisting of Levi Morton and William Mertens, of Von Hoffman's firm, handled the securities exchanges. By that summer enough money had been raised to begin construction and then an eventual arrangement with Charles Morgan enabled completion of the link by 1880.[37]

In the summer of 1881, when Gould's threat in the Southwest had become a reality, Huntington, working through Bliss, bought the completed road to make his connection to New Orleans and Houston.

I have been partly occupied for two days in making a sale to
Huntington of the line from Houston to the Sabine River. Terry
on account of his relations with Gould was unwilling to take any
part in the negotiation. Gould some time ago sent Col. Dodge to
him who told him that they wanted the line—He fears if he
should sell it in Gould's absence without first offering it to him,
it would mar the friendly relations which should exist between
adjoining neighbours. I have now agreed with Mr. Huntington
to sell to him our shares, and do what I can to *give him the control*, at 85, he agreeing to take all the shares at the same price, if
the owners wish to sell. These terms are binding upon me until 3
o'clock tomorrow, and meantime he has telegraphed to his
friends in California and will probably accept them.[38]

Huntington's approval hinged on getting a majority of the
shares. He and Bliss drew up a contract stipulating that Bliss
would deliver the stock at $85, twenty-five percent to be paid in
cash, twenty-five percent in six months, twenty-five percent in
twelve months, and twenty-five percent in eighteen months, with
interest at four percent on the deferred payments.[39] Although Bliss
had only promised to use his best efforts to make up a majority, he
could do this, as he said, "in 45 minutes" since John J. Terry (who
had been won over), Governor Morgan, Oliver Ames, and Morton, Bliss & Company together owned about half the shares.[40] The
rest of the stockholders were similarly pleased with the terms so
that the sale, which had caused Bliss "a good deal of trouble,"
was consummated.[41]

Indeed, these long and complex negotiations for the entire N. O.
M. & T. had tried the patience of the three investment bankers,
George Bliss, Joseph Seligman, and Louis Von Hoffman, all
members of the revamped syndicate which had taken over the
operation and financing of the company. They were the key
figures in drawing final plans for all parts of the property, and of
the three, Bliss was the most active in bringing about the sales to
the Morgan people and to the L. & N., while the agreement with
Huntington had been entirely his doing.

Supple and Johnson's model for investment preferences posits
that opportunistic capitalists seeking quick returns were often
forced by business declines into becoming long-term investors.[42] In
this case, the reverse was true. The backers, private capitalists and
investment bankers, first endorsed developmental building over a
four-state area during the boom partly because of the immediate

returns on building, but also in anticipation of future traffic returns and appreciation of securities. Then as a consequence of the depression, they tightened their criteria for long-term investment. They would, for a time anyway, be more cautious before assuming responsibility for long-range projects which required constant attention and large capital outlays: as recovery returned they would seek instead quick profits from "opportunistic" short-term trading operations.

On the other hand, although they had been reluctant to advance funds for further building during the depression, the property was maintained and new funds were supplied to insure its final disposition.[43] For while separate negotiations took place for individual portions of the line, the through traffic and interregional possibilities were never lost sight of as the major determinant of the road's value. Fresh equity capital had been injected to insure resale and eventually the stock and bonds were disposed of in a fairly favorable set of transactions.

One of the more neglected results of the dramatic oscillations in the business cycle is that it led to reappraisal not only of investment criteria, but more broadly, of business-government relations.

The eventual dissolution of the N. O. M. & T. had proceeded according to the guidelines established by court decisions. Indeed, whatever the plans for extricating distressed property, financial calculations hinged on the compliance of sympathetic judges and the latitude allowed by legal loopholes or insufficient legal precedents. The action of judges could be so significant a factor for potential profits, or for that matter, for actual losses that it led to the persistent labors of Morton and his political associates to name the appointment to the Gulf Circuit Court. Morton's defeat, surprising as it was illuminating, convinced him of the inadequacy of "political business" and helps to explain the larger effort for structural change that received the backing of various business groups in the transitional decades of the late nineteenth century. By the 1890s the shift had been made to "business politics," when the Senate could justly be called a Millionaire's Club "and presiding over [its] activities was Vice-President Levi Morton, who ranked with Belmont and Morgan as one of the greatest bankers in the land."[44] As in the contest with Charles Morgan a decade earlier, the bankers had been again impressed by the limited effectiveness of political influence when the process itself proved so vulnerable to the accumulated pressures of special-interest groups.

From their point of view, a government which promised privilege without restraint fostered excessive competition for favors. Even the separations of powers, intended originally to inhibit special-interest groups, had in a society with an anti-institutional bias the opposite effect, that of encouraging their aggressiveness.[45]

When Judge Woods of the Gulf Circuit Court was nominated to the Supreme Court in 1880, the bankers saw an opportunity to have E.C. Billings appointed his successor. Billings, the judge in the New Orleans & Mobile settlement, had gone South after the war. As a Republican lawyer, he had at first been unpopular with the "old Southern element in New Orleans society" who regarded him as a carpetbag counselor serving carpetbag officials, but he soon cultivated the support of local banking and merchant groups.[46] Billings, it happened, was married to Emily Sanford, a relative of Bliss's wife. The relationship had its business side, too, as Bliss managed their investments.

In December 1880, Bliss alerted Emily to "the nomination soon to be made for the place vacated by Judge Woods," explaining, "I suppose these things are decided largely by outside influences and in many cases for reasons not connected with past experience or ability."[47] Having justified the necessity for political intervention, he assured her that Morton would do all that he could to push the appointment. Morton was an intimate friend of Grant; his election to Congress in 1878 placed him on the Washington scene; he was a loyal supporter of Senator Conkling; and his influence as head of the Republican Finance Committee in the 1880 election would count heavily. Only one problem worried Bliss, sectional loyalties:

> He can do as much as any member of the House. It remains true, however, and there is no use disguising the fact, that Morton's sentiments with reference to the South are not in unison with those of the President [Hayes] and the Majority of the Cabinet. I fancy Evarts, Schurz and the President have more sympathy for an unrepentant rebel, if he happens to be a Southerner, than for a true and loyal man in the South whose fortune (or misfortune) it was to have been born in Massachusetts or some Northern State other than Ohio.[48]

Much has been made of the supposed Republican split between Half-breeds and Stalwarts, but let us just say that Morton belonged to the Conkling faction of the party, which had "never failed to rejoice in the result of his [Billings'] services to his clients."[49] Although Roscoe Conkling, party boss in New York, had little influence with the incumbent Hayes administration, he was unquestionably a power in the Senate and if only the President could be convinced to make the nomination, the bankers were certain of confirmation.[50] Morton planned to reach all factions, including Wayne McNeigh, a former classmate of Billings who belonged to the reform wing: "But a word from him to Secretaries Evarts or Schurz would be useful."[51] When the President in the meantime offered the judgeship to William Hunt of New Orleans, Hunt not only declined, but agreed to argue in favor of Billings. Judge Woods and Justice Bradley of the Supreme Court also gave their backing to Morton's recommendation.[52] Even Evarts "yielded in his feelings in view of [Bliss's] wishes and those of Mr. Morton."[53] Hayes finally made the Billings nomination.[54]

The opposition which had emerged and delayed the nomination came not from the reform wing of the party, but, as the bankers now discovered, from the L. & N. The railroad had attempted to discredit Billings—a lifelong abolitionist who for that reason "was cursed and hated when he went to New Orleans"—by charges that he had removed a black man from office "simply on account of his color."[55] Behind the complaints of "the disaffected colored brother" stood the L. & N., whose campaign intensified after the nomination. The lawyers for the railroad, Foster and Thomson, "were doing all in their power" to defeat confirmation.[56] Charges defaming Billings' character, going back to his school days, were circulated in the Senate and sent to the Senate Judiciary Committee.

Attempts to defeat Billings were so "unscrupulous and persistent" that the bankers mounted a counterattack. Bliss appealed to Noah Porter, president of Yale, whom he had advised in stock dealings for the I. C. & L., asking, "Can you write to the President, especially about his [Billings'] integrity and honor—also to any Senator you know. . . . It would be a great favor to me."[57] Steps were also taken to defuse a report sent to "every Senator and to many others in Washington" of Billings' action awarding undue compensation in the New Orleans & Mobile case.[58] James Raynor, the trustee for the N. O. M. & T., had this in charge and he instructed John E. Parsons, a counsel in the case (who had himself received a $15,000 award), to prepare their version for distribution to the Senators. Bliss also enlisted Edwin Morgan, a powerful Republican presence, to reach Senator Thurman. For Morgan, the co-trustee for the New Orleans & Mobile, more was at stake than the Billings appointment. He had to neutralize charges impugning him personally.[59]

Morgan's influence derived from his contacts as an old-time

party leader and fundraiser. He had been governor of New York from 1859 to 1862 and the first chairman of the Republican National Committee, created in 1856. As national chairman, he had been responsible for financing the successful presidential campaigns of 1860 and 1864. When he was elected to the Senate in 1864, he created a congressional committee which dominated the fundraising efforts for Grant's election. Though he left the Senate in 1869, he again headed the National Committee in 1872 and joined the Republican Finance Committee, headed by Morton in 1880, to elect Garfield.[60]

In addition to the pressure brought by Morgan, friends of friends were also speaking to Senator Bayard. With the nomination now before the Judiciary Committee, Bliss apologized to Emily: "I wish I could render more effective aid. I've worked every accessible lead." And Morton, who was "able to do as much as anyone," was doing "all in his power."[61]

So strenuous had been the L. & N.'s campaign that, rather than face outright rejection, the Morton-Billings group decided to await action by the new administration. As Morton's firm had been the acclaimed leader in the successful federal refunding operations of 1879, he fully expected to be Garfield's Secretary of the Treasury. For that reason he had declined the offer at the Chicago convention of the vice-presidential nomination (much to Arthur's regret, William Curtis assured him).[62] Instead, he had directed his energies to chairing the National Republican Finance Committee, which included private bankers Joseph Seligman, Augustus Kountz, and Pierpont Morgan. He also set up the special "Morton Fund," which made victory possible in the crucial Midwestern states of Indiana and Ohio.[63] Morton had good reason to suppose that Garfield would be beholden so Bliss confidently encouraged Billings:

> I have never felt, as if there would be any question, that, in case your nomination is not now acted upon, it will be repeated by Garfield. I know influences can be brought to bear upon him that ought to influence if not control his action in the case.[64]

When rumors spread that Garfield had chosen elsewhere, Morton discounted the possibility. Judges Woods, Bradley, Hunt, and Campbell all supported Billings. Morton had only to "make the facts known to influential parties."[65] Yet after all was said and done, Billings was not renominated. Garfield proved less susceptible to Eastern interests than suspected. When the President shortly after also refused to appoint Morton Secretary of the Treasury, the rebuff resulted in Conkling's and Platt's famed Senate resignations. Sorely disappointed, but to save party unity, Morton settled for the post of Minister to France.

That April Bliss visited Washington, dining with the new Cabinet, and for the moment "was glad not to have any favors to desire or any claims from Congress or any of the officials." His one consolation, an old and good friend, James Blaine, was the "strong man" in the Cabinet.[66]

As financiers handling the government's funding operations, Morton, Bliss & Company relied upon their intimate connections in Washington to obtain inside information, business favors, and favorable legislation. What is more interesting is the extent to which their economic plans were thwarted when they had to work within the political framework of the 1870s and early 1880s. As their New Orleans, Mobile & Texas experience reveals, for all the influence the bankers could and did wield, they had to contend with too many resistant forces on both the state and federal levels. Bliss complained bitterly of the "stupidity of Congress." In 1881 he wrote what can only seem paradoxical as a description of the Gilded Age: "Corporate capital Congress looks upon as a public enemy and counts it its duty to hit it as hard as it can."[67] And again that year he wrote of executive ingratitude: "It strikes me that this Administration will be famous in history for making War upon its friends. It certainly succeeded in disaffecting a large portion of its warmest supporters and those through whose efforts it was elevated to Power."[68]

By the end of the decade, "business politics" could be more readily relied on. Morton was now vice-president and M.E. Ingalls could call on him with confidence in 1891:

I wish you would use your influence with the President to have Hon. Edmund Waddill appointed one of the new Circuit Judges from Virginia. I can vouch for his integrity and standing and uprightness, and it is an important matter to our property interests in Virginia that such a man should be appointed.[69]

6
Rescuing Foreign Bondholders: The Gilman, Clinton & Springfield

The roads that bankers promoted in the frenzied rail-building years of the early 1870s necessitated increased attention during the subsequent downswing. The inevitable complications of depression certainly did not drive bankers away from the industry or signal the demise of their influence. On the contrary, they coped, mostly because they had to, with constant problems and set out deliberately, as we have seen, to determine policy in order to recover their direct investment. They also found that their role as financial intermediaries, merchandising railroad securities, compelled them to take action to extricate distressed property. The Gilman, Clinton & Springfield is an exemplary case pointing to the sudden, unsought accretion of banker-power in response to investor pressures. Morton's firm originally functioned exclusively as mobilizers of foreign portfolio funds for this corporation, but the partners on both sides of the Atlantic considered their reputation of such priority that they took action to mitigate clients' losses resulting from scandalous construction-company techniques.

By the mid-1870s foreign first-mortgage bondholders had begun to react aggressively to the vagaries of American legal and financial procedures, believing that they had an "absolute right" to take possession of defaulting property.[2] Because of banker intervention, English, Dutch, and German bondholders were not completely powerless. They turned over votes and power of attorney to investment houses which used these voting trusts, not primarily to obtain control, as the device was used in the Morgan era, but specifically to protect injured creditors. In this instance, Morton's New York firm arranged for the road's purchase, ran it as trustees, and eventually disposed of it to a larger system, the Illinois Central.

The foreign affiliations of American bankers virtually forced them to undertake what they considered a burdensome obligation. Such distrust had been created by the Crédit Mobilier Scandal of 1873 that it seriously jeopardized a continued flow of foreign funds for American enterprise. Although similar construction-company financing had been extensively employed since the 1860s, and bankers had themselves participated in shaping the technique, transatlantic investment houses, concerned over their standing in overseas money markets, could not afford to disregard the demands of their clients, especially after exposure of what the public perceived as gross irregularity.

By 1874 Morton, Bliss & Company was laboring on behalf of disgruntled foreign bondholders of the Gilman and of the I. C. The solutions arrived at to satisfy both creditor groups reveal the significance of bankers' intertwining railroad relationships, particularly when magnified by the monetary stringencies of the mid-1870s. What we find is an example of banker protection of creditors, in this instance foreigners, that also attests to the pressure financial intermediaries exerted on executives of a major railroad corporation in shaping expansion strategies. And of particular significance for business history, the negotiations reveal the time and engagement required by the extraordinary difficulties resulting from behind-the-scenes covert dealings and inadequate legal precedents.

The Gilman, Clinton & Springfield Railroad Company incorporated March 4, 1867, in Illinois. Three years later, the president, S.H. Melvin, induced Philadelphia capitalists of the Pennsylvania Railroad to supply venture funds for building a route from Gilman about 115 miles southwest to Springfield and extending to Clinton. The road was to be transferred to the Pennsylvania in 1873 by a 999-year lease to be operated as part of the Pennsylvania system; as a branch of the Pittsburgh, Cincinnati & St. Louis, and as a feeder to the Pennsylvania-controlled Columbus, Chicago & Indiana Central.[3] Additional negotiations allowed I.C. passenger

trains to travel the new road from the junction at Gilman to
Springfield. For the I.C., the track afforded a desirable connection between its main line and the Chicago branch to which the
main-line traffic chiefly tended.[4]

As was typical of the period, the G. C. & S. directors (who now
included Pennsylvania backers) had incorporated as a construction company—the Morgan Improvement Company—to finance
building. Two days before the final transfer to the Pennsylvania,
on July 8, 1873, the McLean County Court issued a temporary
restraining order to prevent leasing and brought to public attention one of the more flagrant examples of construction-company
arrangements. The Morgan Improvement Company stood accused
of receiving enormous and improper profits from construction.
Actual building expenditures for the road were reported at $1.5
million, but the construction company in what smacked of fraud
and chicanery, had charged the G. C. & S. $4 million for purchase;
$2 million in first-mortgage bonds, $1.4 million in stock, and some
$600,000 representing all the bonds subscribed to by the counties
and towns along the way. Yet another accusation in the indictment
of profiteering concerned the road's president and two directors
who owned three-fourths of the stock in the Barclay Coal Company and had a contract binding the railroad to buy coal at a set
rate.[5]

The court immediately ruled that the coal contract constituted a
breach of trust. The more ambiguous, still novel, question
centered on the validity of the $1.4-million stock issued to the
Morgan Improvement Company. Was it legal stock? The court
would decide.

The intricacies and convolutions of the subsequent proceedings,
only briefly outlined here, go a long way to explain the fears harbored by foreign bondholders regarding American legal procedures. The suits, countersuits, and contradictory decisions by
county, state, and federal courts created an extremely complicated
three-year legal battle before a decision defined the standing of
construction-company stock. Moreover, a full year before the
courts' final ruling in the case, the major adversaries, Thomas A.
Scott, president of the Pennsylvania, and Morton's banking
house, had privately settled on a course of action.

Scott's first step had been to obtain a state court order to take
possession of the road, with Hugh J. Jewett (soon after to become
president of the Erie) as trustees under the first mortgage. Since in
the meantime Judge Tipton of the McLean County Circuit Court

had already appointed a receiver, F. C. Hinkley, the trustees filed a counterpetition in federal court to restrain Hinckley from interfering.[6] A fight for control was now underway between the Scott-Morgan stockholder group and foreign creditors acting through Morton's transatlantic banking house. In addition to seeking a federal injunction, the Scott faction had filed a motion in the Circuit Court to discharge Hinckley, calling for the return of the property to a recently elected G. C. & S. board. How, they asked, could the new directorate, purged of construction-company managers, possibly be objectionable to the court? Judge Tipton declined the petition and dismissed the obviously spurious argument noting that the Morgan Improvement Company directors were the voting majority in the railroad's recent elections. The critical issue had been bypassed; the court had still to determine who held the bona fide stock and who could vote. Scott and Jewett, not to be stopped, petitioned again for trustee possession in place of receivership.[7]

Morton's New York firm, representing foreign bondholders, had in the meantime filed a cross-bill which the county court allowed as a separate suit. According to the banking firm, Scott and Jewett could not possibly be trustworthly trustees, representatives of bondholder interests, since they had a $400,000 stake in construction-company stock.[8] In a deliberate countermove to smear the bankers, S.H. Melvin, the recently displaced G. C. & S. president, and a construction-company stockholder, brought suit against the London firm, Morton, Rose & Company, to recover the difference between the price (80) the railroad received from the bankers for $2 million of its first-mortgage bonds and the price (92) at which the bankers sold them. The belated attack questioning the bankers' profits came off rather weakly. Melvin's charges created considerably more of a stir, however, in revealing that, aside from the bonds taken by the Pennsylvania; the half million delivered by the bankers to Holland; and those they sold in London; William Osborn of the I. C. had also taken a portion of the issue.[9]

The news that Osborn had an interest in the feeder line gave rise to repeated speculation that the I. C. stood behind the earlier cross-bill filed by Morton, Bliss & Company. It was rumored that the real object of the various suits, indicated I. C. plans to take control.[10] Actually, the banking house, injured by the scandalous disclosures instigated action. In an attempt to protect both its clients and the firm's reputation, the bankers agreed that the bond-

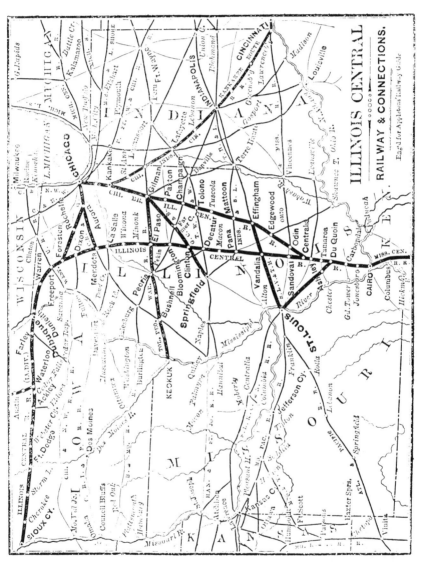

The Illinois Central Railway, 1873.
Courtesy of The New-York Historical Society, New York City.

holders should purchase the property at foreclosure sale. At the same time, Bliss, a director of the I. C., fully expected that some satisfactory arrangement might be quickly worked out with the larger company.[11]

The Scott group received its first severe setback early in 1875 when the Illinois Supreme Court ruled against the construction company. A special report of the Master in Chancery found that 14,000 shares had been fraudulently issued to the Morgan Improvement Company and should be canceled; the G. C. & S. directors were members of both companies; certain lands deeded to the railroad for location of shops were improperly pledged to the Improvement Company for advance of funds; and the contract with the Barclay Coal Company (since abandoned as unprofitable) had been illegal.[12]

Although the decision appears straightforward, something of the ambiguity surrounding business attitudes can be found in the Master in Chancery's explanation to the judge which exonerated the directors' actions while indicting them. Their motives were not questioned since he did

> not think any of the directors or officers intended to do anything wrong, or in any way to defraud the railroad company, but that the Morgan Improvement Company . . . forced them into a position that the law would not permit them to assume; in other words . . . the contract made by them with the Morgan Improvement Company *was a fraud in law,* and *not a fraud in fact.*[13]

The Morgan Improvement Company appealed the decision, taking it to the Supreme Court.

Soon after, Scott and Jewett filed another bill, this time in the Bloomington Circuit Court, again calling for possession of the road under the terms of the mortgage, for foreclosure, and for the removal of Hinckley. The special Master in Chancery—the same man who had questioned the validity of the law, not the behavior of the directors—found the trustee demands justified. No sooner did the Bloomington court order the mortgaged line placed in their hands, to be sold in accordance with the trust deed, than a contradictory order now came from the McLean County Court. Scott and Jewett could replace Hinckley as receiver, but were restrained from selling the road under the provisions of the trust deed.[14] In appointing the trustees as receivers, the court disregarded the most common restriction of the existing legislation—that no interested party be so designated.[15]

This decision was followed in turn by yet another surprising development. In November 1875 the Illinois Supreme Court declared, contrary to an earlier ruling, that the contract with the Morgan Improvement Company was not fraudulent. Nonetheless, a director of the railroad could not legally be, at the same time, a member of the construction company. Consequently, a new G. C. & S. board would have to be elected by bona fide stockholders—that is, stockholders in the construction company could not vote. This significant ruling did not end the court contest. A conflict of jurisdiction now arose between the federal and state courts concerning the varied suits over the G. C. & S. Not until April 8, 1876, did the U. S. Circuit Court order foreclosure of the first mortgage, with instructions for the road to be brought up for sale.[16]

During the delays of the court battle a compromise had already been reached behind the scenes between the banking house and Scott. When Morton undertook litigation in the G. C. & S. case, he did so as a former associate of Scott. Morton had joined the Union Pacific board and his firm had become Transfer Agent for the transcontinental in 1871 when Scott was president. These prior associations made resolution of the current controversy considerably easier than it might otherwise have been. Moreover, poor business conditions in 1875 made the expense of a permanent lease much less desirable than it had seemed just a few years earlier. The bankers convinced Scott to give up his ambitions to use the G. C. & S. feeder as part of the Pennsylvania system and to work out a satisfactory solution for the bondholders. At their request, he agreed to stay on officially as trustee until the settlement of the perplexing lawsuits—with the proviso that the banking house would purchase the road for the foreign bondholders without opposition at a foreclosure sale.[17] In August 1875, when the court had allowed the trustees to take possession from the receiver, Scott had turned the property over to Charles S. Seyton, as the trustees' agent, according to an agreement with the banking firm. Seyton, an Englishman (and a large holder of I. C. securities), was acting under the bankers' instructions for the foreign bondholders and from the time Scott named him General Manager he received all cash advances for restoring the road from Morton, Bliss & Company.[18]

Meanwhile, Bliss had kept in touch with John Douglas, president of the I. C., concerning the forthcoming sale. Both anticipated the road would be bought in the name of the New York banking house, with Bliss and Seyton designated trustees for the first-mortgage bondholders. Much to their surprise, they discovered that the English creditors had instructed Seyton to make a direct purchase in their name.[19] By 1875, foreign creditors suffering default had grown considerably "less patient than formerly." They discussed foreclosure freely as a means of salvaging their investments and were counseled to turn to the courts for possession.

> Our maxim with regard to the defaulting American railroad companies is: Bring suit whenever there is anything to be got, and especially when there is a very valuable and profitable property in question; conclude compromises only when there is little or nothing left to secure. The Rockford suit has shown that in the first case the costs of suit are not money thrown away, in other words, that one can obtain his rights in the American Courts as well as in any other country whatsoever. Rockford had made European bondholders insist more stiffly on their rights. Before they seemed to suspect they would stand a very poor chance in American courts.[20]

Creditors might purchase property at foreclosure sale and then run it for their own account as the German bondholders of the Brunswick & Alabama had done in 1873. The road's inadequate earnings for the next decade suggests the preferable course would have been resale or lease to a larger system.[21] The G. C. & S. creditors favored the second option. The railroad would be put in fair enough running order so it could be disposed of through the mediation of the investment bankers.

A junior partner of the banking house, R. J. Cross—bidding on instructions from Bliss and John Douglas—purchased the road at auction in Springfield on June 10, 1876. To preserve harmony, the property was bought in the name of the bondholders, with Bliss and Seyton taking possession as trustees. The creditors in delivering their votes and power of attorney relied on the banking house to restore the security of the mortgage.[22] The financiers, seeking to protect their reputation, assumed a responsibility which was time-consuming, "vexatious," and without prospect of compensating profit.

Since the summer of 1875 Morton, Bliss & Company had furnished funds for restoring badly neglected rolling stock. Where possible, the bankers had put off Seyton's persistent cash demands, hoping for an early settlement with the I.C. to relieve them from the necessity of improving the property.[23] All they realistically expected was a short-term lease. Rail business across the country continued unsatisfactory and that of the I.C. had been especially depressed. As a director, Bliss well knew the company's financial burden and he feared excessive demands might stir resistance on the board. So a month after the foreclosure sale, Morton wrote Douglas suggesting only that the I.C. work the feeder temporarily under a short-term lease which allowed the bondholders a percentage of gross receipts. Bliss reiterated the limited nature of the proposition. Douglas, however, questioned the propriety of even a short lease based on a percentage of gross earnings and advised them not to press the matter.[24]

The bankers' relations with Douglas are vague, yet the available information is tantalizing for its perspective on the relationship between the president, the board, and the bankers. When Douglas visited Bliss in New York a week after the sale, the firm secretly offered him compensation—which he refused—for all his efforts on their behalf and implicitly for his continued service in the G. C. & S. negotiations. However, in a quixotic move Douglas proceeded to tender his resignation. The bankers were quite furious and to meet their objections he gave Bliss "liberty to withdraw his resignation."[25] The brewing dissatisfaction among I.C. directors over the company's Southern policy apparently precluded such action. After meeting with the board, Bliss tipped off Morton that "his resignation has already been accepted, but this is not known by him or anybody else outside."[26] That same day he chastised Douglas:

> I am sorry to say in reply to your allusion to your letter of resignation that, so far as I can judge, there has never been any doubt that the Directors would accept it since it was received. This on account of the manner of its presentation which you will remember I told you was a great surprise as well as a disappointment to the members of the Board. I fancy the Board deemed the interest entrusted to them so vast and important that they cannot consistently leave them exposed to suffer by action so impulsive as that of your resignation.[27]

In London, Sir John Rose had been busy too, preparing a proposal for a G. C. & S. reorganization. After consultation with H. J. de Mares Oyens, of the administrative office for American railroad securities in Holland, Rose forwarded the plan to New York. Enclosed also were three letters for Bliss to deliver personally: one to William Osborn, who "had almost a controlling influence in the Direction," one to the I.C. secretary, and one to Wilson Hunt, a major shareholder. Bliss expected little from these added efforts to influence Osborn to lease the road, and he explained to Sir John just how poor the prospects were.[28]

Rose needed to placate the bondholders. Bliss, on the other hand, wanted a responsible company to relieve him of the worries of financing and managing the road. He had little faith in Seyton's ability to run the railway to advantage, but treated him "gingerly" for the sake of harmony. Seyton, who lacked experience in operating American railways, called on the bankers for constant advice regarding personnel, legal, financial, and general business problems. Of greater concern still was the large amount the New York firm had advanced. How would they be reimbursed?[29] Despite press reports that the bondholders "who now own the road, have made arrangements to lease it to the Illinois Central, and that the transfer will be made in September,"[30] no such transaction had yet been negotiated.

Morton redoubled his efforts with Osborn in the fall, pressing an alternative lease plan, this time stipulating a guaranteed fixed annual rental. In London, Rose put a tentative proposal to the bondholders: Would they be willing to lease the road for four percent for five years and five percent for the following twenty? Such terms might possibly be acceptable to the I.C. directors, though Bliss himself had little expectation that even these, which he found "onerous" to the bondholders, would pass.[31] But before he had the chance to present the case, I.C. General Manager, James C. Clarke, undertook an investigation which convinced him that the sums needed to put the G. C. & S. in order exceeded Seyton's estimate, and he firmly advised against any lease whatsoever. As an alternative, Vice-President Ackerman, meeting with Clarke and Seyton, worked out a traffic agreement predated as of 1875 to present to the management.[32]

The foreign bondholders had meanwhile revised their demands. Rather than a lease agreement, they wanted to sell the line to the I.C. Bliss so informed the board and when they rejected this latest scheme,[33] Oyens, acting for the Dutch, prepared to petition. He appealed to Seyton and Bliss, asking that they both sign and that Bliss personally present the latest proposal to the board. Sensitive to the pressure he, Seyton, Rose, and Morton had already brought and certain that the purchase demands were unacceptable, Bliss refused to sign and advised Seyton against cooperating.[34]

As liaison between the I.C. board and the G. C. & S. bond-holders, Bliss occupied a dual position. He knew from the inside the severity of the economic problems. As Ackerman later described the period, "1876 brought new misfortunes to the company."[35] Restrictive legislation in Iowa had reduced local rates on leased lines in that state, while crop failures in Iowa and central and north-ern Illinois had reduced the volume of traffic. To make matters worse, the I.C. was crossed at so many points in the most produc-tive part of the state that a large part of that business was in jeopardy. Furthermore, the trunk lines running east had diverted a large portion of the traffic from Chicago. Nor had returns materialized from the Southern connection Osborn had negotiated in the early 1870s. Much to everyone's chagrin, both Southern companies defaulted on interest payments in January 1876, and their operating expenses became the responsibility of the I.C.[36] Considering these difficulties, Bliss deemed it unwise to press fur-ther and perhaps endanger negotiations for a temporary traffic agreement.

In London, Sir John Rose viewed the I.C. with less forbearance and exhibited considerably less sympathy for its problems. Added to the "constant and extreme annoyance" over the G. C. & S., Rose had to cope with irate bondholders of the Southern connec-tion.[37] He had been further embarrassed by Osborn's "manifestly improper" letters to the adminstrative office in Amsterdam con-taining inside investment information. While private cor-respondence between company officials and shareholders, a regular practice, was in no way objectionable, in this case Osborn's behavior had been doubly insulting. His letters had been sent over the signature of the secretary as a formal communication of the railroad and, what was particularly distressing, they had not been simultaneously forwarded to English I.C. shareholders whose aggregate holdings about doubled those of the Dutch.[38]

The bankers customarily supplied inside investment advice on a confidential informal basis. Within weeks of Rose's criticism of Osborn, Bliss had written a long explanation of the company's un-satisfactory condition to a large shareholder, Hugh Glenn. He cautioned Glenn against selling and added, confidentially, "I own as much of the stock as when it was worth Par, and I do not think the Directors, with one exception have reduced their holdings."[39] Besides providing similar information to other friendly private banking houses and to their own firm in London to manage their portfolio there, Morton, Bliss & Company also supplied Osborn with the latest information on the London market. In the summer of 1876, Bliss had advised Sir John of how anxious Osborn was "to know how nearly through our people were with New Illinois Fives; if there were to be a panic in this market and a decline in first class securities he might desire to make a change by selling there [in London] and investing in something here."[40]

As the bankers had curtailed their own dealings in I.C. shares to prevent straining their relationship with the board until a resolution of the G. C. & S. matter, they had good cause for resentment.[41] Sir John's irritation derived also from Osborn's disregard of the Southern problem.[42] Rose's suggestions to move quickly to pacify foreign creditors of defaulted Southern securities had brought no response. As a result, a group of English bondholders, after learning of misuse of funds by Henry McComb, president of the consolidated Southern connection, the New Orleans, St. Louis & Chicago, had decided to take action on their own and to bring suit.

Faced with Osborn's continued indifference, the bankers took the initiative. Early in December 1876, Bliss requested that McComb meet him privately regarding "a matter of mutual interest." Bliss had prepared—unknown to the I.C. board—a cash settlement plan to end McComb's claims and facilitate foreclosure.[43] When Bliss later presented this agreement to the directors, they dropped further litigation, which at best would have been tedious and slow. He also saw to the further details, reporting to the board on December 20 that McComb would accept $150,000 for his $228,115 of unpaid I.C. coupons. By the end of the year, he had paved the way to purchase the lines in receivership.[44]

English I.C. stockholders remained anxious, nonetheless. Not only did they believe that the cash outlays for the Southern tie were lost, but they blamed the complications over this connection for the decline in I.C. securities. So on January 26, 1877, while perturbed over the G. C. & S. and piqued by Osborn's behavior, Sir John Rose presided over a meeting of irate I.C. investors where "some unnecessary denunciation was indulged in."[45]

At Rose's suggestion, the English shareholders and Oyens, representing the Dutch, named a joint committee to select two delegates to investigate I.C. operations. (It hardly appears a coincidence that one of the committee members happened to be Charles Seyton, the trustee and general managaer of the G. C. & S.) The delegates were to confer with I.C. directors, examine the company finances, personally investigate the lines in the West and the South, and then prepare a report on their findings. Captain Douglas Galton, who had served as official investigator of American roads for the British government in 1857, was named to represent the British.[46] Oyens, who had been urging the I.C. directors to take over the G. C. & S., was named representative for the Dutch I.C. creditors. "I do not think a selection could have been made by a Committee that would be more satisfactory to the Illinois people on this side," Bliss wrote Sir John. That the selection had been carefully made for their own interest needed no comment.[47]

While the delegates investigated, the bankers shaped another reorganization plan for the G. S. & C. One drawn up the previous summer by Rose and Oyens had been unsatisfactory to Bliss. He objected to the proposed bond issue of $2.5 million and the large amount of stock. The plan would only foster doubts as to the road's ability to pay.[48] A scaled-down version, fixed by March 1877, called for $300,000 of first-mortgage bonds (which Bliss and Seyton had the power to execute), payable by installments over an eighteen-month period. Afterwards a $2-million loan could be considered; the excess of earnings over interest on this issue would, hopefully within a year or eighteen months, pay off the floating debt and leave a surplus to put the road in good order. Placement of the $300,000 again provoked annoyance since Osborn and the I.C. unexpectedly refused their share of the new issue, obliging the banking house to take the allotment. The security was now so good that Bliss believed his firm's position was "much better than . . .in the past."[49]

Because of the constant friction with Osborn, intensified by his refusal to participate in the G. C. & S. reorganization, Bliss stopped attending I.C. board meetings. But with Galton's and Oyens' visit coming to an end, he feared such overt hostility might adversely influence a G. C. & S. settlement. "I shall be glad," he reassured Sir John, "to do whatever I can do to facilitate the object of Captain Galton's visit, and hope to avoid giving offense to the Illinois Company."[50] He subsequently met separately with Osborn and then with the delegates before they left for England to prepare their recommendations.[51]

The *Report of the Delegates*, issued on April 27, 1877, was replete with reassurances. It attributed declines in I.C. revenue and dividends, as well as in stock prices, to the diminishing proceeds from land sales. Earnings had, of course, decreased because of growing competition, the immediate effects of the panic of 1873, and crop failures. If only the company had been more aggressive and sought control of the local traffic in the West instead of allowing rivals to acquire the business, revenues might have been better. To rectify the directors' conservatism, the delegates prescribed their remedy—"the absorption of the Gilman, Clinton & Springfield, and of the eastern section of the Toledo, Peoria & Warsaw Railroads."[52]

The rest of the report focused in detail on the Southern connection. Indeed, one-half the bonded debt of the I.C. consisted of the $4.8 million of consolidated bonds of the Mississippi Central and the New Orleans, Jackson & Great Northern, purchased with the proceeds of the five-percent sterling loan of 1874. For the most part, the delegates approved the steps which the company had taken. In March 1877, the I.C. bought the New Orleans, Jackson & Great Northern on account for the consolidated bondholders. (Stuyvesant Fish, who had been with Morton, Bliss & Company since 1872 and at the same time had worked for the I.C., was the treasurer and the agent for the Purchasing Committee.)[53] While the purchase of the Mississippi Central was temporarily delayed, the delegates noted that arrangements could be worked out with holders of the second-mortgage bonds and the "necessary legislation for the consolidation of the two companies" would be effected. Since the I.C. planned to advance money to improve and modernize the Southern route, management confidently expected "that a great portion of the Western trade [would] return in its natural course towards the South" once proper rail facilities were available. This policy received wholehearted endorsement. Oyens and Galton assured the shareholders that the new traffic would be more than enough to pay interest on the money advanced and add to earnings.[54]

Osborn's confidence in the potential traffic from a direct north-south route was in every way justified and did prove advantageous. The decade of the 1880s, one of rapid development in Southern and Southwestern trade, revived New Orleans as the commercial outlet of the lower Mississippi. Shipments from that city of cotton, rice, and tobacco rose from $80 million in 1886 to

$130 million by 1891. Not only did the I.C. possess the shortest, most direct, route from Chicago to New Orleans, but it exchanged goods with the fifty-two roads which crossed its lines south of Chicago.[55] The "banana specials" advertised it as the carrier of more import-export traffic with South America, through New Orleans, than any other company in the 1890s.[56]

Acquisition of the G. C. & S. appears in the company's *Centennial Report* as part of a long-range plan similarly devised for new traffic possibilities.[57] As we have seen, however, the decision to acquire the line reflected unflagging pressure by Anglo-American and Dutch bankers. It is highly tempting to speculate that an agreement, prearranged, between Osborn and the bondholders' representatives—Oyens, Seyton, and the Morton firms—to secure their backing for the Southern policy explains the purchase. The delegates had reported that at least $1.5 million had to be advanced for the Southern property; a new mortgage executed on the line; and new bonds sold to repay the I.C. To accomplish this, Osborn clearly needed the continued cooperation of foreign capitalists. With the dullness of the investment market at home in 1877, he could not continue to risk alienating irate foreign creditors or their representatives. The evidence suggests that the sudden reversal in Osborn's and the board's position on the G. C. & S., coming as it did immediately after the *Report of the Delegates*, was in return for their endorsement of the Southern policy.

Through the summer of 1877, Bliss awaited definite news of a purchase plan. By September there was still "no visible indication of its being soon reached."[58] Copies of the Decree of Sale arrived in London in October and a notice of the event appeared in the *Herald*. That December, the I.C. counsel left a deed of conveyance for Bliss and Seyton to execute. But rather than close negotiations, the deed proved unacceptable to Bliss, who refused to sign. He was to have "a world of trouble . . . with the title to the Gilman line."[59]

The deed as prepared constituted a warranty deed rather than the trustee deed customary in such sales. The Illinois Company, Bliss argued, bought the road from him and Seyton as trustees. They therefore held the powers of attorney under which the trustees acted, and which, with the order of the court, constituted the trustees' authority. The line had been originally transferred to Seyton and Bliss as trustees for the bondholders and as such they had sold it. However, the warranty deed would make the trustees personally responsible and liable in the future for any adverse claims.[60] He cautioned Seyton:

You and I may die in a fortnight and our heirs or executors might be annoyed and perplexed, not being fully acquainted with the fact and not having a document in hand with which to defend our Estates—The Illinois Central is aware of the delivery of the bonds to the Clerk of the Court; is aware of the terms of the Decree, the particulars of the Sale and of its confirmation, and the Company holds the authority under which we have acted, which accompanied in each case the bonds to which the several powers of attorney refer. Moreover, the Corporation lives forever and can defend itself—has directors and Executive Officials to protect its interests. The more remote the possible contingency of trouble the more reason why it should be met by the Company and the less why you or I should incur the possible chance of trouble.[61]

Bliss continued adamant in his refusal to sign unless a discharge could be obtained from the owners of the bonds. He warned the London office that he would not sign "even if my objection should defeat the Sale."[62]

In an effort to work things out, Ackerman, who was now I.C. president, and Randolph, the treasurer, came to New York. Both men hoped to expedite the business and Bliss admitted to Morton he would probably, though reluctantly, yield to save time: "If I were the only person interested, and neither the firm here nor you in London were concerned in it, I would not execute the paper now or hereafter."[63] Under the circumstances, he modified his objections and by April 1878 notified Morton: "I think that we shall all rejoice more and more that this vexatious matter is out of the way."[64]

But the matter was still not closed. Minor claims for lawyers' fees and suits had to be settled by the banking firm. Not until the Supreme Court compelled Hinckley to "disgorge" in September 1881 could the last of the old bonds be forwarded to the Clerk of the Court at Springfield.[65] In November, Bliss sent Ackerman the statement of the account with the closing entries. The compensation to the trustees, to be paid by the I.C., remained to be decided, but Seyton and Bliss would receive equal payment.

For all the difficulties, the outcome was satisfactory. Five years after George Bliss and Charles Seyton assumed operation as trustees for the bondholders, Bliss wrote:

I am much gratified at the result of this whole business and, in view of the difficulties which we encountered, think the Bondholders should be well-satisfied. It should be remembered that

the G. C. & S. bonds were originally put upon the market at a
low price for a 7 percent security and allowance made for the
high interest so long as it was paid, and also that, taking into account the premium upon the Illinois bonds, *the loss to the investor has been small.*[66]

In retrospect, after time had healed the hard feelings between Bliss
and Osborn, the banker reflected that not only had Osborn
"rendered important aid to the Trustees," but that "in fact" he
did not "know if the settlement finally could have been accomplished without his assistance."[67]

There were, as we have seen, distinct advantages for foreign investors purchasing American railroad securities from a house
whose New York office had intimate, intertwining ties to railroad
management in the States. As a director of the I.C., Bliss could
bring pressure on the board and, as important, keep his partners in
London informed of likely options. He had concerned himself
with the affair considerably more than he wanted, to facilitate a
settlement which would relieve London from embarrassment. The
bondholders did fairly well as a result. He would hardly have
bothered with the long, troublesome negotiations except for the
responsibility the copartnership imposed. If, for instance, the New
York partners had to arrange with a foreign house to place
securities in England—as Kidder, Peabody did when working with
the Barings—it is doubtful that they would have burdened
themselves to a similar extent, or gained as a by-product, the experience and expertise.

The dilemma for the rail industry in the mid-1870s was how best
to utilize the track constructed during the period of boom, how to
rationalize the rail system. The *Railroad Gazette* delineated the
problem, suggesting that bankrupt feeder roads could now best be
used if arrangements were made to incorporate them into the interregional traffic strategy of larger systems.[68] In other words, combination, so feared in the late 1860s, seemed by the late 1870s an
acceptable solution to the unplanned construction of earlier years.
However, in a society where private gain predominated over the
public good, the benefits of combination, like those of competition, frequently accrued to special interests. Certainly the best
solution for the G. C. & S. bondholders was to sell the property to
the I.C., but the resulting consolidation emanated from particular
pressures which had little to do with rationalizing the railroad

system, as the inadequate traffic for the line made clear.

When E. T. Jeffery, the general manager of the I.C., spoke before the Board of Railroad and Warehouse Commissioners in 1887 describing the trunk-line competition of Eastern roads as the cause of ruinously low rates in central Illinois and as a factor in explaining the many railway bankruptcies, he used as his example the old Gilman. Now known as the Springfield division, this line, although it crossed good agricultural country, registered a loss of $97,000 in 1884, $75,000 in 1885, and $53,000 in 1886. According to Jeffrey, the property did not have the traffic or revenue it ought and if "operated independently, not as part of a large system, it would be still less productive than under present ownership."[69] As part of the larger system the losses of the old G. C. & S. were minor compared to the disastrous condition of Illinois roads in the mid-1880s, but the acquisition clearly did not conform to a deliberate strategy to secure new traffic possibilities as management claimed.

In all of their dealings with Osborn and the I.C. board, the bankers had acted as representatives for their clients, that is, as financial intermediaries. Nor was the G. C. & S. the only instance of private bankers being called upon by bondholders actually to operate railroad property. The South, which suffered the highest incidence of default (forty-three percent of the 127 lines were in default by 1876), offers several unexplored examples of banker management and control. When the Mobile & Ohio defaulted in 1874, William Butler Duncan, the recently elected president, was designated receiver; he retained both positions until 1883.[70] The Alabama & Chattanooga, after several years of litigation which delayed bondholder possession, was sold in 1877 to Emile Erlanger of London (the banking house which had handled the Confederate war loan). "The new English management renamed the road the Alabama Great Southern and soon added it to other roads controlled by their English corporation, the Alabama, New Orleans, Texas and Pacific Junction Railways Company." The holding company also obtained control, by 1882, of the New Orleans & Northwestern, the Cincinnati Southern, and the Vicksburg & Meridian.[71] Or to take another instance, when the Chesapeake & Ohio defaulted in 1873 and then again in 1875, the plan of the Bondholders Committee headed by financier A.S. Hatch and C.P. Huntington became the basis for a reorganization with Hatch as vice-president. Similarly, the Atlantic, Mississippi & Ohio, the Virginia road of William Mahone, also passed from the hands of a receiver into the control of a private banking firm—E.W.

Clark—which, with the aid of Drexel, Morgan & Company, refinanced the road.[72] The specific circumstances of these as well as other cases deserve further study as examples of institutional adaptation in a vulnerable new industry under the pressures of the first great depression.

PART III

Business Instability And Bankers' Investment Preferences

Introduction to Part III

By the late 1870s, private bankers had experienced virtually every possible pitfall of railroad finance and administration during a long-term depression. The combined pressures of oscillating government support, opposition from local entrepreneurs, prolonged litigation, fierce trunk-line competition, and harsh public censure of financial practices in the rapidly growing industry had heightened the cares and complications of railroad enterprise. At the same time, with the magnitude of the monetary contraction that followed the panic of 1873, the financial community had been severely affected, more than either manufacturing or commerce. Price deflation, limited borrowing, and low interest rates added up generally to bad business for investment bankers.

Instability and price deflation generated caution, especially when it came to undertaking major new railroad affiliations in the later 1870s. Still, bankers' unabated eagerness for profitable railroad transactions constitutes the more noteworthy characteristic of their investment preferences, since it reflects the larger dilemma financiers were facing. Opportunities for lucratively using capital in the transportation sector remained sharply curtailed for as long as the depression continued, but aside from federal government refunding operations, they found it exceedingly difficult to find alternative employment for funds.

In 1877 and 1878 such firms as Morton, Bliss & Company; Drexel, Morgan & Company; J. & W. Seligman; and August Belmont competed vigorously for the few bond contracts offered by reputable railroads. There was little chance of adequate business since most corporations issued bonds only to replace those scheduled to mature. The public would not touch construction loans for new companies. Remembering the recent fate of many such roads, investors required evidence of completed track or a lien on physical assets to secure mortgages. Having been victimized by its earlier enthusiasm, the public carefully scrutinized rail offer-

137

ings to insure also that earnings covered fixed charges. With loan contracts in the doldrums, bankers tried to supplement their own holdings of depreciated rail issues, and they actively searched the industry for participation in favorable reorganization plans that would bring future profits.

Until the return of full recovery, finding employment for capital outside the rail industry or government refunding transactions posed problems, and the income from governments similarly, was too small to satisfy. Except for the pressure of periodic crop movements, which normally brought forth an active demand for money, the complaint shared by the investment community until 1879 was that "it was so difficult to find anything to put money into."[1]

By the spring of 1879 a second boom was under way. Investor confidence quickly rebounded when heavy crops were earmarked for export to make up for failures abroad. Railroad freight returns climbed from a low of $347.7 million in 1877 to $386.7 million in 1879. In 1880, when freight revenues reached $467.7 million, railroad managers rejoiced. As a further indicator of economic recovery, the number of miles in receivership declined from a peak of eighteen percent in 1878 to below ten percent by the summer of 1880. With confidence restored, frozen assets quickly thawed and the capital stock of the industry soared. Total capital stock of $2.3 billion in 1878 had jumped to $3.2 billion in 1881 and to $3.7 billion by 1883. The nominal increase of some $1.4 billion between 1878 and 1883 was greater than in any other five-year period between the Civil War and 1890.[2]

From 1879 into the early 1880s banker activity featured significantly in what Poor's viewed as the "immense increase in fictitious capital."[3] In the reorganizations of those years, bankers attempted to keep down fixed and floating debt. Instead, to allow for greater working capital, they urged increased stock issues as compared to bonds. With the return of what contemporaries believed to be unparalleled prosperity, they also advocated stock increases to finance continued interregional expansion. And as in no previous period, bankers also became involved in large-scale market operations which induced the public to take up these new share issues. The sale of 250,000 of New York Central stock in 1879 by a syndicate composed of Drexel, Morgan & Company; August Belmont & Company; Morton, Bliss & Company; and Jay Gould signaled that investment bankers were challenging individual promoters in engineering stock operations for quick profits. Transatlantic firms had emerged as syndicate organizers to make a market for volume stock sales requiring delicate manipulation. The extent to which such volume transactions, shifting funds between two continents, contributed to extreme fluctuations can be gauged by the speculative fever of these years and the instability of the averages. When the Drexel, Morgan syndicate sold New York Central stock abroad without depressing consequences, the event was hailed as a grand success. By 1880, however, the shares had begun to return and caused a severe downturn on Wall Street.

Since loan volume kept pushing upward too, bond syndicates offered bankers another source of safe and quick profits. The public was eagerly buying first-class bonds and even issues that had never paid a dividend could be quickly sold. An 1880 Northern Pacific syndicate contract to take $40 million in bonds set a record for the largest single flotation in railroad history. It would have been unthinkable just eighteen months earlier for bankers to place a loan of such magnitude, yet Drexel, Morgan & Company; Winslow, Lanier & Company; and August Belmont unhesitatingly joined in managing the issue and interested their immediate associates: Drexel & Company, Philadelphia; J.S. Morgan & Company, London; and Drexel, Harjes & Company, Paris. New York parties who participated included J. & W. Seligman & Company; Kuhn, Loeb & Company; Woerishoeffer & Company; L. Von Hoffman & Company; J.S. Kennedy & Company; Speyer & Company; the National Bank of Commerce and the Third National Bank. Lee, Higginson & Company and Brewster, Basset & Company in Boston, as well as Johnston Bros. & Company in Baltimore, completed the investment group.

Syndicate operations can be counted as the single most important innovation in security sales to be introduced after the Civil War.[4] Bond syndicates, as in the Northern Pacific instance, allowed financiers from many firms to share risks while amassing long-term capital in volume. By the early 1880s competition for a host of attractive contracts encouraged ever more sophisticated appraisals of potential business. Prospective syndicate managers pondered the extent to which the market could be advanced, while calculating the possible bids of other contenders. Money-market conditions, the amount of funds to be raised, the demands of prospective members, whether the issue could be merchandised abroad, the nature of the security, all received scrupulous attention. By no means were all bankers equally aggressive, but the business had become so profitable in the early 1880s that even the most conservative suspended their more stringent criteria of the late 1870s to participate in group transactions.

The high volume of securities trading in the early 1880s came to an abrupt halt with the panic of 1884 and did not resume until the end of 1887. Again as in 1873, the failure of New York banking firms sparked the run which observers attributed to the overextension of railroad building and borrowing. From 86,556 miles of track operated in 1879, the system had expanded to 125,345 miles by 1884. The year-by-year additions had been nothing short of phenomenal, climbing from 6,706 miles in 1880 to 9,846 miles in 1881, to a peak of 11,569 miles in 1882. Then in response to growing investor unwillingness to finance still further construction, the amount of new road operated began to decline. Why, with five trunk lines already competing for New York to Chicago business, build two more? New milage dropped to a still impressive 6,745 miles in 1883, but declined once again in 1884 to 3,923 miles. In

	Mileage		Investment (in millions of dollars)	
Year	Road Operated (Dec. 31)	%Change from Preceding Year	Capital Stock & Bonded Debt	%Change from Preceding Year
1878	81,747	+ 3.4	4,772	− .7
1879	86,556	+ 5.9	4,872	+ 2.1
1880	93,262	+ 7.7	5,402	+ 10.9
1881	103,108	+ 10.6	6,278	+ 16.2
1882	114,677	+ 11.2	7,016	+ 11.8
1883	121,422	+ 5.9	7,477	+ 6.6
1884	125,345	+ 3.2	7,676	+ 2.7
1885	128,320	+ 2.4	7,842	+ 2.2
1886	136,338	+ 6.2	8,163	+ 4.1
1887	149,214	+ 9.4	8,673	+ 6.2
1888	156,114	+ 4.6	9,369	+ 8.0
1889	161,276	+ 3.3	9,680	+ 3.3
% Change 1878-1889		+ 97.3		+ 102.8

Railroad Mileage and Investment: 1878-1889

SOURCE: Adapted from U.S. Bureau of the Census, *Historical Statistics of the United States, Colonial Times to 1970* (Washington, D.C.: Government Printing Office, 1975), part 2, pp. 731, 734.

1885 additions hit a low for the entire decade, totaling only 2,975 miles.[5]

Following the panic, investors had had to adjust to another element that further inhibited the flow of funds and accounts in large measure for the mid-decade construction trough. The public needed time to adjust to the restructuring of the industry's credit terms. Up until May 1884, seven to eight percent had typically been offered for long-term rail loans, and the minimum inducement had never fallen below six percent. These returns, already substantially lower than the ten percent possible before the 1873 panic, contrasted sharply with the common yield of four and four-and-a-half percent in 1885. By then hardly a road of prominence issued new mortgages at higher than five percent and only an exceptional company offered as much as six percent.[6]

The *Commercial and Financial Chronicle* took great pains to justify the lower rate structure in such a way that would restore investor confidence. It explained to its readers that reduced interest reflected reduced risks; the industry had survived the experimental stage. Certainly, the expanding system had more than demonstrated its ability to supply quick and cheap transportation for the country's "gigantic" internal and external trade.[7] The question was no longer whether railroads would succeed as a transportation form, but rather whether a particular company would succeed. Lower rates, especially for the developmental projects being planned would, it was argued, actually protect investors. By reducing fixed costs, companies moving into relatively unsettled areas could hold out for profitable returns, lessening the likelihood of default.[8]

If the long-term analysis convinced some investors, the fresh wave of receiverships in 1885 and 1886 testified to the immediate fragility of the industry's financial structure with all the attendant risks. The rapid pace of construction, much of it in parallel entries to markets east of the Mississippi, had imposed unprecedented fixed costs that could not be supported by existing traffic returns even with the introduction of lower interest rates. By 1887, however, despite the risks, investors settled for lower returns for the use of their monies because they had little choice; the industry's credit arrangements had been uniformly altered.

From the first quarter of 1887, when business conditions showed signs of stabilizing, the *Commercial and Financial Chronicle* repeatedly highlighted the role of powerful banking syndicates in carrying through reorganizations and combinations.[9] Except for the belated entrance of Brown Brothers, these were the very same firms, doing exactly what they had done a decade earlier, now using well-tested methods. In 1885 bankers found themselves in much the same position as in 1875. Faced with shortages of available portfolio funds for new building, bankers had sustained expansion programs undertaken during the boom. By 1886 they were again seeking to recover their losses through reorganization plans that would be implemented as business revived. These tactics were applied now on what seemed a grander scale only because of the growth of the network and the persistent trend, in evidence since the early 1870s, toward interregional combination.

Increase in Railroad Mileage and Investment: Selected Years, 1867-1889

Years	%Increase Road Operated	%Increase Investment
1867-1874	85.4	260.2
1874-1878	12.9	13.1
1878-1889	97.3	102.8

SOURCE: Adapted from U. S. Bureau of the Census, *Historical Statistics of the United States, Colonial Times to 1970* (Washington, D.C.: Government Printing Office, 1975), part 2, pp. 731, 734.

7
Criteria For New Business: 1877-1878

As Levi Morton and George Bliss surveyed the investment scene in the first quarter of 1877, they looked expectantly to new deals in government refunding transactions as "the best and about the only good business now being done"[1] The firm had managed the federal refunding loan of 1873 and then that of 1876. Owing especially to Morton's standing as "the representative of Wall Street in the Republican Party,"[2] they felt fairly confident of again winning syndicate management, for as Bliss observed in appraising the competition, "So far as regards political influence, I believe we are stronger today than at any former period, and I am satisfied that Belmont, Drexel, and Seligman are aware of this."[3] His evaluation proved fully accurate. Morton, Bliss & Company became the acknowledged leader in the Treasury's end-of-decade loan operations.[4]

Not surprisingly, some four years of difficult negotiations to resolve railroad tieups had bred suspicions of large projects requiring direct responsibility. On the other hand, the depression experience in no way diminished their enthusiasm for railroad investment. Quite the contrary, the partners kept an active eye on new opportunities in anticipation of an imminently expected business upturn.[5] They complained repeatedly because of the dearth of good railroad business.[6] The firm had "not made a large amount of money" during the mid-1870s, but it had "more than provided for the shrinkage in values," and Bliss reported to London in 1877: "On the whole I think the firm here are in a better position than at any former time."[7] Anxious to put monies to use, they wanted safe and short-term railroad business, especially as capital middlemen.

Public demand for first-class rail bonds stood in relief against the prevailing investor apathy of 1877. The partners expected such issues would become increasingly popular as the severe squeeze for funds passed and as the silver discussions in Congress directed attention to railroads. Contracting for and quickly merchandising these blue-chip bonds offered the perfect solution to strengthening liquid assets until the return of better times.[8] Their forecast, at least concerning investor response, had been confirmed by the summer of 1878; "Approved bonds of old, dividend paying companies which had passed through the fire, as it were unscathed, never were so much in demand."[9]

Yet here lay a dilemma. Insistence on safety and an eschewal of risk limited options. Eager for more business, but inhibited by the stringency of investor criteria, the firm restricted new commitments to contracts for first-mortgage bonds of established companies at a time when very few were available. They refused to negotiate loans for new lines, believing that the public would not lend money as they had in the early 1870s on the promise of future construction. "The halcyon days for railroad projectors, when they could borrow money in advance, and satisfy the lenders by a mortgage on what was bought with a part of the loan, had not yet returned."[10] Such bonds were sceptically regarded in the States and in the London market as well, where little had been done in railroads for a considerable time. All in all, exchanging capital for securities earmarked for distribution did not provide adequate business for financial intermediaries in 1878. But until full recovery, Morton, Bliss & Company shied away from direct finance which entailed managerial burdens plus questionable long-term liability. Not all bankers were as hesitant, as we shall see in the St. Paul & Pacific negotiations.

Since safety constituted an overarching concern in 1877 and 1878, the security of mortgages figured as a primary criterion when accepting bond contracts. To cater to investor preference, the house insisted on loans for completed road only, secured by good mortgages, or at the very least, they wanted issues with interest guaranteed. In no other way could they achieve their goal to convert securities to cash in the shortest possible time—in no longer than one year.

Morton and Bliss readily agreed when in October 1877 their neighbor, Perkins, Livingston, Post & Company, invited them to share in a contract for $1 million of Buffalo, New York & Erie bonds on which they had options for $2,380,000. Both firms anticipated a no-risk short-term outlay. This road possessed valuable real estate in Buffalo, and was leased to the Erie for a sum sufficient to pay interest on shares and bonds. (For all the changes in Erie management, interest had been regularly paid by court order.) Moreover, holders of $1.5 million of the road's bonds, scheduled to mature in December, appeared willing to reinvest. Hopefully, the securities would be taken nearly as fast as the bankers received them. The amount to be made was small; still there were "no risks except advancing money."[11] As expected, the original investors responded enthusiastically to a seven-percent first-mortgage issue, a first and only mortgage on a company without a floating debt, which for many years had paid an annual seven-percent stock dividend.[12] Demand proved so brisk that nine months later Morton, Bliss & Company held only nine bonds while the joint holdings of both firms totaled eighteen.[13]

Unexpected difficulties could complicate even a so-called safe issue, like those encountered in handling the Syracuse, Binghamton & New York first-mortgage renewal seven-percent bonds. Bliss, who was a director of the road and the parent company, the Delaware, Lackawanna & Western, had kept in constant communication with Samuel Sloan during 1876 and 1877 anxiously awaiting an expected combination of the coal roads which would advance security prices. By the end of the year, when combination appeared imminent, plans matured for the bankers to take the bonds.[14] Their preferred tactic, to bring out part of the issue in London, raised a delicate problem. To secure a quotation on the London Exchange, a prospectus had to be submitted containing data on gross and net earnings. Such information had never been required by, or disclosed to, the New York Exchange. Repeated conferences with Sloan convinced Bliss that publication would do more harm than good, yet in London their omission would certainly induce negative remark.[15]

The partners decided first to place some of the bonds with other bankers at home. Priced at par plus interest, here was an attractive offering: seven-percent bonds, with interest guaranteed by the Delaware, Lackawanna & Western under their lease, as minimum rental.[16] However, when the money discussions in Congress in February 1878 temporarily "paralyzed business of every kind," and especially that relating to securities operations,[17] the firm had little success in sharing the contract.[18] Morton's difficulty in obtaining a quotation in London soon convinced him the firm had better divest itself of this issue and disassociate itself from the offering as quickly as possible.[19] In March, Morton, Bliss & Company made application to have the bonds admitted for listing on the New York Exchange. Bliss persuaded Perkins, Livingston, Post to participate in distribution, but he refused to advertise subscriptions in the press. Instead, circulars were mailed to private and institutional domestic investors, offering the bonds for over-the-counter sales at par, plus interest, less one-half-percent commission.[20] Once they obtained a New York Exchange listing in May, the market price advanced to 101, and then rose to 103, though the securities continued to be sold to clients discounted to par.[21] By June, 565 bonds remained, by July 403, one-third of the entire issue. Though the bonds were advertised subsequently, only Perkins, Livingston, Post were identified on the financial pages.[22]

All in all, the loan had been a success. They closed the account in April 1879, happy that the securities had gone into the hands of investors, rather than speculators, always an important consideration. It would be some time consequently before they came back on the market.[23]

Another negotiation, involving J.P. Morgan, a junior member in Drexel, Morgan & Company and the son of Morton's former partner, reveals the nascent rivalry for position within the investment-banking community, a rivalry fated to intensify as railroad opportunities expanded during the next several years. In the summer of 1877, J.P. Morgan invited Morton, Bliss & Company to join the Drexel firm in purchasing a $5-million Delaware & Hudson bond issue. The business appeared so safe and prospects so good that, even before consulting with Morton, Bliss agreed to take $500,000. "I am sorry," he wrote his partner, "to owe so much money but believe the loan is good, and the pay so satisfactory that I could not resist the temptation."[24] The bonds, secured by a first and only mortgage on all the property of the Pennsylvania, had to be attractive, while the contract contained a favorable option: it allowed for a mortgage covering everything the D. & H. owned, including all coal lands. The bankers signed the contract and paid the company by January 1878.[25]

As late as April, however, Pierpont Morgan had not yet taken steps to dispose of the bonds. Instead, he went off to Europe to consult his father and urge a sterling issue to sell at or over par. (He hoped to avail himself of the privilege in the contract to buy additional bonds of the same issue and convert them to sterling.) Bliss now feared that Pierpont would persuade Morton, who was in London, to sell them their interest. He strongly advised his partner against any reduction of holdings, suggesting that he and Morgan promptly fix a plan of issue.[26]

During the slight flurry of railroad bond activity of 1877 and 1878, Bliss came thoroughly to dislike the younger man's manner, which he found arrogant and indiscreet, not to say overly ambitious. He complained that when John Ellis of the long established firm of Winslow, Lanier requested that their name appear in advertisements offering the D. & H. bonds, Morgan improperly "manifested considerable annoyance."[27] As for "the privilege of having [their] name added," as Bliss sarcastically put it, he preferred anyway to decline. Whatever the irritations of the alliance, in July 1878 Drexel, Morgan & Company and Winslow, Lanier & Company advertised the issue at home for public sale—"We recommend these bonds to investors desiring a security of undoubted character"—and a year later the account was closed.[28]

Despite these successful contracts, never had business been so dull for the Morton firm as in the summer of 1878.[29] With the exception of a few older companies, railroads had stopped borrowing to increase equipment, track, or siding. With investors afraid of companies carrying large funded debts, railroads had turned conservative. In 1870 and 1871, when construction and money were both dear, projects abounded; now, when both were cheap, companies could "hardly be got to touch them."[30] The loans being taken paid off old maturing credits and none of these were coming due on the market for some time.

Faced with the paucity of safe bond contracts and on the verge of an expected business resurgence, the bankers moved to increase their own holdings. They purchased securities for individual or joint account with partners; for the firm or joint account with the partner firm in London. Such holdings were distinct from those taken for merchandising, as were the decisions which governed their acquisition.

As shareholders, financiers became entitled under calls to their proportion of new bond issues—usually at discount. In the case, for example, of the Manhattan Elevated, the New York rapid-transit project, Morton and Bliss could take new stock at $100 a share equal to the amount they already held and as a bonus receive a $1,000 bond, with only twelve-and-a-half percent payment called in, for every seven new shares of stock purchased.[31]

In addition to taking such designated allotments of new issues, the partners wanted to buy depreciated securities of roads in default coming up for reorganization.[32] Other financiers looked likewise to enlarge their railroad holdings through reorganization settlements as prospects for business began to improve. In January 1878, the Funding Association, U.S.A. Limited, advertised for holders of defaulted bonds to contact the association, whose board included Louis Von Hoffman and William Mertens of L. Von Hoffman & Company; John W. Ellis and Charles Lanier of Winslow, Lanier & Company; and Francis O. French and Hugh McMulloch of the First National Bank.[33] The anticipated rise in market prices would be the source of returns, or as Bliss later wrote identifying a larger context: "I was in for a large loss [in the Indianapolis, Cincinnati & Lafayette] and hoped by taking an active interest in it and putting in a large sum additional to recoup myself."[34] Then again, the exchange of depreciated securities for new ones, issued according to favorable reorganization agreements, would multiply potential profit-taking.

George Bliss made repeated inquiries in 1878 for news of reorganization plans. But like his attempts to join the Atlantic, Mississippi & Ohio reorganization, he found that coming in from the outside did not offer adequate advantage. He complained to Morton that it was cheaper for them to build new roads in such cases than to refinance old ones.[35] Aside from Bliss's heavy purchases of Indianapolis, Cincinnati & Lafayette securities, and some first-mortgage bonds of the St. Louis, Council Bluffs & Omaha and the Central of Iowa prior to reorganization, Morton, Bliss & Company made small purchases of Western securities.[36] In general, however, defaulting roads did not provide the opportunities they hoped for.

So strict were the firm's criteria that they lost out on a venture, the St. Paul & Pacific, which reputedly brought a fortune to its backers. The failed negotiations are doubly instructive, first, in revealing the concerns freshly wrought by the lessons of depression and, secondly, in pointing to the formation of a Canadian-New York-London financial nexus which soon after proved vital to the completion of the Canadian Pacific. The episode, crucial in opening an international route for capital, attests to the significance of personal contacts in overcoming geographic barriers to the flow of funds.

The ingroup ties contributing to the success of the American business elite were even more pronounced in Canada.[37] Since they extended in the 1870s to a transatlantic community of wealth, it was not at all surprising that when George Stephen, the president of the Bank of Montreal, needed aid for the St. P. & P., he turned to Morton, Rose & Company. Rose and Stephen, both Scottish immigrants, had settled in Montreal and had been closely associated for at least a decade.[38] Their intimacy continued after Rose resigned as Minister of Finance in 1869 to accept Morton's offer to become a senior partner in the London banking house. Rose was on the London Committee of the Bank of Montreal when Stephen became a director of the Bank in 1871, vice-president in 1873, and president in 1876. It was at Rose's suggestion that the Bank of Montreal made its first "excursion" into investment banking in London. In collaboration with Morton, Rose & Company, the bank in 1874 underwrote a sterling loan for the provincial government of Quebec and another for the city of Montreal.[39] Stephen had translated Rose's advice into policy. While he was vice-president, and then as president, the bank continued to increase its involvement in the bond market, concentrating on governments, and purchasing and underwriting issues for New York as well as London.

In addition to these intertwining interests, Rose also shared mutual affiliations with Donald Smith, who is credited with originating the S. P. & P. plan.[40] Smith was chief commissioner of the Hudson's Bay Company from 1871 to 1874, while Rose became a director in 1872—the same year Smith became a director in the Bank of Montreal.

It was Smith who first encouraged the idea of a Canadian rail link to the United States extending from Manitoba to St. Paul. In 1870 he had discussed the possibility with Norman Kittson, a former agent of the Hudson's Bay Company and operator of a steamship line on the Red River. A year later, Smith and Stephen were among those who applied for a charter to build a road from Fort Garry to the United States boundary at Pembina or St. Vincent. They apparently envisioned an eventual connection with the St. P. & P., a Minnesota line designed to stretch to the British possessions in the northwest. Their proposal, which threatened competition to the projected Canadian Pacific, was rejected, but by the time the government introduced legislation for a C.P. branch to the international boundary three years later, financial failure south of the border preferred an alternative. Since the St.

P. & P. had passed into receivership in 1873, as had the controlling corporation, the Northern Pacific, Smith considered the possibility of acquiring the road.[41] He found willing allies in Kittson and his partner, James J. Hill, who had investigated the line going north in the direction of the Hudson's Bay property at Smith's suggestion.[42] After some persuasion, Stephen, president of the Bank of Montreal, agreed at least to talk with the New York bankers in control of the road.

These talks should be placed within the context created by the depression of the 1870s, when creditors of defaulting United States railroads turned to private banking firms to salvage what they could of their investments. As heads of Bondholders' Committees, through trustee and receivership arrangements, and by becoming directors and executives of railroad corporations, private bankers attempted to recoup not only their clients' investments, but also their own. In this instance, Stephen first began negotiations with the New York firm of J.S. Kennedy & Company, with the result that John Kennedy was to figure in the reorganization forming the St. Paul, Minneapolis & Manitoba—acting as a director for the next decade—and was also to join the syndicate which financed construction of the Canadian Pacific.[43]

In 1876 Kennedy and his partner, J. Sanford Barnes, president of both the St. Paul & Pacific First Division and the First Division, Branch Line, had good cause to listen carefully to the associate's proposals. The bankers had forced the road into receivership in August 1873, in order to oust the management and acquire working control for the bondholders.[44] Kennedy, it may be recalled, had utilized this legal device earlier to gain control of the Indianapolis, Cincinnati & Lafayette in 1870 and the technique so employed had created a sensation in business circles.[45] Jesse Farley, the receiver of the St. P. & P. since 1873, had been operating the road for the bankers and his petitions to the Minnesota Railroad Commission reveal their desire to complete the Canadian connection, but also reveal those problems which made the bankers sympathetic to an outside offer.[46]

For three years while the property had deteriorated for lack of funds, the bankers had vainly tried to secure legal possession in the Minnesota courts for the bondholders—most of whom were Dutch—who had already supplied an estimated $9 million for construction.[47] The delay, caused by unsettled title disputes between the Northern Pacific and this company, had so demoralized the Dutch creditors that they refused to furnish advances for completing the vital St. Vincent extension.[48] In June 1876, the Minnesota railroad commissioner, William Marshall, under pressure, as he said, from "great commercial interests," appealed to Governor Pillsbury to "remove all hindrances" and facilitate bondholder possession. Marshall argued that the "company proper" would not finish the northern link but he hoped the bondholders would "take hold and complete the road, and make the capital invested productive." The alternative would be to declare forfeiture of the franchise and rights to the unbuilt lines and to seek new parties to complete it—these, he feared, "could not be found."[49] However, by the end of the year Farley reported: "We have assurances from parties interested that, as soon as the title to the lands and the 140 miles of road can be secured, a new organization will be effected, and they will place themselves in condition at once to go on and complete the lines."[50]

The Dutch creditors, rather than risk additional capital for developmental building and then run the road for their own account, were as willing to consider a sale of the property to restore their losses. Discussions of the tentative terms for sale or exchange of senior securities were held in the winter of 1877, when Johan Carp, a bondholder representative, came over to meet with the bankers, empowered as trustees to arrange matters, and with the prospective purchasers represented by Hill and Kittson. Stephen and Smith deliberately stayed in the background, but Hill and also Barnes later met them in Montreal and it was decided to purchase the Dutch bonds for cash and then obtain the road through foreclosure proceedings. The immediate problem was the cash and at this point Stephen suggested he might secure purchase funds in England from "parties known to Mr. Smith and himself."[51] Consequently, his understanding with Hill, Kittson, and Smith allowed for English parties to be admitted to a one-fifth interest and, furthermore, Stephen could "concede any reasonable terms" to obtain the loan.[52]

As noted earlier, Stephen brought his proposition to Morton, Rose & Company, the firm which had recently collaborated in successfully merchandising government issues and had been involved in Canadian railroad finance ever since Rose left Ottawa. In extensive testimony some years after relating to the financing of this railway, Stephen did not identify the bankers he had contacted between September and December 1877. Nor did his hazy recollections, meant to justify his own behavior, reflect the nature or dynamics of the subsequent interchange. "After considerable negotiation I utterly failed. Nobody believed—or at least I failed to induce anybody to believe—that the property was good for anything."[53]

In fact, both Rose and Morton, who happened to be in London, were much interested. But in keeping with policy, whereby all investment decisions had to be approved by the senior partners in both firms, the papers were sent to George Bliss in New York. Bliss was still studying the scheme when he saw Stephen immediately on the latter's return in the last week of December 1877. Though Bliss's own inclination had initially been "against taking an interest in enterprises of this sort," his interview with Stephen, he assured John Rose and his partners in London, increased his "willingness to look into the matter carefully."[54]

Bankers had become considerably more cautious since the carefree days before 1873. Less sanguine, their insistence upon detailed knowledge tempered the "young America spirit" which had characterized much of the decision-making of the earlier boom. Bliss in particular demanded more specific information and he wrote Stephen in mid-January that he would undertake further investigation "without exciting remark."[55]

As he studied the map, he pondered the problem of passenger and freight traffic. The risk of new building in sparsely settled territory worried him especially. What was the potential business from the section through which the road passed? What would it be from Winnipeg once the Canadian Pacific branch was completed? The long-range possibilities of the road depended, as he cautioned his London partners, on the construction of the Canadian Pacific—"were the Canadian Pacific finished to a point far West of a junction with this I would expect a considerable business from the Western Extension of this line."[56] Besides immediate and prospective traffic returns, a major consideration was the one and a half million acres of unsold land belonging to the company. The sale of these was essential. While it seemed to Bliss that the section of the country covered by the land grant was too far north for emigration, he had also heard that the Valley of the Red River all the way up to Winnipeg was a good wheat-growing section. How much the lands could be sold for—that was the question. He instructed Edward F. Winslow, whom he often turned to in such matters, to find out.[57] These questions of potential income had also to be balanced against expenditures, which Stephen tended to underestimate. Among other costs, interest had to be paid on a bonded debt of from $12,000 to $15,000 a mile and the iron rails

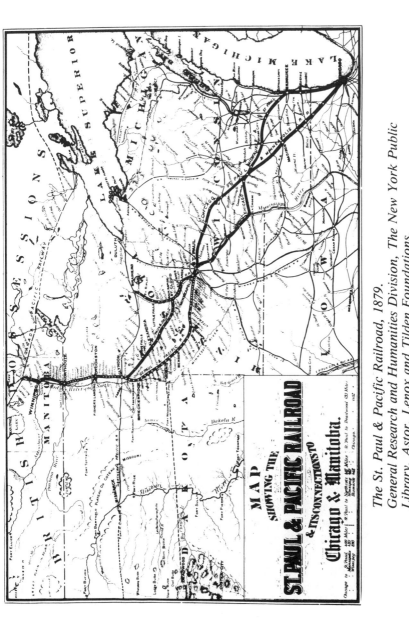

The St. Paul & Pacific Railroad, 1879.
General Research and Humanities Division, The New York Public
Library, Astor, Lenox and Tilden Foundations.

on the whole road, some 552 miles, would probably need to be
relaid; judging from experience with English imports, they needed
constant replacement.[58]

Although ostensibly Bliss was not nearly so favorably disposed
to Stephen's project as Morton or Rose, in part, he was playing
devil's advocate, as he usually did when faced with his partners'
enthusiasms. In fact, his main complaint, shared by other bankers
in 1877, concerned the lack of new railroad business. As for that
requiring venture capital, however, he needed to be convinced of
the safety and profitableness of the transaction and he hoped that
Stephen would answer his objections "satisfactorily," at their next
meeting.[59]

Stephen, accompanied by Richard Angus, general manager of
the Bank of Montreal, was in New York again in January 1878
conferring with Bliss and also with Kennedy. According to a new
proposal, determined on for the Dutch, the bonds would be
bought at the stipulated price, but on credit, part payment to be
made before purchase and the rest after the foreclosure sale, from
the proceeds of a new bond issue. Kennedy agreed to the plan,
considering it "the best thing for the Dutchmen" and "a good
thing for Kittson and Hill and their friends."[60]

Despite these credit terms, the larger problem of construction
funds still remained unresolved even by early March. Stephen had
decided, he told Bliss, to "go into the thing in any case," but
before presenting the matter to the bankers again, he wanted, as
Bliss explained to Morton, to ascertain the exact resources of his
"Minnesota friends," that is, of Hill and Kittson.[61] In the meantime, on March 13, 1878, the Dutch signed the agreement although
Stephen had not as yet arranged an outside capital commitment.
Conferences held with Stephen in late March had convinced Bliss
that Hill and Kittson were unable to furnish cash and that Stephen
would have to supply their share. Barnes was of the same opinion:
"Now I have personally the highest regard for both these
gentlemen, and I would take their word as soon as that of any man
of whom I know so slightly, but except that I have a general notion
that some Canadian gentlemen stand behind them, and who are
able and willing to furnish the large sum mentioned, I can say
nothing which adds strength."[62] Barnes' veiled allusions to Canadian backers were also echoed by Farley, who also doubted the
resources of Hill and Kittson. "His [Kittson's] friends who is [sic]
expected to furnish the money has unlimited control of Canadian
Politicks, It might become a Canady projeck [sic] but that would

be a matter of no moment to me if we could make some money."[63]

Where then was the money to come from and how would liability be distributed? This was a developmental project requiring a considerable amount in excess of a million dollars. Besides $280,000 for expenses and costs of the Dutch Committee, the legal charges up to that date came to $150,000 and substantial lawsuits might have to be compromised to avoid delay in selling and completing reorganization. Also a "large sum" had to be paid as "compensation to the Trustees under the Mortgages and to the Receivers Messrs. J.S. Kennedy." Furthermore, the sixty-four miles of road to be built, even though mostly graded, would cost about $600,000 if constructed, as Stephen intended, with steel rails. Then, if business increased because of good crops and the new link, at least $200,000 more would be necessary for additional rolling stock.[64]

Stephen's vagueness created a major uncertainty. He still had not indicated by late March whether the bankers were to be admitted on the basis of his interest, if they were also expected to furnish a proportion for Hill and Kittson, or if they would be partners on signing a contract with Stephen alone. What therefore would be their liability? Since the insecurity posed by a contingent liability with Stephen and his partners could be eliminated by joint liability with the Bank of Montreal, the bankers viewed such a connection favorably.[65]

On March 28, the associates signed a new agreement apportioning two-fifths of profits and losses to Stephen and one-fifth each to the other three members. This agreement further stipulated that Stephen could use his two-fifths in any manner necessary to carry out plans for purchasing and made him responsible for all financial arrangements for further construction.[66] He had thus increased his ability to secure capital just when reports of emigration pressing into Manitoba, and of improved demand for land, spurred Bliss's enthusiasm. Bliss came to look favorably on Stephen's latest suggestion that, if interested, the banking house take a one-fourth proportional share, which would come to, from the incomplete information provided, about $400,000. Thus, when May passed without word from Stephen, Bliss inquired anxiously, assuring Morton, he had "never indicated any indisposition to Stephen to take an interest in his Northern Pacific enterprise, but strangely enough . . . had not heard from him."[67]

Faced with the financiers' hesitation, with their demand for time and assurances, Stephen had turned in March to his own bank for a loan of $280,000 to pay off the Dutch Committee and then for additional funds that raised the total to $700,000. It has been argued that he urgently needed capital by the spring to complete the line from Melrose to Sauk Center by August 1, and to Alexandria by December 2, to earn the land grant and to ward off the newly reorganized rival Northern Pacific from any attempt to force a bankruptcy.[68] Yet whatever the immediate basis for his decision, and even allowing for reluctance on the part of Bliss, at no point between September 1877 and June 1878 did the bankers in London or New York reject his proposal. Actually, the partners, unaware of the Bank of Montreal arrangement, had continued to debate terms for their participation into June; Morton preferring a straight $100,000, while Bliss, the most recalcitrant, initially called for a proportional one-fourth share of $400,000.[69] Although the partners had dallied, it was Stephen who left off negotiations. And whatever his prior efforts, he had refused to clarify adequately the exact amounts necessary or, more importantly, the liability of those to be involved.

As for the loan from the Bank of Montreal, the *Times* called it "very ill-timed, coming as it did on the back of a scare in banking credit that . . . very nearly involved the temporary suspension of half the banks in the Dominion."[70] Questionable also was the collateral, the exact nature of which was never disclosed to the bank's shareholders. Bliss agreed with the critics who charged the loan would never have been made at all had not Stephen and Angus been personally concerned. "An advance such as the Bank of Montreal made to Stephen and his associates would never have been made by a national bank or, if made, not meet the approval of the Banking Department—In fact a bank that made such an advance would be put in the hands of a receiver."[71]

The St. P. & P. problems were resolved shortly after the road was reorganized as the St. Paul, Minneapolis & Manitoba in 1879. Stephen became president of the new company, a consolidation of the St. P. & P. and the Red River & Manitoba road, including all branches and extensions; but it should also be noted that J.S. Kennedy & Company were the financial and transfer agents for this road and that Kennedy, a member of the first directorate, became vice-president in 1884 and held both positions till the end of the decade.[72] These continued affiliations in the decision-making hierarchy strongly suggest that this banking firm had increased its direct interest in the enterprise, and what evidence there is supports such an assumption. To begin with, it should be noted that the entire physical property consolidated by the 1879 reorganization had been in the hands of the banking firm since 1877. Kennedy and Barnes had applied for a charter to incorporate the Red River & Manitoba line in 1877, with capital reported at half a million, in order to build and operate the road connecting the St. Paul to the St. Vincent extension. Farley, whom they appointed general manager of this line, continued at the same time as manager and receiver of the St. P. & P. companies.[73] Moreover, from 1877 until the St. P. & P. was obtained at foreclosure in the spring of 1879, Kennedy, as trustee, "had full authority to take action as he thought best," and had been purchasing Dutch bonds at prices ranging from fourteen to seventy-four percent of face value.[74] While the bulk of these were slated for the associates—since bankers commonly relied on the reorganization period to acquire depreciated securities for their own account—it is likely that the firm increased its security holdings at this time in order to exchange them for new issues on reorganization. And since the $700,000 Montreal loan Stephen had obtained was nowhere near the million or more estimate Bliss calculated as necessary, we might also speculate that the Kennedy firm supplied part of the additional venture funds needed for the project. Indeed, some thirty years later Stephen was to acknowledge that as a "reward" for Kennedy's usefulness he had given him a one-fifth interest in the enterprise.[75]

This business, although it eluded the Morton firm, had focused attention on Canada as a field for capital employment. In July 1878, just a month after learning of the Bank of Montreal loan, Bliss urged Charles Rose, Sir John's son and replacement in London: "Come over, Canadian railroads are not yet in favor, yet I think if you were to take a run through the Dominion it would do good."[76] Of course, the road, which would require enormous outlays of both venture and loan capital, was the Canadian Pacific. When Sir John Macdonald returned to power in 1879, he announced the completion of the transcontinental as a keystone for his National Policies. Both the Prime Minister and Stephen, despite the avowed anti-Americanism of the new economic policy, called immediately, as we shall see, on the Morton and Kennedy firms to provide both high-risk equity and loan capital. By then Morton's firms in London and New York had altered criteria for railroad investment.

8
Looking To Market Returns: 1879-1881

In their search for new business in 1877 and 1878, Morton, Bliss & Company had focused on contracts for well-secured first-mortgage bonds and government loans. Such transactions, promising to be short-term and devoid of risk, met the partners' criteria for safety but not for profits. Returns had been limited, since good rail contracts had been hard to come by and in the case of governments, "the margin ha[d] always been narrow until either by manipulation or otherwise, prices advanced."[1] The partners awaited recovery for the return of viable railroad business which promised more varied and satisfactory sources for profits.

After the successful resumption of specie payments in January 1879, business confidence gradually revived. The stimulus came from agriculture. Exceptionally abundant spring crops, coming at a time when those in Europe were unusually poor, accounted, by September, for foreign shipments of a million bushels of grain a day; cotton exports reached an all-time record; and large harvests of corn found a ready market abroad.[2] Since depression prices for supplies and labor, coupled to cutbacks, had enabled railroad managers to reduce costs "below all previous levels,"[3] the large agricultural freight increases produced a net result in real earnings beyond all expectations. By the second quarter, rail stocks, even shares of companies previously in default, as well as bonds of all sorts, spiraled so rapidly that Wall Street was taken by surprise. The marked advance in the averages, especially for securities of financially discredited companies, dismayed the most experienced observers.[4] As rails replaced governments, the bankers judged, "We shall be content for a long period of time re: gov'ts with whatever sum we can make out of those in which we now have an interest."[5] Having moved from governments to railroads in 1869, the firm repeated the same pattern a decade later.

Morton, who had been elected to Congress in 1878, stayed in Washington for much of the time and then went abroad after his appointment as Minister to France in 1881. Bliss wrote him regularly, at least once a day, detailing their operations and seeking approval of major decisions. This correspondence is laced with hints, tips, and gossip of securities operations. Inside knowledge of earnings, traffic, leases, and the prospects of individual companies provides another theme. The resident partner always relayed news from "the street," but he regarded his exchanges on a regular basis with intimates in various enterprises as a somewhat more reliable source.[6]

Expanding opportunities now introduced a plethora of options, compounding the problems of decision-making. In an era deficient in institutionalized arrangements for publicizing business operations—when cost-profit data and capitalization figures were withheld at will or frequently inaccurate when supplied even in annual reports—incomplete evidence was often gathered through an informal network consisting of railroad personnel, financial intermediaries, large investors, corporation lawyers, and judges who passed on selected information which became the basis for investment decisions. Carefully worded confidential requests such as the following abounded:

> I want to inquire of something you may feel constrained to decline to answer. If not and you feel at liberty to give me the information I desire I shall feel obliged by your doing so. Are the Rochester and State Line Bonds a good security and if arrangement with the Central are of a permanent character. . . . In case you give me the information and wish so I will consider your answer confidentially.[7]

Under such constraints, decision-making demanded constant sifting of material and evaluation of sources. The motives and veracity of informers necessitated continuing assessment. In practice, the secrecy shielding business activity, which the bankers themselves insisted on, had the effect of complicating and occasionally impeding rational investment behavior.

It was particularly difficult in 1880 to draw upon the lessons of past experience, for as Henry Clews recalled, "So numerous were the combinations, consolidations and extensions of railways that in many cases the analogy with former periods was lost, and comparisons as to earnings were of little value."[8] Still, so rapidly did the Morton firm expand its commitments that the possibility of inadequate cash reserve replaced the former concern over inadequate business. The offices on Nassau Street filled with a steady stream of visitors outlining "new schemes constantly." Bliss held as steadfast as circumstances allowed to a set of cautious

criteria and deliberately guarded against Morton's renewed
enthusiasm. He skeptically questioned the terms of any large-scale
direct involvement, reminding his partner that not only had
building costs begun to rise, but that financing construction
directly required "constant attention."

> The building of a road requires constant attention and a con-
> siderable period of time. . . .Buying stocks for a short term
> soon works itself out, but the building of 70 miles of railroad,
> or more, is a pretty long strain! I haven't discouraged these
> people but spoke pretty well of their enterprise.[9]

Here is the key to their investment policy as money eased and
security prices crested. No longer did they discourage direct
financing, but they still preferred to limit their involvement to
short-term transactions and to reap quick returns in the advancing
market. For a fast turnover the firm concentrated on stock
syndicates and bond contracts. In this more restricted business as
financial middlemen, they had only to turn securities to cash. And
in response to lively investor demand they could relax their
priorities for safety. By late 1880 the partners accepted loan
contracts on projected track so long as traffic appeared assured.
Stock trading for their own account supplemented profits from
securities contracts until the market levelled off in 1882. The firm
and the partners bought and sold, unloaded depreciated shares,
and with an eye on market returns, intervened to effect combination of smaller roads in which they had substantial interests.
While profits could be made with but minor risk in the bull
market, bankers appraised more demanding ties for proportional
returns.

Of all the stock syndicates of this period, perhaps the most
famous is the sale of a portion of Vanderbilt's New York Central
& Hudson River shares. The size of the stock transaction, when
news of the agreement first became public, created enormous
excitement. Sales of 250,000 shares could depress the market.
Historians have presented the operation as "J. P. Morgan's first
major venture in corporate investment banking"[10] or as initiating
a new phase in railroad-banker relationships which led eventually
to "finance capitalism." Contemporaries, on the other hand,
identified this as a syndicate operation headed by Drexel, Morgan

& Company and credited Junius Morgan with overseeing sales in the London market.[11]

From a banker's perspective, the operation, well managed, represented exactly the kind of short-term, high-volume transaction deemed desirable. Morton, Bliss & Company readily bought 15,000 shares and the individual partners also took portions of the 250,000 purchased by the syndicate in November 1879. By the end of January 1880, Morton's firm had already received twenty percent on par for sales of the 15,000 shares, and soon after, in March, they sold off a thousand more at 132.[12] The negotiation had gone so smoothly that Morton, Bliss & Company secretly agreed to take an interest with Sage and Gould of purchases by a "new ring" working the market to buy the balance of the syndicate holdings.[13] When J. P. Morgan, unaware of Gould's plans and so far "very happy over the result," left for London that month to confer with his father, he was not about to sell off and he advised Bliss, " 'Don't you sell any shares. I know what I am talking about, it is going much higher!' "[14]

The profits from the New York Central syndicate, even before they were realized, were already slated for Huntington's Central Pacific stock syndicate. Huntington, hoping to make a market, was arranging a purchase of 50,000 shares to encourage frequent and easy trading. If he could impress the public at home with their value, he planned to use Central Pacific stock as collateral to borrow three or four million for building the Southern Pacific.[15] Bliss judged that "well managed, it should be very safe, especially if the outside holdings are in good hands."[16] Although the affairs of the company were actually "a sealed book," investors seemed favorably impressed with both its financial condition and prospects. After much discussion, however, Bliss refused to have his firm manage the issue because of its liability feature.[17] Shareholders' traditional liability for all company obligations had in this instance been circumvented by the issuance of stock certificates with coupons attached numbered one to twenty for the semiannual dividend. These coupons could be separated for presentation and the owner remain conveniently anonymous. Bliss feared that this "contingent liability" might, if disclosed, cause concern which would depress the shares' marketable value.[18]

The Speyers, less agitated by the device, agreed to manage the issue, but pressed for a major share reallocation. In the opening conversations, Morton, Bliss & Company had been promised 5,000 shares, Kuhn, Loeb & Company, 5,000, and Russell Sage

5,000; the remainder would go to Darius Mills, W. Flower, J. D. Prince, and Speyer & Company. Coaxed to relinquish 1,000 shares, the Morton house succeeded in keeping their interest at 4,500 and squeezed Kuhn, Loeb the less powerful firm, to 2,000.[19] The entire 50,000 lot, purchased in mid-January for seventy-five, was sold in the domestic market within the month. With the plan to push them to par, at a market price of eighty-four, they were a "great buy." Morton even considered the possibility of a new pool[20] and Morton, Rose & Company declared their interest, believing they could market additional blocks in London.[21]

Inevitably, the return of a bull market, which made short-term stock syndicates profitable both at home and abroad, intensified competition among private bankers for new bond contracts. Rivalry flourished among the handful of firms recently involved in refunding transactions, as rails bearing six and seven percent became more attractive to investors than government four percents.[22] In shaping syndicates and winning contracts, Morton, Bliss & Company was challenged repeatedly, especially by J. & W. Seligman, Drexel, Morgan & Company, and by the upcoming Kuhn, Loeb & Company. As a result of competitive maneuvering, aspects other than the character of investor demand began to emerge more prominently in bond syndicate operations. Tactical problems such as market manipulation, the possible bids of other groups, and relations with railroad executives took on increasing importance as the volume of business and the contest for it accelerated. Skirmishes for business fostered unaccustomed situations and strained relations within the banking community.

Bitter infighting demanded skill and sophistication, as seen in the bankers' negotiations which began in November 1879 for an issue of Metropolitan Railway bonds to finance New York's elevated system. Morton's interest in urban rail systems dated back to 1870, when as a member of a New York Chamber of Commerce Committee he had investigated their feasibility. Like August Belmont and William Butler Duncan, he joined the board of the New York Viaduct Railroad in 1871 with high hopes for improving local passenger service and for linking interstate through systems to city terminals. Engineering and legal impediments to construction temporarily delayed financing of such projects, but in the later 1870s, still confident in the potential of these ventures, Morton's firm joined syndicates financing both the New York Elevated and the Manhattan Elevated. In the boom of 1879 bankers believed investment capital would be attracted, after its initial hesitancy, to support urban transit projects that extended the residential perimeters of the city and added even further to rising real-estate values.[23]

Josiah Fiske, chairman of the Metropolitan's Executive Committee, had confidentially informed Bliss and Morton (his associates in Manhattan Elevated) that Jacob Schiff of Kuhn, Loeb planned to bid for the $4-million issue. On the added tip that the railroad wanted par or over for the bonds, Morton's firm immediately invited Drexel, Morgan and the Seligmans to join with them, only to discover that both these houses were already committed to Winslow, Lanier.[24] They failed further in repeated attempts to interest Louis Von Hoffman & Company, Harris Fahnestock of the First National Bank, Vanderbilt, and John A. Stewart. The prospective party Morton, Bliss & Company finally gathered included private capitalists Darius Mills and T. B. Musgrave, each for a quarter interest, and their London firm for an eighth. Morton, Rose & Company especially favored these bonds since they were payable in London at the option of the holder and at a fixed rate of exchange.

Formal written agreements with financial intermediaries were still relatively new. In this case, a clause unnoticed by Fiske in an earlier contract restricted all the railway's new issues to Kuhn, Loeb & Company until January 1, 1880. When rumors reached Kuhn, Loeb of Morton's intent to bid a little over par, Schiff threatened an injunction if the railroad delivered the bonds to another banker. Fiske and Bliss regretfully decided, and the Executive Committee agreed, temporarily to delay the issue.[25]

The tentativeness of financial and political arrangements complicated matters further. Just two months later, when Fiske announced bids would be taken, the bonds had fallen in esteem. Doubts had already spread among insiders concerning the finances of the Loan and Improvement Company, the construction company behind the loan. In the interim, too, a bill in the New York Legislature reducing fares to five cents publicized government control over rates. Prospective London syndicate members feared negative effects in the foreign market. The contract's appeal diminished, but the amount of the issue had been increased from $4 to $6 million; $1 million cash delivered at the option of the purchaser, $1 million successively thereafter for three months, and $2 million when the road was completed, as scheduled, in mid-August.[26] With the general waning of enthusiasm, Kuhn, Loeb now announced they would not even bid.

Twice in one week Fiske came in to reassure Bliss of the safety of the issue; he swore the security was beyond doubt.

Once Kuhn, Loeb withdrew, the competition took another turn. The Seligmans—counting on Drexel, Morgan; Winslow, Lanier; Hallgarten & Company; and John A. Stewart—announced their interest. And in order to forestall an independent bid, Seligman offered Morton, Bliss & Company a joint share of $1 million.[27] Since Morton and Bliss had resolved to manage their own syndicate for the entire $6 million, they rejected the proposition.[28] Bids were to be delivered on the eleventh, and on the ninth Bliss had an urgent message from Joseph Seligman: would he come by after closing? His syndicate, Seligman confided, "would be glad to fix it" so that Morton, Bliss & Company would not bid separately. Drexel had agreed to reduce their share to $1,750,000; Ellis of Winslow, Lanier would reduce theirs to $475,000; and the Seligmans in New York and abroad would take only $750,000, leaving $500,000 each for Hallgarten and John A. Stewart. The remainder would be given to Morton, Bliss and "their friends." Bliss again refused, insisting that since each had its own group, the proper division, if they were to unite, would be $3 million apiece.[29]

Determined to take the business, Morton and Bliss persuaded their associates to approve a high bid of 98.56 for $6 million, or 99.07 for $4 million with an option for the remaining $2 million. (In either case accrued interest would add three-quarters of a point.) Pointing to J. P. Morgan's success the preceding day with L. & N. six percents, they argued that he naturally would be anxious to win the Metropolitans. Furthermore, rumors of their earlier plan to make a high bid against Kuhn, Loeb would certainly inflate Seligman's offer. They felt the bonds would reach 102½ without any effort as soon as the sale was made and the price could be advanced still further without risk.[30]

Notwithstanding protracted negotiations with numerous parties, an inside contact, and a considerable effort to anticipate their rivals, the Morton firm lost the contract. At the reading of bids, Fiske appeared very pleased and the board of directors were equally delighted with Morton, Bliss & Company's offer. When the Seligmans' was opened, it far exceeded all expectations. The railroad became the beneficiary of the skirmish.[31]

Railroad executives, well aware of the scurry for good business, deliberately used it to advantage in securing loan capital. The Chicago, Milwaukee & St. Paul, considered a first-class investment even when extending road somewhat in advance of settlement, made it a policy to invite bids for their securities. So varied were the C. M. & St.P. negotiations with the banking community that, while the Morton firm fought for one issue, Winslow, Lanier & Company and J. S. Kennedy were selling the corporation's six-percent Southwestern bonds and Kuhn, Loeb was handling its five-percent Milwaukee bonds.

The railroad played one house against another, as in the complicated negotiations for their Iowa & Dakota extension bonds. Julius Wadsworth, banker-vice-president of the road, called on Bliss in the spring of 1879 to discuss plans for selling $2.5 million seven-percent bonds secured by a mortgage on the Iowa & Dakota Division. Wadsworth proposed to deliver a half million July 1, a half million August 1, and a half million September 1. The last million was to be issued on unbuilt road, and if the line was extended still further, the corporation would issue yet another million.[32] Both partners favored the business for, as Bliss noted, he didn't "know any bond that promises so well for those Trust and Investment Co.'s for which inquiry has several times been made."[33] However, before speaking with Bliss, Wadsworth had already partially committed the first half million—with an option on the rest—to Jacob Schiff. Kuhn, Loeb had then allied with Winslow, Lanier and Woerishoffer & Company.[34]

Morton's firm and Kuhn, Loeb now matched offers. Since Schiff would take the first shipment at 97½, plus the accrued interest, if the bonds were delivered before July 1, Bliss met this price and offered somewhat more for those deliverable in August and September. He also persuaded Wadsworth to delay all negotiations until he conferred with Morton for their best terms. "I don't like it," Bliss nevertheless complained. "It leaves them the final chance—I would like to have the final chance after he [Wadsworth] has seen K. L. & Co."[35] When Wadsworth subsequently offered Morton, Bliss one and a half million with the option on the remainder, Bliss insisted on a written agreement. Despite the formalized precaution, Schiff reaffirmed his syndicate's claim to the first half million. A compromise allowed Morton, Bliss & Company to retain one million at 97½ with an option on the second million at the same price, but allowed the Kuhn, Loeb group immediate delivery on the first half million.[36]

At the time of the I. & D. negotiations in April, Morton, Bliss & Company expected to realize 102 on the bonds. In view of the strong market, this estimate was soon revised to 105. Even if demand did not continue into the autumn, even if they had to carry them over into the early part of 1880, the firm expected to realize a profit of more than five points on the funds supplied to the railroad.[37] The issue did even better than predicted. In January 1880, the bankers advanced the price to purchasers to 107½ and two weeks later to 108½. When their holdings dropped to $600,000, the price was again advanced to 110. As orders rapidly continued, they estimated the $2 million of bonds would bring a return of $200,000.[38] The final statement, prepared in April 1880, just a year after the purchase agreement, showed a gratifying net profit of $227,709, of which Morton, Rose & Company received $56,927.[39]

The return to London reflected the New York firm's policy of sharing contracts to bolster the London company's business or, more frequently, to take advantage of intermarket sales. For some time prior to 1879 so little had been done in the way of U. S. rail offerings in London that Morton, Bliss & Company gave its transatlantic partners a one-fourth interest in both the definite I. & D. purchase and the option. Although the bonds were merchandised domestically, the London house, having been brought into the purchase syndicate, received a proportionate share of the profits.[40] In contrast to Kuhn, Loeb & Company, which frequently sold an entire allotment abroad, Morton's New York firm preferred to divide merchandising when money-market conditions allowed.

While infighting for contracts encouraged railroads to spread their business rather than rely on one investment house, banker reluctance to accept contracts functioned similarly to diversify capital alliances. For example, when in April 1880, Alex Mitchell, president of the Chicago, Milwaukee & St. Paul, had difficulty selling $3 million six-percent bonds to Drexel, Morgan for the newly purchased Chicago & Pacific line, Wadsworth approached Morton, Bliss & Company. Bliss felt as hesitant as Morgan, for in April 1880, monies going into bonds had for the moment dried up. "I don't want to load up and be compelled to borrow largely to carry them unless there is good profit. There is nothing to indicate London can sell them."[41] Within a week Mitchell sold Kuhn, Loeb the whole three million.[42] A month later, Morton, Bliss & Company received a cable from London—Could they get $2.5 million of the bonds the C. M. & St. P. were issuing on their newly purchased Minnesota Southern line? Morton, Rose had a buyer for a half million at ninety-six. Bliss now doubted they could get the business. "If Schiff of K. L. & Co. succeeds in selling the 3 million Chicago & Pacific Div. bonds readily on the other side he will no doubt take the balance of the Minnesota Southern division issue, and if he don't, he won't."[43]

Such anger is indicative of the growing threat posed by Kuhn, Loeb & Company in the highly active private banking community. After 1875, when Jacob Schiff joined, the firm vigorously and quickly became a major railroad investment house. From the late 1870s they were distributing bonds of both the C. M. & St. P. and the C. & N., major competitors in the Northwest. They then enlarged their business further by becoming the principal bankers for the Pennsylvania. Besides Schiff, J. P. Morgan also emerged as a particularly aggressive contender for railroad business in the late 1870s. Bliss disliked the "young" Morgan intensely, finding him arrogant, impulsive, and dyspeptic. With the Seligmans, on the other hand, who belonged to the same generation and had shared a similar apprenticeship, moving from retailing to import-jobbing to banking, relations were always cordial. In the refunding syndicates of the late 1870s, Morton served as a buffer to shield them from the active disdain of the Rothschilds. From time to time, Jesse and Joseph inquired after political favors and information which Morton could provide better than any other investment banker of the day. In the matter of the Panama Canal, for example, they asked if Morton would especially intercede with Secretary Evarts, who, they thought, preferred the Nicaraguan scheme over the Lessups plan, for which they were arranging the financing.[44] Their associations in railroad financing dated back to 1870 in the Katy and the New Orleans road, while in the late 1870s they cooperated in syndicates such as that for the St. Louis-San Francisco first-mortgage bonds.[45]

The growth of syndicates for purchasing and retailing bonds is attributable to the magnitude of transactions and the need to share risk.[46] At the same time, consolidation within the industry brought bankers of previously separate properties into working alliances. Keen competition among investment bankers also encouraged participation, for rather than chance underbidding, they found that cooperation proved finally more profitable. Still, rivalry and personal dislikes affected syndicate groupings so that in the late 1870s and early 1880s loose clusters formed with certain associates favored over others, and by the end of the century specific groups had emerged in syndicate operations.

When stock prices fell in May 1880, large operators such as

Vanderbilt began unloading. The decline continued into mid-month, abetted by the return of New York Central and Erie shares from abroad.[47] Worried by the risks of an inflated market and the frequent oscillation in stocks, investors began transferring funds, stimulating a further demand for bonds. But the fate of new companies during and after the panic had not been entirely forgotten and the public looked for tangible completed property or some evidence that earnings covered costs.[48]

Long-term capital once again, as in the early 1870s, began to move into government-guaranteed issues in South America. When Morton, Bliss & Company concluded a contract for $4 million six-percent Panama Railway bonds in October 1880, the partners decided against sending any to London knowing they could be closed domestically at par in just a few days. The bonds, purchased at ninety-five in equal portions for the New York firm, for the London office, and for Trenor W. Parks, American president of the road, were quickly sold to friends at 106 and to outsiders at 110.[49]

So many new issues were widely advertised by the fall of 1880 as to to remind observers of the days before the 1873 panic. Although these bonds were for the most part secured by line already built and were issued or guaranteed by established companies, still the *Railroad Gazette* warned—"It will be very easy for us to build too much railroad these days: money is easy to get, and the cost of construction since iron went down is quite moderate."[50]

Even Bliss began more and more to revise his investment criteria. His steadfast caution had been appropriate to the prevailing mood of 1877 and 1878, but the mounting demand for securities now tempered his requirements for safety. When stock incentives redeemed risk, he reconsidered his objections to bonds on unbuilt roads. He became positively enthusiastic about a $3.5 million issue of six-percent bonds of the Massachusetts Central Railway. This company had contracted for the completion of a line to the Hoosic Tunnel and for a spur from Amherst to North-hampton. The road and spur totaled 117 miles, financed at $30,000 a mile. According to the proposition offered by S. B. Welsch, Welsch thought he could get the bonds at ninety-two and a half and in addition have $1 million in stock "thrown in." He would take his compensation in stock and the balance would go to the bankers with the bonds.[51] Though the scheme seems not to have come to fruition, it highlights the behind-the-scenes incentives which make it so difficult accurately to estimate investment returns.

Small companies in particular had difficulty finding loan capital and typically offered bankers stock incentives. When the Wisconsin & Minnesota Railroad proposed to build fifty-four miles of track to connect with the Wisconsin Central line, it called on Morton, Bliss to take half the issue, $405,000 in bonds at eighty-five, and offered them $45,000 in stock. The risk was minimal since the seven-percent gold interest bonds were to be delivered by the United States Trust Company—trustees under the mortgage—on certificates of the engineer, guaranteeing the completion of sections of not less than three miles, attested to by a person to be selected by the purchasers of the bonds. As further reassurance, the company agreed not to lay more than a quarter of the line with iron rails and pointed to arrangements with the Wisconsin Central which virtually assured traffic for the completed road.[52] But Bliss had heard reports that these negotiations wouldn't succeed and so, despite the incentives, his firm took only a third of the issue, which came to $271,000; part went to Morton's account, part to a joint account, and on Morton's request, his close political associate, New York Senator Roscoe Conkling, was given $21,000 of the bonds.[53]

From 1879 to 1882 speculation was the order of the day. Market manipulations puffed prices, created an irresistible demand for bonds and shares, and eventually brought public censure of the better-known and bolder jobbers. Investment bankers, more careful of their reputations, were more covert in their methods. However, they were heading the more important syndicate operations and for as long as they anticipated continued advances, active trading offered an attractive source of profit. Reflecting on the market drop in May 1880, Bliss regretted their lack of surplus funds on hand—it was a good time to buy more.[54]

In addition to trading on the New York Exchange, American bankers with partner firms abroad increased their intermarket dealings in 1879 and 1880. Just as Morton, Bliss & Company handled securities trading on the New York exchange for Morton, Rose & Company, so the London house handled trading for the New York firm in London. Neither firm served as brokers; rather, orders were executed through brokers in the same manner as they were for national banks, savings banks, and trust companies. Buying and selling might be done for the firms' accounts, for the partners' personal accounts, for joint accounts, or for those of favored clients. Railroad associates such as William Osborn of the Illinois Central and Josiah Fiske of Manhattan Elevated, and Morton's political associates such as Roscoe Conkling and James Blaine, with accounts in London, were kept informed of trading opportunities, much as Simeon Chittenden was about Erie:

> Seligman told me the other day that his brother in London was still holding Erie Second Mortgage bonds. They have been dealing largely in Erie Stock between the two markets, and also in Erie Second Mortgage bonds, most of the time holding considerable sums, for several years past. We have had more or less to do with them in & out, from the time bonds selling in London at 32½—out while large advance in price was made. Our London people now hold some which cost less than present rates, & we incline to wait certainly till present issues are exchanged for the new bonds. . . .Jewett has great confidence in the ability of the road to provide interest on the new exchange issue to be made—Gov. Morgan also thinks well of the securities. It is stated confidentially that California Keene is a very large holder, having gone in when the price was about 60/62. I do not know whether the Convertible issue—in dollars—can be purchased in this market. We have never dealt in either save in London. If you want some bought M. B. & Co. will do it by cable & either bring the bonds here or retain them in London. The exchange for the new bonds is to be made in London and they can be carried there afterwards in case you desire. I want to correct your guess as to our holdings —you say ½ million—that is very excessive though no doubt bold stock operators would be willing to hold to such an extent.[55]

Although bankers usually benefited by their access to inside information, their role in management could inhibit trading activity. This had been the case in 1877, when Bliss refused, though urged by John Rose, to deal in I.C. shares:

> I do not think we have any possible motive for dealing in Illinois Shares; and with our present relations, and especially in view of those which we hope to sustain with the Company, our proper course is to abstain from any dealings, unless in the way of investment.[56]

Similarly in May 1879, Bliss's place on the board of the Burlington, Cedar Rapids & Northwestern, restrained the firm's market operations. In August the road's executive committee called Bliss from Saratoga to work out details of a lease with representatives of the Chicago & Northwestern. Before the conference closed, the shares advanced from fifty-one to fifty-eight. The day after, they hit 60 on news that the C. & N. would take a lease in perpetuity, paying a sum sufficient to meet bonded interest, as well as three percent on share capital for five years, and five percent thereafter. If, as Bliss expected, the executive committee convinced the board to accept the arrangement, shares might advance to sixty-three, bonds to ninety.[57]

Higher prices created a twofold problem. Apologies had immediately to be sent to London in defense of earlier sales of both firms' holdings. Morton hoped to close out New York's remaining interest (2,000 shares, plus $100,000 in bonds), but had to balance the proprieties imposed by an official tie to the corporation. As Bliss had to remind him, "Perhaps it would not be entirely respectable to sell our shares entirely while I am in the Direction. In fact, I don't think it would be: perhaps better a hundred shares—act as you deem best."[58]

As the year closed the large demand for rail stocks and bonds continued both at home and abroad. "Such investments seem[ed] wise, considering the price of Government bonds and the almost certainty that the outstanding five and six percent bonds of the Government [would] be refunded into three percents during 1881."[59] Looking back at their profitable rail business and ahead to the future, financial intermediaries could anticipate continued quick rewards in an active market.

Stock speculation was one thing, bond contracts another, but for the bankers to become a major source of continuing funds they had to enter into much more detailed appraisals. After careful consideration Bliss refused to become a director in the reorganized Iowa Central because of his negative estimate of long-term traffic. He had increased his holdings and then sold off in the advancing market, rejecting the advice of Russell Sage and the rest of the board to hold out for even higher returns after reorganization, to join the directorate, and to service the road's financial needs.[60]

On the other hand, structural changes in the industry opened special opportunities for rewards from direct investment. The days of short lines serving local needs were rapidly coming to an end. In Eastern business circles it was agreed that such companies could

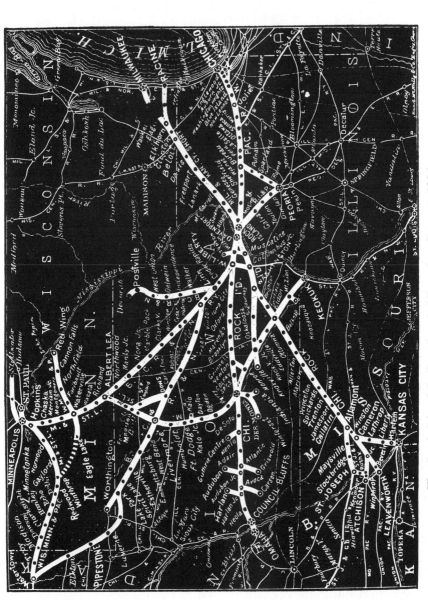

The Rock Island Railroad and Albert Lea Routes, 1886.
Courtesy of The New-York Historical Society, New York City.

not be satisfactorily worked under separate organizations to attract adequate traffic. If combinations could be arranged, bankers saw the chance to sell shares in the bouyant market or to balance whatever losses had been sustained during the depression in such investments. Their varied contacts resulting from overlapping managerial positions, given the force of their security holdings, plus access to specialized channels of information, put them in a key position to accomplish such goals.

These considerations, intertwined with political factors, induced Morton, Bliss & Company to support William Washburn and construction of the "millers' road," the Minneapolis & St. Louis. In 1879 Washburn had brought his proposition to Levi Morton, a major financier of the Republican Party, an old friend of his brother Elihu (former Minister to France), and a fellow congressman.[61] A year earlier, Washburn, "the millers' choice," defeated Democratic candidate Ignatius Donnelly, and took his seat along with Morton, the new congressman from New York's silk-stocking district. These political and personal ties made the Morton firm a likely choice, especially since Morton's partner, George Bliss, was on the board of neighboring roads such as the Des Moines & Ft. Dodge and the Burlington, Cedar Rapids & Northwestern.[62]

After five years of depression, supplying loan capital in 1879 to such a needy and as yet unestablished company posed risks. While bonds of established dividend-paying lines were in great demand, the public remained reluctant to lend monies to new companies for unbuilt track unless there were certain guarantees of safety. It might turn out that money would be easy and the bankers could turn securities to cash in a short time, but the reverse was also possible, and Washburn wanted them to buy a million in Iowa extension bonds immediately to build a southwesterly line from Albert Lea to Fort Dodge.

Washburn's proposal provoked a revealing discussion between the partners testifying to just how instrumental political and personal contacts could be in overcoming geographic barriers to capital flows.[63] Viewing the state of the capital markets, Bliss felt reluctant to take up the business and wanted to put Washburn off for six months. Morton, calculating the political as well as economic returns, continued to press. Bliss reconsidered the options, realizing that if terms could be concluded to effect a combination with the Des Moines & Ft. Dodge (in which the bankers had suffered considerable losses during the downswing), they might very well recoup their investment.[64] The merger would increase traffic for both roads and even its announcement would immediately boost share value.[65]

No sooner had the firm agreed to float Washburn's loan than Bliss instructed him to take possession of the Iowa road. As a director, Bliss knew the finances of the company, and he suggested that Washburn propose a lease agreement of $75,000 a year as the best means for the merger.[66] Within the month an even better alternative became likely. As Transfer Agent for the Des Moines & Ft. Dodge, the banking house handled coupon payment on bonds. When unknown parties presented $6,000 in coupons at their office in January 1880, the bankers began a private inquiry among the members of the informal network of lawyers, railroad directors, large investors, bankers, and brokers that acted as the repository for business information. Bliss reported to the Des Moines board that he had reason to believe that the "Rock Island was endeavoring to gain control."[67] And to Morton he confided that if the Rock Island did take over the Des Moines & Ft. Dodge, it might very well want the Minneapolis & St. Louis to add to an interregional system.[68]

So with their eye on market returns and awaiting the prospective mergers, the financiers continued to aid Washburn. In December 1879 they had made an initial advance of $110,000 for bonds, plus $10,000 for iron rails. In January 1880 they advertised sale of Minneapolis & St. Louis seven-percent gold bonds secured by a first mortgage on the extension to Ft. Dodge. Some two months later poor sales vindicated apprehensions about selling bonds for this company; however, when Washburn's requests continued to mount they agreed to advance $20,000 for iron and supplies and shortly after underwrote a loan for construction to Lake Superior and Taylor Falls.[69]

Much as they had anticipated, Hugh Riddle of the Rock Island approached Charles Whitehead of the Des Moines & Ft. Dodge with a plan for alliance. As these negotiations broadened to include Washburn's road, the banking firm decided in January 1881 to increase its share interest in the millers' road. The line was still lightly charged with bonded interest so that if taken over by a larger system "it should be done," Bliss reflected, "on terms that would make the share capital valuable after a little."[70] Eager to increase their stock holdings, Morton pressured Washburn to have his "local friends" sell "at a low price."[71]

Having enlarged their direct interest, the bankers became

increasingly apprehensive about the road's financial management. They had advanced $250,000 to carry the company through the winter, in addition to a large sum for steel rails. The money had been put in without absolute security and the larger the amount became, the greater their inducement to increase it, to finally realize returns on previous advances. They had begun to discover, too, that they had been misled when they bought into the company and that Washburn had withheld information on the floating debt. Moreover, to lessen his constant calls on the banking firm he had been carrying other loans by notes and putting over payment of payrolls and supplies.[72]

The bankers' assessment of Washburn's practices derived from their dealings with larger systems where the rate wars and financial distress of the seventies had brought improved accounting procedures to determine what it really cost to run a railroad. In keeping with the ideas set down by Albert Fink in 1874, in a model of modern accounting methods, the chaos of individual, undefined criteria for decision making was being replaced by the early 1880s by precise guidelines of accountability that could be applied to the performance of men, money, and machines. Throughout the industry, and particularly in the case of through systems, costs were carefully analyzed and classified according to distinct types of expenditures for an inclusive range of daily operations. The crucial distinction between fixed costs and those that varied with the amount and type of traffic carried had been assimilated by accounting departments that monitored internal corporate spending and by treasurers' offices more concerned with long- and short-term debt operations.[73]

By these standards Washburn appeared a "wholesale sort of man in his way of doing business," ordering supplies and stocks without knowing where the money would come from and, what was even worse, without a notion of how vulnerable his financial position had become.[74] The bankers were amazed that "he seemed utterly oblivious of impending troubles," although the company was indebted to banks in the West, to his brothers, and to friends, and by 1882 Washburn had borrowed $200,000 for his personal account from Morton, Bliss & Company.[75]

The banking firm, having decided to "carry the Company" in any case, did not have to wait long for a change in managerial control. After the October 1881 board elections, Ransom Cable, vice-president of the Rock Island, replaced Washburn as president of the millers' road. As an experienced operating manager, Cable concluded that the road "had never been worked properly nor would it ever have been with Mr. Washburn at its head."[76] He had insisted that Washburn step down and in addition to Washburn's ouster, the local directors were also turned out in favor of R. I. associates.[77]

Until the financial arrangements could be settled, Morton, Bliss & Company took over all decisions, normally made in the treasurer's office, as the official financial agent for the company. That December Bliss summoned Washburn to New York to approve a mortgage for a one million issue of consolidated bonds. The following month the bankers instructed the reconstituted board to pass a resolution offering $800,000 of the new issue to preferred stockholders.[78] In May 1882 the bankers organized a stock pool to boost share value. The plan for stockholders to part with half of their preferred and common at $40 and $12.50 respectively provided the final solution for extricating the property from local control. It allowed the bankers to increase their holdings and enabled the Rock Island to gain share control.[79]

For the bankers, the merger they had counted on and helped negotiate paid off. By 1882, they had collected their large advances plus back interest on bonds and could dispose of securities at a profit.[80] Under Cable's management the business of the road improved, and its securities came to be better regarded by the public. In measuring risks against stock averages, which had been the bankers' primary criteria, they had behaved as "opportunistic investors" and reaped short-term returns. Yet, as far as they were concerned, they had done Washburn and the millers a service by sustaining a property desperately in need of funds and by pressing for its consolidation with a stronger, better managed corporation.

Whatever hesitancy the depression induced, by 1880 it had vanished. The widening demand for rail issues, competition for profitable short-term syndicate operations, and the rewards of stock trading reshaped the outlook of even the most cautious private bankers. The losses of the depression, they found, had been recouped with interest in most cases. As criteria altered, private bankers renewed, on an even larger scale, their commitments to direct investment. Morton's firm, one of the more conservative, had only gradually added more demanding ties to short-term transactions. Nevertheless, by 1881 it too embarked, with Bliss's approval, on as ambitious a direct investment policy as had characterized the early 1870s. Bliss, the most wary member among the New York and London partners, shed his usual restraint. He went so far as to proclaim to John Rose, "You must be surprised at the wonderful prosperity of our Country for the past two years. I judge it to be unprecedented in the history of the world," and he then predicted that the "nation must gain in wealth rapidly for many years."[81]

Such optimism was ill-founded and short-lived. Partly as a result of trunk-line competition, and partly owing to the anxieties created when companies with large capitalization began canceling dividend payments, there had been a slow decline in stock prices from May 1881. The return of New York Central stock from abroad had further depressed the market. Continued losses eroded investor confidence so that the bond market, too, was in the doldrums on both sides of the Atlantic by 1882.[82] Demand for good first-mortgage bonds continued, though loans to newer roads, those undertaken since 1879, could not attract funds. The one bright spot, ironically, was that, for a time anyway, dangerous competition from more new building declined: "There is probably no way to get on with any new schemes now except from the parties interested to put up their own money."[83]

From 1883 until 1887 Morton's firm again, as in the mid-1870s, faced shortages of portfolio funds that strained their ability to complete expansion programs started during the boom. The recurring pattern and their responses can be traced in affiliations to the Big Four, the Kentucky Central, Huntington's roads, and the Canadian Pacific.

9
Morganization in Perspective: The Big Four

The reorganization of the Chesapeake & Ohio and its consolidation with the Big Four in 1888 is a frequently cited illustration of Morganization. The corporate restructuring joining the Western and Southern roads is presented as an early example of J. P. Morgan's determination to replace competitive inefficiencies with system building. Much has been made of the use of voting trusts and banker directorships, which supposedly introduced the more rational management methods that would come to typify the period of banker-control in the 1890s. Regarded as a landmark in Morgan's career as a consolidator, it has also come to symbolize the industry-wide advent of banker strategies calculated to rescue the railroads and place them on a more viable financial footing.[1]

If the focus shifts from Morgan to a study of the corporations, a different view emerges. Bankers had managed the Western road since 1870, when they took control specifically to implement interregional alliances. They continually improvised new techniques to overcome legal restraints or to mitigate financial burdens accentuated by unstable business conditions. Despite receiverships and bankruptcies, they pursued their plans for expansion. The eventual consolidation brought to fruition a southern strategy envisioned as early as 1874, which became a major policy goal during the recovery of 1879. The C. & O. figured as the vital link for a projected southern system for more than a decade before Drexel, Morgan & Company reluctantly entered the affairs of both companies.[2]

The emphasis in what follows, therefore, is on banker participation as it shaped the expansion of the Cincinnati, Indianapolis, St. Louis & Chicago—the Big Four—before Drexel,

Morgan had to be called on for aid. Neither the context for the ensuing negotiations nor the subsequent relationship between the old and new groups in control of the property substantiates the commonly accepted depiction of Morgan's singular accomplishment in effecting the consolidation or introducing new strategies or innovative techniques.

As was frequently the case, rail syndicates formed to operate and finance lines during the postbellum boom were reconstituted in the crises of the later 1870s and subsequent reorganizations often opened possibilities for new alliances. By the time the I. C. & L. reorganized as the Big Four in 1880, the original banking group that had taken control a decade earlier no longer dominated decision-making. By 1877 John Kennedy had turned his attention to the reorganization of the St. P. & P. and relinquished his very active role of the early 1870s. Of the Boston bankers, Thomas Perkins increased his holdings in the new company but did not join the directorate, and Joseph Fay held a seat on the board for only two years beginning in 1882. George Bliss, on the other hand, assumed leadership in the late 1870s and, after the reorganization, held his place in every election. Bliss, together with Melville Ingalls, who had been renamed president, and Collis Huntington of the C. & O. became the controlling stockholders. The trio dominated policy determination until the problems of the mid-1880s necessitated new capital alliances and a new division of control.

Bliss could have remained aloof in 1880 and, as he said, watched his "shares work," for he had high hopes for the property. It was scaled down from the inflated condition of 1870 and well situated to share in the general traffic increase.[3] Linked to water communication by lake and canal, it could accommodate eastbound traffic from Chicago expected to come that way. It could also count on westbound freight, the bulk of which went by rail, and on large numbers of immigrants going West. To the south, the opening of the Cincinnati Southern had already proved an advantage and could be counted on to add considerably to business. Moreover, Huntington's promised connection to the C. & O. was in the offing.[4]

Rather than prompting Bliss to retire, his holdings in the Big Four served instead to insure his continued participation, especially when the demands of Cincinnati investors almost immediately threatened the financial and administrative structure of the corporation. As part of the recurrent pattern of the period, local interests attempted to regain control. Whatever the specific issues in individual cases, these pervasive contests reflected a constant dilemma. The crux of the matter was always the same. What decisions should be made and who should make them? At stake was the satisfaction of local, more immediate aims or those of outside directors whose views were shaped by broader perspectives encompassing more complex criteria and commitments. The outsiders generally had the access to funds, the expertise, and the contacts which allowed them to win out.

In the summer of 1880, ambitious Cincinnati shareholders pressed a plan to increase share capital from $4 million to $10 million.[5] Bliss immediately enlisted Huntington's aid to limit the capital increase. Prior to the scheduled board meeting, Huntington personally intervened to urge a more conservative plan on local backers. Arguing that so substantial an increase would excite public suspicion about the financial practices of the company and "injure the interests of all concerned,"[6] he forestalled the possible realignment behind the move. The directors limited new capital subscriptions to $2 million, with six-percent stock offered to original holders at seventy.[7]

Despite the considerable holdings of its local members, behind-the-scenes persuasion and pressure frequently abrogated formalized board procedures.[8] Bliss, Ingalls, and Huntington (who did not join the directorate until 1882) determined the expansion strategy of the early 1880s. Ultimately their power derived from their share control, but it was enhanced considerably by their intertwining interests and access to confidential information. In addition, their insistence on secrecy, endemic to business operations, served similarly to restrict the policy-making base.

Conspiratorial attitudes, so typical of the period, flourished in the business community. In the absence of institutionalized communication channels, secrecy intensified distrust and fostered a "paranoid style" of business behavior. The discussions to take control of the Indianapolis, Decatur & Springfield, a first step in the triumverate's expansion program, are a good instance of the extent to which these attitudes permeated the decision-making process. During lengthy conferences in New York, Bliss and Huntington debated whether to take an interest in the I.D.&S. Bliss spent considerable effort puzzling over the list of directors to

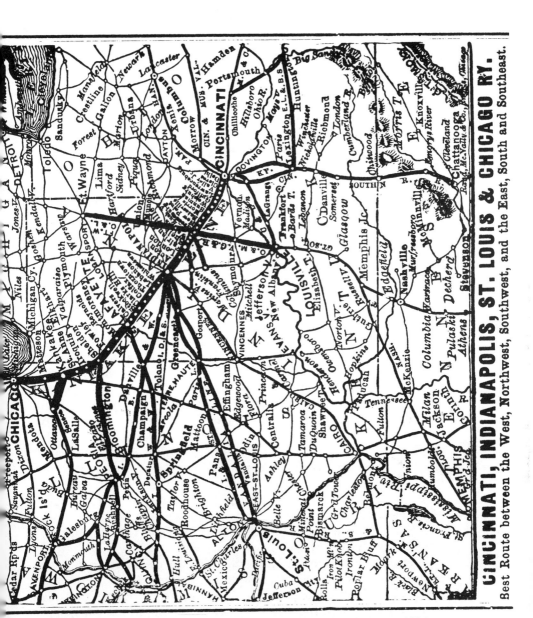

The Cincinnati, Indianapolis, St. Louis & Chicago Railway, 1886.
Courtesy of The New-York Historical Society, New York City.

identify who held the road's income bonds. Drawing on hints and suggestions that he picked up on the "street" and among his friends, he guessed which parties would be willing to sell.[9] Huntington, meanwhile, secretly obtained a traffic agreement between this line and the Wabash. After close scrutiny, Bliss decided the contract contained no legal force. It was so loosely drawn it could be easily disregarded. However, without the assurances of a Wabash connection, the I.D. & S. could not control business for its eastern line. Bliss instructed Ingalls to inspect the road—of course without letting anyone suspect his real motive.[10]

Huntington was ready to buy. Bliss wanted a moderate interest and Ingalls could have persuaded the Cincinnati people to assume a share. Then Huntington heard confidentially from his broker that the Wabash planned to obtain permanent control. If he acted immediately, the broker promised enough of the I.D.&S. bonds at sixty to guarantee Big Four control. Bliss discounted the advice, suspecting a maneuver by the broker to drum up business. According to his sources, the Wabash was reluctant to make any but the most imperative commitments. He figured control would have to cost at least $1 million, but if news got out, it might be even more. If the Wabash was really interested in buying, he and Huntington had to work quickly and quietly. Instructions to Ingalls were changed. There was too much "danger" in Ingalls going over the line or talking to anyone in Cincinnati. Someone else should be sent, or if Ingalls made the trip, he was cautioned to "go as an ordinary passenger in such a way as to prevent suspicion."[11] In a milieu of such pervasive suspicion, constant fear of disclosure went hand in hand with secrecy to complicate effective decision-making. Distrust coupled to fragmented information finally impeded their ability to act.

The plan to acquire the I.D.&S. reflected the larger policy of continuing the expansion interrupted in the mid-1870s. Although Bliss typically advocated caution and was a frequent critic of his more aggressive partners, and of younger ambitious financiers such as J. P. Morgan and Jacob Schiff, he championed growth during the upswing of the early 1880s. When appraising costs of further extensions, he sanguinely concluded, "We are always likely to be in debt, as our energy and ambition are, and will be, greater than our means."[12] Sorry as he was at the prospect of owing so much, he nevertheless continually encouraged Ingalls. If they were to build elevators and stations and complete the projected branches, there would naturally be a debt balance against the company. It was unavoidable.[13]

There is little here, or indeed in these bankers' other dealings, to substantiate any overarching claims that "powerful bankers on the board gave the president a sense of financial security, but by the eighties these 'finance capitalists' were beginning to intervene in favor of economy as against what the president might regard as the best interests of the growing road."[14] Prospects of profits to come from expansion appealed to financiers as well as railroad presidents during the boom of the early 1880s. If anything, in this instance, Bliss advocated new spending for new connections much more enthusiastically than Ingalls.

Amongst his various projects, he supported proposals for a Kankakee extension, for a Greensburgh & Rushville extension, and for another line from Greensburgh to Columbia. In the spring and summer of 1881 Bliss persistently pushed Ingalls ahead: "How soon will the Vernon, Greensburgh & Rushville line be finished— when will you commence on the line to form a junction with the Rock Island?"[15] He called his attention to a smaller road, the Indianapolis & Springfield, which planned to build first from Bainbridge to Montezuma, a distance of forty miles, and then twenty-seven miles further into Indianapolis, and forwarded a letter from Senator Hendricks speaking well of the local coal traffic.[16] Toward the end of the year, he called for completion of the Kankakee & Seneca line: "If you can get enough men to push through the Kankakee & Seneca line before the frost you will I'm sure. . .I have great hope that in connection with the Rock Island people it will be done. Have plans been fixed upon for the new Union Depot & for building it?"[17]

By 1882 the Vernon, Greensburgh & Rushville, run in connection with the Ohio & Mississippi Railroad, gave the Big Four a line between Louisville, Indianapolis, Chicago, and the West. The northern section from Greensburgh gave the company a line from Cincinnati to Fort Wayne and the North. The Kankakee & Seneca, a feeder which opened in March, established a valuable connection with the Illinois Central, the Wabash, the Chicago & Alton, and the Rock Island. In addition to the branches, a new hay warehouse had been erected, a new passenger station almost completed to enlarge depot facilities, a grain elevator started, and a coal elevator built.

Although ideally Bliss desired to avoid inflation of the company's capital base until justified by earnings, even with the enlarged debt he favored new stock issues and he argued that shareholders would also take new bonds. In June 1881, he took his proportion of a \$2-million stock increase (paying \$174,387 for 2,500 shares, less than seventy cents on the dollar). He took his proportion also of another million issued to the stockholders at ninety so that by June 1882 his quarterly dividends came to \$11,250.[18]

Besides these purchases, Morton, Bliss & Company advanced funds to pay creditors for \$100,000 Cincinnati & Indiana bonds coming due January 1, 1882. The banking firm had paid for the maturing issue, receiving five percent for the advance, plus a \$500 commission. So the railroad could repay the banking house, Morton, Bliss & Company also undertook sales of \$100,000 Big Four consolidated bonds and disposed of them rapidly for 101 to 103 plus interest.[19]

In addition to supporting western and northern traffic ties, Bliss finally convinced Ingalls to embark on new acquisitions for the southern system. He had in mind several ideas for a new trunk line more direct than the Cincinnati Southern for reaching the seaboard, but settled on a proposal of Huntington's. Together the three would acquire the Kentucky Central so that the northwest business of the C. & O. could reach Cincinnati and connect with the Big Four. To compensate for the meager local business of the K. C.—a road from Covington to Lexington—they would build a southern extension to meet the East Tennessee & Virginia and Huntington would arrange for a traffic agreement.[20]

The burden of the new venture worried Ingalls, who reluctantly agreed to help finance the project and consented to become president only to insure its success. Huntington's affiliation would be kept secret.[21] Ingalls with some Cincinnati backers would make the purchase and would then turn over share control. Accordingly, the press was informed that a syndicate of twenty Cincinnati capitalists, represented by Melville Ingalls and Albert Netter, had purchased a controlling interest in the K. C. of some 30,000 shares at forty. The new route to the seaboard would, it was reported, be built immediately.[22]

Bliss, Ingalls, and Huntington soon set about figuring the necessary financing for building a link to the E.T. & V. Huntington, who had sold bonds abroad through the Speyers, suggested that they handle the \$3 million loan.[23] The banking house was offered one million at ninety plus interest, an option on the second million at ninety-five plus interest, and an option on the third million at ninety-seven and a half. Since Speyer wanted the bonds at eighty-five, the deal fell through.[24] Interestingly, Bliss raised no objection to giving them the business instead of his own firm. In fact, he regarded the Speyers as a particularly good office through which to place bonds. They did not advertise or seek stock exchange listings, but rather, because of their extended connections, sold over the counter in London and on the Continent. Moreover, their clients usually held bonds for long periods, in contrast, as Bliss noted, to the typical pattern. "In most cases, when bonds are sold they are taken largely by speculators and come back upon the market."[25]

While he had no objection to Speyer, Bliss preferred another alternative. He argued that it would be more desirable, in order to keep interest payments at a minimum, to allow shareholders an option to take their proportions of at least $2 million worth of bonds. They would hold these (without payment to the railroad) until monies were actually needed. His proposal was in fact followed[26] and gave shareholders unpaid-for collateral for securing other loans.

The southern line under construction, linked to the C. & O., was expected to furnish such substantial traffic to Chicago and the Northwest that Bliss remained optimistic. There was no avoiding the fact that east-west through rates for freight and passenger traffic on the Big Four declined substantially in 1881 and 1882, but gross and net earnings remained unaffected because of tonnage increases. Gross earnings, which had climbed from the $1.3 million figure of 1877-1879 to $1.8 million in 1880, rose to $2.4 million in 1881 and then to $2.5 million in 1882.[27]

These favorable returns of the Big Four, the effect of new ties, were atypical. By the beginning of 1882, trunk-line competition had made railroad through business "more unprofitable than at any former period"; projections for the spring also appeared poor. Wabash suffered particularly and could not earn its fixed charges. Although not quite so adverse, prospects were poor for the Chicago, Milwaukee & St. Paul; the Chicago, Burlington & Quincy; the Rock Island; the Illinois Central; and the Union Pacific.[28]

Continued prosperity for the Big Four depended, it was quite clear, on Huntington's promises to supply traffic via the C. & O.; on a completed southern connection; and on a tie-in to the E.T. &

V. By 1883, these goals remained still unfulfilled, forcing Bliss to admit apologetically to Ingalls—"You are doing quite right in running the Kentucky Central in its own interest. The interests of the C. & O. are not more than secondary. I am greatly disappointed that we have not derived more business from that line. Certainly Mr. Huntington encouraged us to expect a very different result."[29]

Bliss redoubled his efforts during 1883 and personally intervened in 1884 to make the needed arrangements. Business for the K.C. languished and, although building costs turned out higher than anticipated, he called continually for its completion so that freight could be exchanged with the E. T. & V.[30] He also pressured Huntington while simultaneously stirring Ingalls to boost C. & O. business to Chicago. In addition, he stayed in constant communication with the new K. C. president, B. S. Cunningham, stressing the urgency of the E.T. & V. traffic agreement and offering his services.[31] As a last resort, he threatened to refuse additional monies, even to cover K. C. interest payments, unless Huntington worked out the traffic ties.[32] After instructing Cunningham to raise money among the large K. C. shareholders, he finally convinced Huntington to put up $75,000 for K. C. interest coming due in January 1884. He added only $25,000 to emphasize his exasperation, but let his own coupons go unpaid.[33]

Since Huntington's supply of C. & O. traffic could not even help cover the fixed costs of the K. C., Bliss decided not to wait any longer on the E. T. & V. arrangement. Early in 1884 he worked out a stock deal as the prerequisite for the E. T. & V. traffic tie. He had been particularly concerned that Bryce and Thomas, who controlled the E. T. & V., would negotiate an interchange with Erlanger & Company, the English bankers in control of the Cincinnati Southern. Should that happen, K. C. traffic would be dependent on local business and the road would prove nothing but a liability.

This concern over the C. & O. traffic and the southern connection related directly to Bliss's shareholdings. With K. C. earnings so low, the stock had been disappointingly depressed. Much to his chagrin, Bliss had been unable to repay monies borrowed for the K. C. But with a reorganization ahead, he planned still further outlays to average out his investments and compensate for his losses. For the stock to rise, however, he had to secure the traffic tie. As a consequence, he willingly furnished Thomas and Bryce with 1,000 of his own shares to cement the deal. All in all, they would receive 2,000 shares at $10, the price he paid, and in common with all shareholders, they would pay a $10 assessment per share. As he told Huntington, "The sale of these shares at so low a price will enhance the value of the balance of my holdings."[34]

In describing Huntington's strategy for building the eastern end of the transcontinental system, Grodinsky concluded that: "Huntington then bought the Kentucky Central stock, and this road, together with some short construction, gave him a route to Cincinnati."[35] Although Huntington held a majority of the stock, in fact the actual working of the line was in the hands first of Ingalls and then of Cunningham, one of the Cincinnati group heavily invested in the Big Four. Under their management the K. C. operated independently since Huntington's C. & O. had not even provided adequate business to cover interest. Bliss made the matter bitterly clear to Cunningham:

I went into the scheme [the K. C.] supposing that we were to work in harmony with the Chesapeake & Ohio and thus secure for the line a large increase in business. Then the plan of extending South was brought forward. . . .I am sorely disappointed that we get no benefit from either of these sources, and the earnings of the Line, to me, are very disappointing.[36]

By the mid-1880s the banker's disappointment with the southern system paralleled his rising concern over the needs and prospects for the Big Four. He had encouraged substantial expenditures to enlarge the road from 300 to 411 miles, which burdened the company with a heavy fixed debt. To add further to its problems, flooding of the Ohio River three years in succession had caused heavy damages necessitating costly repairs.[37] The southern system hardly furnished adequate traffic to offset the dire affects of east-west trunk-line competition, and between 1883 and 1885 the road's earnings had been insufficient to cover July dividend payments. Concerned too over his banking firm's increased outlays to Canadian enterprises, Bliss reluctantly agreed to a $100,000 repair loan in 1884 after he convinced Huntington to put up an equal amount. He gave notice that he was unwilling, or at best would be unhappy, to make any additional advances, yet he did not want the company to "suffer."[38] He counseled the "utmost economy," and advised Ingalls to defer expenditures. As for a long-term loan, he saw little possibility of success considering the condition of the money markets.[39]

Such distrust had infected the money market by 1884 that it was nearly impossible to float issues on their merit. A great many corporations badly in need of funds had been unsuccessfully competing for loans. Few private investors, it seemed, were left with either the desire or the ability to increase their holdings after the shrinkage in bonds and shares which had been underway for almost eighteen months. Then came the 14th of May, a day of intense panic in the financial community. "The crowd in Wall Street, from Broadway down nearly to William Street, and in New Street and Broad, from Wall to Exchange Place, was almost as dense as in the worst days in the Autumn of 1873."[40] The "storm had been brewing," wrote Henry Clews, "for nearly three years, but it was in no sense a commercial panic. Stock-exchange values had shrunk to an unparalleled degree, and the crash was precipitated by the developments regarding Grant & Ward, John C. Eno, Fish of the Marine Bank and a few others."[41]

Morton, Bliss & Company had not been directly affected; still the partners remained adamant that it would be useless to offer rail bonds.[42] During the last week of June Bliss met with major Western railroad managers. He heard the views of Cable of the Rock Island, the managers of the Chicago, Burlington & Quincy, and among others, Wadsworth of the Chicago, Milwaukee & St. Paul. All agreed that nothing could be done while the depression continued despite the substantial reductions in operating costs and the promise of good crops. On the "street" most men acted "as if they had lost a large portion of their fortunes and didn't intend to lose more."[43]

The winter of 1885 saw some improvement but the demand for shares remained dull; only first-class bonds could find a market. Bliss again refused to back a bond issue or put further money into the Big Four. "Today I have no money to invest," he told Ingalls. "Besides, the amount of my interest. . .is now as much as I ought to make it."[44] Both the financial condition of the road and the condition of the money market continued to account for this decision. While he believed the company sound, he wanted it back on a regular dividend-paying basis. July dividends had been omitted three years running and until the road could earn dividends for several years in succession, he doubted the general public would have confidence in its securities. In 1885, moreover, the rates on east-west traffic were so low that the directors withdrew from that business entirely. The year's end showed a reduction, compared to the previous year, of eighteen percent in average rates per ton mile of all freight carried. According to Ingalls, everyone suffered from "the apparent insane attempt of the trunk railways of the company to destroy themselves."[45]

By 1886 Bliss and Ingalls were at loggerheads over the best means to secure funds. Ingalls' solution was simple. They would reduce their fixed outlays by refunding the $9 million, seven-percent, bonded debt by a new $10 million consolidated mortgage bond, paying only four percent. Bliss had little faith that "outside investors" would take such a low-interest issue and he did not want Morton, Bliss & Company to handle the business.[46] His continued unwillingness to invest further in the company or to have his firm assume sole responsibility for flotations led him to seek alliances in the banking community.

Economic recovery in 1886 had not yet alleviated investor suspicion. Distrust fluctuated almost on a day-to-day basis generating a highly volatile climate which discouraged bankers from undertaking flotations. When Bliss offered the business to his aggressive competitors at Kuhn, Loeb & Company, they were every bit as guarded and would not consider it unless Morton's firm agreed to cooperate.[47] Matters remained unresolved into May, when Bliss, to placate Ingalls, offered to see his former partner, George Bowdoin, who had recently joined Drexel, Morgan & Company. He very much doubted the outcome and warned Ingalls: "I am sure it will not lead to business. There has been a great increase in distrust & it has been far more difficult to make transactions in bonds than a few days ago."[48] Announcement of a large French loan had further limited available loan capital for low-interest rail bonds. As Bliss expected, Drexel, Morgan & Company declined the contract.[49]

A small syndicate, finally gathered in June (limited to Ingalls; Morton, Bliss & Company; and Vermilye & Company), took $1 million of new consolidated four-percent bonds. A few months later $2 million more were exchanged for an equal amount of the old bonds. This left $7 million of the company's bonds outstanding.[50]

Both Ingalls and Bliss continued to appeal to the Drexels, but not until some nine months after their initial refusal did Drexel, Morgan reverse themselves and decide to proceed with the flotation. The contract of 1887 specified, first, that a syndicate under their management would make the exchange and conversion of the remaining bonds "for themselves and friends"; and secondly, that they would act as agents of the Big Four for a limited period of five years.[51] "This is a very valuable contract," Ingalls reassured the stockholders in his annual report, "as the high credit and financial standing of that house insures its successful completion, thereby reducing the fixed charges of the bonds and also giving great strength to the proposed new four percents." As a sweetener, $1 million new stock had been issued which new shareholders received at thirty-five-percent discount and older shareholders at forty-two-percent discount.[52]

Bliss welcomed the alliance with Drexel, Morgan for several reasons. He felt great uncertainty about the four-percent flotation. Also, into the third quarter of 1887, despite business recovery, the market dragged and he and Morton expected little advance and little investment. The anxiety and distrust which had continued so long among investors had still not abated, with trading chiefly among speculators.[53] The construction of 12,000 miles of railway had meanwhile been pouring out bonds that in some way had to be provided for. "No one can foresee when the change will come with any certainty," Bliss told his friend Perkins; "I think that at least 40% of the Year's railway construction, amounting with rolling-stock to 225 or 250 millions, has yet to be sent West from Boston, New York & other Eastern towns & cities."[54]

Besides the lack of investment demand, Morton, Bliss & Company had made such large advances to railway contractors and to railroad companies that they held back on new obligations. Their outlays, added to the bonds they were carrying, prompted Bliss to complain to Morton early in the new year that "we have not made any progress in liquidation, on the contrary our interest in some enterprises has increased considerably."[55] The firm had, in fact, been borrowers themselves.[56]

Largely owing to the capital straits of Morton, Bliss & Company, Ingalls approached the Drexels to handle the C. & O. reorganization that became the prelude to the later consolidation with the Big Four. Huntington's enterprises numbered among the various projects tying up the Morton firm's capital in 1886 and 1887, after Bliss backed the promoter's plans for a connection to Cincinnati by means of his Ohio River line. Bliss considered the river road an "absolute necessity" to insure C. & O. traffic, and he convinced his partners to finance construction.[57] He also enlarged his own holdings in the K. C. during the reorganization of 1887, again hoping for increased C. & O. traffic for the Big

Four.[58] Huntington, however, continually disappointed him, and Ingalls felt certain that he would never complete the River Line. Since the C. & O. had defaulted on bond payments since 1885, Ingalls wanted a reorganization that would include the new extension and serve as a first step to the larger merger.[59]

The Drexel firm had insistently limited its Big Four contract to a five-year period and felt as reluctant as Bliss about becoming further involved in a larger undertaking. Ingalls barely persuaded the Drexel house to reconsider the C. & O. reorganization by offering a "partial promise," as Bliss explained to Morton, that he would assume the presidency.[60] Although the financial plan had still not been made public, by February 1888 the *Commercial and Financial Chronicle* reported that it was "accepted as a fact that M. E. Ingalls of the Big Four will be president or general manager."[61]

The syndicate finally formed to handle the C. & O. refinancing, and headed by Drexel, Morgan & Company, also included Morton, Bliss & Company; the important Anglo-American firm of Brown Brothers; and Huntington's old connection, the Speyers. As they had in the 1870s, Morton, Bliss & Company resorted to its persistent policy of increasing investment during reorganization to "recoup" prior losses. In this instance, the partners could not afford a full share, and they had enlarged outside support because of the accumulated outlays poured into "Huntington's enterprises."[62]

Following the C. & O. reorganization came plans for its consolidation with the Big Four. With this in mind, Bliss journeyed west in late 1888 on an inspection tour. In Chicago he met with Cable of the Rock Island and Jeffrey of the I. C., both of whom had joined the board of the Big Four when connections had been made with those roads earlier in the 1880s. All agreed that "the Big Four was exceptional among western lines" in now earning regular dividends. They anticipated a large increase of business from the C. & O. after the completion of the new bridge being built at Covington for traffic to Cincinnati, and from the line south to the Ohio River.[63] By contrast, Morgan's reservations with regard to the larger combination still lingered and had to be overcome:

It is probable that Mr. Morgan, when he has had bad digestion, has sometimes wished that he had never had anything to do with the Big Four or the Huntington line, but, now that his books are balanced to the 1st of January and the outlook is rather improving, I think your letter will tend to make him comfortable and happy.[64]

After the Big Four consolidation, Bliss continued as a director. His son, George Bliss, Jr., entered the executive ranks as vice-president of the C. & O. and also served as a director in the newly formed Ganley Mountain Coal Company, along the line of the C. & O., even though for reasons of propriety the elder Bliss had suggested his son-in-law as a more suitable candidate.[65] Bliss continued to shape policy, convincing Ingalls to extend the C. & O. to the coal mines at Hawks Nest and to take over Austin Corbin's Ohio, Indiana & Western Railway. Drexel, Morgan & Company managed that reorganization, but Morton, Bliss & Company made sizable purchases of its securities and Bliss took some personally. As he insisted, the road was leased.[66]

The C. & O. reorganization and the combination with the Big Four have served typically as symbols of Morgan's innovative techniques and his system-building strategy.[67] However, the reorganization had hardly been Morgan's idea and Drexel, Morgan agreed to handle it only if Ingalls consented to assume executive responsibility. As for the techniques employed, such as voting trusts and banker-trusteeships, they were hardly innovative. Both had been utilized since the early 1870s as concomitants of banker control and alliances. And in this case, Drexel, Morgan had been called on to join a banker whose influence in the Big Four dated back two decades and who had long advocated the traffic benefits of the larger system. Morgan emerges as a reluctant reorganizer, who hesitantly agreed to structural consolidation.

Similarly, there is little indication of Morgan's dominance in the new organization. Rather there were two groups formulating policy. On the one side power was in the hands of the Vanderbilt clique, including Morgan—the Grand Central people, as Bliss called them. Bliss and Ingalls acted as a separate faction, retaining their identification with the particular properties they had been and were now directing.[68]

Seen against the events of two decades, the new system represented not the beginnings of banker-induced combinations and control, but the culmination of a continuing process conditioned by institutional forces.

10
Direct Investment in Canada

At the start of the 1880s major Eastern investment-banking houses were actively engaged in managing the nation's transcontinentals then underway. Drexel, Morgan & Company and Winslow, Lanier & Company became "the guiding force" in the affairs of the Northern Pacific.[1] Kidder, Peabody & Company functioned as the principal bankers for the Atchison. The Seligmans defined policy for the St. Louis-San Francisco Transcontinental and were aiding Gould in his Southwestern designs. Morton, Bliss & Company and J. S. Kennedy & Company turned to a foreign enterprise, the Canadian Pacific. Their participation, particularly the sustaining role of Morton's firm in 1884, proved crucial to completing a Canadian transcontinental.

The activities of American financiers, but briefly alluded to in the many accounts of the C. P.,[2] further substantiate the recent revisionist redating of direct American investment in Canada in the 1880s.[3] New York private bankers were original stockholders in the railway and worked closely with the road's president, George Stephen. Their considerable influence on policy and their vital role routing venture and loan capital across international boundaries supplies further evidence for the current questioning of Sir John Macdonald's brand of economic nationalism. The Prime Minister depended from the start on this American alliance to make his "Impossible Dream" a reality. Yet, whatever Macdonald's politically motivated insistence on a veil of economic chauvinism, it does not fully account for the obscurity of American participation. Ironically, the Americans, even more than the Prime Minister, feared disclosure of their engagement in developmental enterprise across the divide. The partners in Morton, Bliss & Company repeatedly rejected invitations to join the directorate. Not until the road was completed 2,900 miles to the Pacific, did they relent and then only to satisfy the demands of their London firm for fuller information.

To explain American participation in the venture, we must look first to the intertwining economic and political ties which bound the New York-London-Canadian business elite. John Rose, Morton's partner in London, had been John Macdonald's most intimate friend for over twenty years, his Solicitor General (1857), Receiver General (1858), Minister of Public Works (1859-62), Minister of Finance (1869), and the architect of his National Policies. Rose was also an old friend of George Stephen, and in the 1870s had been a member of the London Committee of the Bank of Montreal when Stephen was president of the bank. Because of these Canadian connections, Morton's New York and London firms, in collaboration with the Bank of Montreal, had underwritten Canadian municipal bonds in the transatlantic market. When Stephen hesitantly agreed to head the trans-continental railroad, he counted on the cooperation of Morton's Anglo-American house, and that of J. S. Kennedy & Company, New York bankers who had been instrumental in his acquisition of the St. Paul & Pacific and held a one-fifth interest in that property.

From the bankers' perspective, the more centrally directed Canadian economic milieu appeared to offer more stable investment opportunities, especially after their problems with unreliable state aid at home. Discounting the fact that commercial success had often been subordinated to political goals, they were impressed by bureaucratic controls and government development of transportation closely linked to fiscal policy.

Only Bliss, the most skeptical of the group, questioned the government-sponsored venture, doubting whether investors in the international money markets would furnish the massive support for constructing such large-scale enterprise in relatively thinly populated Canada. As we shall see, changes in government policy and money-market conditions brought "surprises and disappointments" which dimmed the originally "brilliant prospects" of the syndicate. For a time it seemed that the risks and uncertainty attending long-term developmental construction differed little whether across the divide or in the States. For all the Dominion's largesse in the forms of cash subsidies, land grants, and interest guarantees, the Yankees found themselves as readily vulnerable to external variables. Forced by shifts in government policy and investor response to revise continually their calendar of profit expectations, the Americans supplied considerably more capital than they intended. All in all, their experience in foreign direct investment paralleled that at home.

More than a decade before the 1881 charter to the Canadian Pacific Railway Company, Rose and Macdonald had been working for a transcontinental as the best instrument for politically unifying the Dominion. Rose never lost sight of the goal even after he resigned from the government in 1869 and left for London to become a senior partner in Morton, Rose & Company. When construction of a continuous overland route, from the eastern provinces to the Pacific, became a condition for the entrance of British Columbia into the Confederation in 1871, he saw the opportunity to secure Imperial funds. He used his rather unorthodox role as unofficial high commissioner for Canada, negotiating the Alabama Claims, to begin separate talks pressuring Lord Grey. Rose promised Dominion support of the *Alabama* settlement in the Treaty of Washington in return for a Colonial Office guarantee of an internal improvements loan containing a specific transcontinental allocation. His two-pronged diplomacy brought a £2,500,000 loan, conditional on ratification of the treaty.[4] Meanwhile, to secure private funds, he cooperated with the transatlantic syndicate headed by a Canadian, Hugh Allen, until the revelation of American capital involvement and campaign payoffs to the Prime Minister brought Macdonald's resignation in the Pacific Scandal of 1873.[5] Rose persisted under the succeeding Mackenzie regime, and Morton, Rose & Company tried, though fruitlessly, to mobilize foreign capital.[6]

When Macdonald returned to power in 1879, completing the Canadian Pacific as an all rail route wholly on Canadian soil remained central to his National Policies. Although Rose had by then resigned from the Morton firm, he again offered the Prime Minister his services: "If I can be of any use whatever to you or Sir Charles Tupper in supporting any scheme likely to be acceptable, from a market point of view, for the Pacific Railway, pray command me." He anticipated difficulties attracting loan capital, realizing that should an Imperial guarantee be lacking, it would "require delicate manipulation so as not to weigh down the general credit."[7] But first they had to resolve the more immediate problem of venture funds. Rose judged that his former banking partners and his son, Charles, who had succeeded him in London, might well be interested in direct investment in Canadian roads—provided the terms were right. The New York firm had already become involved in C. P. construction in 1879, having taken a share of the government's Onderdonck contract for the difficult building in British Columbia. Here was business they had considered "legitimate" and "perfectly safe" because of the government guarantees. And for some two years Bliss had been pressing both father and son to come to Canada to renew old acquaintances and explore further possibilities.[8]

When Macdonald visited London in the summer of 1880, he had, as he told Goldwin Smith, "three substantial offers for the C. P. R." Since he intended to reverse the policy of the Liberal government and place the business wholly in private hands, he sought a group which would finance the project and, more importantly, would build, manage, and assure its completion.[9] On his return to Canada in September, news leaked out that the Prime Minister had been successful. Although the contract had still to be settled and would then need approval of the Privy Council and Parliament, it was rumored that Macdonald had come to satisfactory terms with Canadian entrepreneur, George Stephen, and his associates Norman Kittson, James J. Hill, and Donald Smith, who had recently made a fast fortune on taking over a distressed Minnesota road, the St. Paul & Pacific. No mention escaped of American private bankers.

Stephen understood the risks of developmental building. As president of the Bank of Montreal and then of the reorganized St. Paul, Minneapolis & Manitoba road, he had acquired considerable railroad expertise. He knew from experience that securing risk and loan capital for the delayed transcontinental posed formidable problems since, as he warned Macdonald, "no one can be sure [it] will earn enough to pay working expenses."[10] However large the resources of any individual or group, they would in any case need to be externally supplemented by monied institutions. Despite the avowed anti-Americanism of the new economic policy, both he and Macdonald relied on Morton's firms to join the company. Besides supplying risk capital, in Stephen's opinion no firm was in a better position to handle a Canadian loan abroad.[11] He turned also to J. S. Kennedy & Company, his secret partner in the Manitoba road.

From the start, conflict within the Morton firms marked their affiliation with the enterprise. While Macdonald was still in

London in the summer of 1880, the English partners, Charles Rose and Pasco Du Pré Grenfell, forwarded his proposition to Bliss. The senior partner in New York, in his typical fashion, raised objections. There loomed the magnitude of the enterprise, the uncertainty, the lack of time for properly estimating building costs, and his personal reluctance to take part in a project which could hardly be completed, he felt, for some ten or fifteen years. But above all, the major and most problematic factor would be mobilizing outside loan capital, especially in the States, until construction could be completed. Even the Northern Pacific, considered a much better route, would, he judged, "have great difficulty in placing bonds outside the circle of Shareholders until the line ha[d] demonstrated its ability to pay."[12] Instead of involving the New York firm, Bliss much preferred to have Morton, Rose & Company ally with the Barings and Glyn Mills & Company (joint agents for the Canadian government), to merchandise the C.P. issues in Europe.

Nevertheless, and though it was contrary to their established policy, Morton and the London partners made pledges that summer of which Bliss was unaware.[13] Personal and political relationships had figured so prominently in their decision that when Bliss subsequently conceded, it was, as he said, to protect the firms' reputation and sustain the ties on which it rested. "Rather than give the slightest chance for criticism," he preferred "to lose the entire amount of [his] personal prospective interest in the undertaking."[14]

The demands of Bliss, in particular his insistence on safeguards for the participating members, had their effect outside the firm in determining the railroad company's proposals to the Canadian government. In his judgment, two problems of paramount importance had to be resolved. One concerned the amount of share capital; the other, closely related, the right to dispose of shares. The senior financier feared that the project required considerably more funds than share subscriptions provided. Constant requests would be made on the banking house to accept bills for rails and for supplies "under the pretext that the money will be refunded as soon as a proportionate subsidy was obtained from the government."[15] To guard against this eventuality, and with an eye on market returns, he wanted the right to dispose of shares before, or at least after, they were fully paid so that the banking house would be relieved of continued responsibility.

When Bliss discovered that after his approval of the twentieth section of the proposed charter it was later amended to restrict share transfers, he demanded further discussion. This new provision, he angrily pointed out to the C. P. syndicate, prohibited subscribers from selling shares until the road was finished and worked for ten years. Moreover, the shares of a subscriber, if he died, could not be transferred or sold except with the consent of the directors. He now insisted on transfer privileges after fifty percent of the capital was paid up.[16]

As to the other issue of contention—the amount of the capital subscription—the syndicate agreed that stock subscriptions should be set at $10 million. Bliss argued for limiting the initial amount, since it would have to be taken at par, to $5 million. Then the remaining $20-million share capital could be issued and discounted at the board's discretion. His persistence necessitated continued conferences between himself, Stephen, Grenfell, Kennedy, and Duncan McIntyre of the Canada Central into November of 1880.[17]

Grenfell, who came over from London as the banking firm's representative to fix the details of the contract, finally returned on December 7 after substantially gaining the concessions Bliss demanded. On December 10, Parliament met to consider the ten-year contract for construction and operation of the Canadian Pacific Railway. The signatories included George Stephen; Duncan McIntyre of the Canada Central; John S. Kennedy of the New York banking house; Richard Angus and James J. Hill of the St. Paul, Minneapolis & Manitoba; Morton, Rose & Company of London; and Kohn, Reinach & Company, bankers in Paris and Germany who were brought in to mollify the French in the Dominion Parliament.[18] (Grenfell had signed the contract for them as their representative.) Among the unlisted parties who had an interest were Morton, Bliss & Company of New York, Donald Smith, Norman Kittson, and Sir Henry Stafford Northcote, Stephen's son-in-law.[19]

The major features of the contract need to be at least briefly reviewed, particularly those affecting financing. The authorized C. P. capital stock was set at $25 million, with initial subscriptions, as Bliss had insisted, limited to $5 million. The personal liability of the company members was limited to $1 million and this sum had to be deposited with the government in either cash or securities, as a building guarantee. On completion of some 1,900 miles, the deposit, with accrued interest, would be repaid to the company. The government further agreed to provide a cash subsidy of $25 million, as well as 25 million acres of land. Both the money and the land were to be apportioned between the central and eastern sections of the road and earned as the construction of twenty-mile lengths was finished.[20]

After vigorous resistance by the Opposition in Parliament, the Canadian Pacific Railway Bill became law on February 15, 1881. In the months that followed, Bliss, his London partners, and Angus, McIntyre, and Stephen planned strategy. The group agreed to purchase McIntyre's Canada Central and then to build necessary spurs, as well as a branch to Spanish River, and one from Winnipeg southwest to a junction with one of the Manitoba branches.[21] They deliberately declared their intention to build other branches, "solely with reference to making it possible to secure good lands under the Land Grant to the Main Line." During 1881 the Morton firms also took an interest in the Credit Valley and the Toronto, Grey & Bruce.

As early as April 1881, the partners in Morton, Rose & Company, desiring a regular source of information and closer attention to decisions, pressured Bliss to join the C. P. board. He refused, questioning the wisdom of the move for the New Yorkers. How could they identify publicly with a Canadian venture? If their interests absolutely demanded, he would have R. J. Cross, his junior partner, named in his place. In light of the crucial decisions to be made for the company, Bliss did attend the May share-holders' meeting in Montreal.[22] Under consideration were the board's terms to take over McIntyre's Canada Central and a construction company plan for further building. In addition to positive action on these matters, the shareholders approved an issue of C. P. mortgage bonds secured by the land grant.[23]

Although Morton, Rose & Company could place the loan in London, Stephen quickly concluded a contract with J. S. Kennedy & Company and the Bank of Montreal. Stephen supposedly wanted to demonstrate Canadian confidence: to prove that "Canada has faith sufficient in the enterprise to buy the bonds."[24] Actually, Morton, Rose & Company wanted the bonds, but at too low a price. In reaction, Stephen had asked Kennedy and the Bank of Montreal to manage the $10 million flotation of fifty-year, five-percent bonds, secured on the land. For this syndicate operation, Charles Rose, with New York approval, agreed to take a half million for the London house.

It would not answer for them [London] not to take any part in it, as of course, it would to some extent, influence others.

Kennedy expects to retain one million himself and the Bank of Montreal 2½ millions, and I [Bliss] understand the rest are placed with the exception of half a million reserved for the Paris parties till they can be heard from by cable—which should be tomorrow.[25]

Historians have puzzled over the relationship of Morton's firms to the C. P. and concluded that "it was really, however, the New York end of that firm, Morton, Bliss and Co., which was interested. Contrary to the general impression, the fact is, that though most of the shares when issued eventually drifted into English hands, no English financiers shared in the building of the Canadian Pacific until it was within one hundred days of completion."[26] This was not quite the case. Selling and registering bonds, paying interest in London, their large stock holdings, and the London partners' continual pressure on Bliss did indeed give Morton, Rose & Company a share and a say in "the building of the Canadian Pacific" from the beginning.

The earlier impulse of Morton and his London partners to participate in the venture seemed certainly to be vindicated in 1881. Even Bliss no longer complained of the impulsive tendencies of his associates. The flow of immigration and the reports concerning land sales had increased the value of the company's securities. By the year's end C. P. prospects were more promising than he had ever anticipated and he took to favorably comparing its condition with projects in the States. Investors had become suspicious of new building there, believing that construction was again going too fast and too far. The demand for first-mortgage bonds for new schemes had dropped considerably and the decline in share values had been severe since the summer.

By contrast, C. P. securities were well received in a strong market. In the spring of 1882 the insiders regarded C. P. stocks as a far better purchase than they had been at par when the company was formed. "No one can tell," Bliss happily noted, "how long the rush of immigrants will continue, but the demand for lands and the increase of population are far greater than the most sanguine could have expected. The general estimate of the value of the subsidies and concessions is greater than at any former period."[27]

The bankers were further encouraged by the formation of the Canadian Northwest Land Company, which planned to purchase 5 million acres from the railroad at $3 an acre. The successful operation of the land company (which sold $8 million of its stock immediately after it was announced) would enable the railroad substantially to retire its bonded debt, giving another boost to the value of shares.[28] And not least among the reasons for the bankers' enthusiasm had been the board's decision in May 1882 to sell the remaining $20 million original stock—*for twenty-five cents on the dollar*—to "those friends of the Company" who had purchased the original issue at par. The directors decided also to give new parties, "whom it was desirable to interest," the opportunity of taking 5,000 shares each.[29] Without hesitation this time, Morton, Bliss & Company not only took its allotted proportion, but purchased those of some small French holders. Before departing for London in June 1882, Bliss wrote confidently to Stephen: "I hope to hear soon after my arrival on the other side, of the completion of the purchase by the new Land Company of five millions of acres of land from the Canadian Pacific; and I shall be glad to be kept informed of everything relating to the interests of the several companies in which we are concerned."[30] Besides investments in the C. P. and the Canada Central, the New York firm gave approval for London to take a one-fifth interest in the projected Ontario & Quebec line from Montreal to Toronto to connect with the Credit Valley and the Toronto, Grey & Bruce.[31]

By 1882 Bliss agreed with Stephen that new capital and traffic arrangements should figure in the larger strategy of opening cross-border gateways. By then Americans and Canadians were vying for the grain trade of the American West destined for East Coast international ports from Montreal to Baltimore. Vanderbilt had been an active competitor for the business since the Canada Southern had been built across the Ontario Peninsula in 1873 and joined his New York Central lines to Michigan. In 1882, when his Canadian rival, the Great Western, passed to the Grand Trunk, he foresaw an even greater threat to control in the Great Lakes. As a countermove, his Michigan Central had leased the Canada Southern.[32]

Knowing Vanderbilt's interest in a route from Chicago going east through Canada, Bliss volunteered to enlist his support for the C. P. and he arranged a traffic exchange for the Credit Valley at St. Thomas with the Vanderbilt system. As a result of his inter-vention, the possibilities for C.P. grain traffic were enhanced and a new route opened to increased financial aid. As Bliss predicted to Stephen—"If Vanderbilt should decide to become interested applications to share with us would no doubt be pressing and abundant."[33] By the year's end a New York-based syndicate was organized to take an interest in new C. P. construction.

With the availability of New York capital assured, the authorized stock of the C. P. was raised to $100 million in December 1882. *Thirty million dollars* of the increased share capital, placed in the hands of the syndicate for fifty-two and a half cents on the dollar, were disposed of by February 1883 "at a favorable price."[34] At the same time, another organization was formed, the North American Railway Contracting Company, made up of Drexel, Morgan & Company; Winslow, Lanier & Company; Kuhn, Loeb & Company; J. & W. Seligman; William L. Scott, a member of the stock syndicate; and the Amsterdam banking firms Boissevain & Company, and Oyens & Company. The latter had close working ties to Morton, Rose & Company. Supposedly, the syndicate and construction company acted as separate entities; in practice, the two groups were functioning as one—with the members of the construction company working to sustain the market in New York and abroad.

After the fresh infusion of capital, the C. P. appeared to be in an even stronger position. A seventeen-day inspection left Bliss favorably impressed and his on-the-scene account in the summer of 1883 ended in affirmation:

> When I contrast the condition of the Canadian Pacific with the Northern Pacific I cannot but believe that its prospects are far better. The N. P. has a large bonded debt, with interest maturing semi-annually, its Preferred share capital & then its Common shares. Then its connection with the Oregon and Transcontinental and the Oregon Improvement Companies, accounts representing a large capital causes more or less of distrust. The Canadian Pacific has agreed to pay 5% until the line is completed. When this is done, the Company can omit dividends, if necessary so that it will have no fixed charges except the current expenses. The impressions of the Englishmen who were of our party, as well as the Germans so far as I could judge, were extremely favorable to the Company.[35]

The Morton firms' capital tie-up in the C. P. and other Dominion Railways had become by 1883 quite substantial, but according to their timetable they would realize profits in the spring of 1884. Their proportion of $4 million of the bonds for the new line of the Ontario & Quebec alone came to $1,059,000 (for which they paid $740,682 or seventy), but they planned to exchange these profitably for debentures guaranteed by the C. P. As always, Bliss reminded Morton of the risks. "Till an issue can be made of Debentures or some other security to reimburse us for the Credit Valley and Ontario & Quebec, the amount cannot be reduced, and it really seems quite too large."[36] Hopefully, this issue would be made by the spring and by then too the Ontario & Quebec would be in operation and adding to the traffic of the Credit Valley. For the time being, Bliss cautioned Morton against any other ventures, desiring to avoid direct commitments "in view of the constantly increasing amount that we find it necessary to put into the Canadian Lines."[37]

The fall of 1883 marked a new phase in the company's fortunes and a change in the bankers' behavior. In late October, Stephen embarked on a policy that caused considerable dissension among his Yankee financial supporters. He had applied to the government to guarantee a fixed rate of three percent for ten years upon the already-issued and to-be-issued stock of the C. P. The guarantee brought an immediate attack in the hostile press as "simply a scheme for raising money on the Government's credit." The *Globe* went on to charge the company with inappropriate profit-seeking:

> They may be assured that already there is widespread suspicion that the real purpose of the arrangement is to enable them and their associates to realize profits of the prairie section of the road and to escape with them.[38]

The action, according to Gilbert, was taken to assure the company funds at a time when a market decline had created capital difficulties.[39] Yet another version is offered by Skelton, who concluded that, on the advice of "New York and London financiers," a new policy was adopted to make a market for the unissued stock by promising a ten-year three percent dividend based on the deposit the company would leave with the government.[40]

What in fact was the bankers' response to Stephen's plan? For the original stockholders, the guarantee linked to a ten-year restriction would actually limit potential profits. They strongly opposed and argued against implementation. Stephen had pursued the course contrary to their interests and adopted it, Bliss believed, to satisfy the government's desire to eliminate "everything connected with the construction company."[41]

> The Government has never been satisfied with the Construction Company plan; and this concession is renewed or obtained with an idea of making all the issued Stock stand upon one basis, thus blotting out the distinction between the original 25 millions & later issued stock & cancelling everything connected with the Construction Co. Of course, this cannot be done without securing the assent of the holders of all of the 250,000 Shares. It will strengthen the position of the Company. It will solve the financial question & provide, so far as I can judge, for all money contingencies; but it changes the brilliant prospects of profit that have been entertained by the holders of the $25,000,000 Original Stock.[42]

At a meeting in Kennedy's office, "when all were present," Bliss complained that it "was a strange proceeding when the Company wanted a moderate sum of four or five millions of dollars, to undertake to deposit so large a sum with the Government to obtain a guarantee of interest for ten years to come."[43] He instructed Grenfell to work out an alternative plan with Stephen for raising funds—"one that will not go back upon the original parties in interest." Certainly, the friends of the company could loan the amount needed to tide over work until the spring. Although the government three-percent guarantee on par value for ten years would be four percent on seventy-five (the anticipated market price), if the road proved anything of a success it could earn dividends beyond that a few years after completion.[44]

It was, then, in the face of the objections of financiers in New York and London that the government passed the interest guarantee, in somewhat modified form, on November 5. The government fixed the amount of the company's deposit at $8.6 million and limited the guarantee to *issued stock* instead of the whole $100 million. In other words, the guarantee was made applicable to $65 million; the original $25 million, the $30 million turned over to the syndicate, and a new $10-million share issue. The government retained the option to guarantee the remaining $35 million, but Stephen assured Bliss—in strictest secrecy—that he was negotiating with the Dominion to keep these off the market for at least a year.[45]

Bliss and Morton remained furious with Stephen, especially for his refusal to explain the reasons for his action. "I don't attempt to justify the course taken when asked by friends to whom we were instrumental in giving an interest, nor to explain it. I can only reply that this course has been taken by Mr. Stephen, without consultation, sanction or approval.''[46] The financiers half expected that those similarly disappointed would bring suit to secure their rights under the contract.

Surprisingly, neither the guarantee nor the encouraging reports of the company's condition succeeded in attracting the investing public.[47] The low prices for shares evident since October continued. Stephen was forced to rescind the authority he had given Kuhn, Loeb & Company to deal in shares in London, for sales there were precipitating declines in New York. About the only bright spot for the insiders was the report that Kuhn, Loeb had sold 24,000 shares more than they had purchased, which, if accurate, would "so largely reduce the Construction Co.'s holdings.''[48]

At the close of 1883 Morton's partners faced a quandry. They aimed to unload their large holdings in C. P. shares and to transform their interest in the Credit Valley and the Ontario & Quebec into easily negotiable securities. As the depressed condition of the market did not allow this course, their only option was to hold on. Negotiation of C. P. and O. & Q. debentures appeared impossible, and an advance in C. P. shares no more likely. Their large holdings of these, upon which they had expected to realize a good profit, now became a burden that might have to be carried into 1885-1886.[49]

By 1884, the Morton house had become a source of C. P. emergency funds. Stephen, under pressure for ready money, had already put up all his securities as collateral and so had Donald Smith. To cover the company's one-percent semiannual dividend on stock already issued, he appealed to Morton, Bliss & Company for a $650,000 deposit in the Bank of Montreal. Though reluctant, the bankers finally agreed to a 60 day advance. Bliss estimated that the demands of the company were fully $7.5 million. He blamed Stephen for improperly appraising the road's capital needs and for relying on Angus, who in "his easy going way" had only accounted for a small portion of the company's wants.[50] Bliss hoped for at least partial clearance of the road's debts after passage of a railway relief act in March. Aware of the bankers' criticism, Stephen commented somewhat ironically: "The Yankees are all happy now, having got their money from the C. P. R., but somehow the stock both in New York and London is *dead*.''[51]

Not all the Yankees were happy. Morton and Bliss remained convinced that their earlier expectations for profits would not be realized and that they would best divest themselves of their holdings. More distressing still, they knew that of the original syndicate only their firm could be relied upon in case of sudden monetary need. "The circle of friends who can aid, in case of necessity is too small. Mr. Stephen, Donald Smith, M. R. & Co. & ourselves comprise the whole." Hill had sold out by 1883 and resigned from the board. Kennedy had become disaffected. McIntyre could not be called on. Angus "lacks both the brains and money to be very valuable, and I think would be very glad to be out."[52] Paradoxically too, the government's relief act, implying a possible government takeover, had weakened rather than strengthened credit.

These circumstances prompted Bliss to insist that they reduce their interest to the smallest possible sum.

> The surprises and disappointments of the past have been extreme, and I fear they will continue. Since the arrangement with the Government, by which 3% is assured for ten years to the Shareholders, I have felt that the stock was intrinsically cheap & that the public would learn to think well of it. Such has not been the fact. *Long* stock comes upon the market & "bears" attack it with success, while there is nobody ready to support it. Many a time lately have I thought that no present anticipated profit could compensate us for the risk & anxieties attending it. I have manifested confidence & readiness to do our share in assisting; and this the first communication to any person living from me of such feelings.[53]

Even with prices depressed to the low thirties, Morton, Bliss & Company began selling C. P. shares in the London market (in small amounts) and advised London to do the same.

When payment of the August dividend came under discussion, Stephen complained to Macdonald that Morton, Rose & Company was "perfectly cowed" and unwilling to aid. "We must get into connection with a stronger and more courageous firm over there without delay. . . .I wish we had a firm like Barings to represent us in London."[54] Both Stephen and Macdonald tried unsuccessfully that fall to persuade Baring Brothers and Glyn, Mills & Company to replace Morton, Rose & Company as the C. P.'s Financial Agents. The Barings, viewing the distrust in both London and

New York toward older transcontinentals, could not be convinced to take C. P. business.

Since the international banking community refused to come to the rescue, Stephen prepared a relief plan which he put to the Dominion government in the spring of 1885. Morton's New York firm now decided to put off further sales; they would await Stephen's success in securing government aid.[55] While Morton, Rose & Company sold gradually to reduce holdings to 15,000 shares, Morton, Bliss & Company, acting under Stephen's instructions and reporting to him, attempted to hold up the market in New York.

> Since my letter earlier in the afternoon Can. Pac. has been sorely [?] raided. At a moment when we had no orders in the room, 100 shares were sold [?]. We bought several hundred shares @ 37 & 500 @ 36½ which was all we could get.
>
> We are bidding 36 7/8 and hope to close it a little higher.
>
> I hope you will telegraph us tomorrow morning whether everything is going satisfactorily & giving us as definite an idea as you can of the situation.
>
> There was some excitement in the [?] and a great many brokers were endeavoring to sell. My present belief is that it was a preconceived movement to depress it as far as possible.[56]

Passage of the new relief plan could reverse things. Investors who had placed a high value on the company lands had been distressed by the earlier act of 1884, pledging the entire property to the government for the $30-million loan. The new proposal canceled, in effect, $20 million of the loan and might raise the credit standing of the company.[57]

While pressing for new government aid, Stephen had again tried to effect a reorganization of the railroad's board to include the Yankee banking firms which were the largest stockholders in the States. In 1885, these included J. S. Kennedy & Company, Morton, Bliss & Company, and Drexel, Morgan & Company. (Drexel, Morgan and J. S. Morgan in London probably held 2,500 to 3,000 shares.) When Stephen reverted to his long-standing arguments for Bliss to join the board, Bliss reiterated his unchanged objections:

> The considerations which have governed us hitherto still exist in regard to a member of our firm here assuming the responsibility

of being a director in your Coy. While the connection would be a pleasant one on many accounts it would at the same time be an improper one for us to make. We are prosecuting a business of such a kind that it is desirable to avoid identifying ourselves before the public in any large outside enterprise.[58]

Instead, Bliss did the best he could to convince a member of the Drexel firm to take a directorship (a possibility Stephen favored), only to be met with an absolute refusal.[59]

New aid for the Canadian Pacific received Royal assent on July 21, 1885. Three days later Baring Brothers reversed themselves and agreed to take the entire $15-million first-mortgage bond issue called for by the act. By the end of October, the bonds, which the Barings were selling slowly but steadily, had advanced to almost ninety-nine, and the shares of the company had jumped from thirty-seven and a half to fifty-two and a half. On November 5, Stephen cabled Macdonald, "Railway now out of danger," and two days later the last spike of the main line was set by Donald Smith, marking the completion of the company's contract with the government. By 1886 train service was inaugurated 2,900 miles from Montreal to the Pacific.

With the project completed and the shares steadily climbing, Bliss, from the beginning a critic of Stephen and his policies, softened his appraisal. The London partners, who had lost out to the Barings, harbored considerably more resentment.

I have been inclined to feel aggrieved at times at the way C. P. business has been done by Mr. Stephen. His choosing J. S. Kennedy to arrange Syndicates, to take stock, & paying a commission therefore—& especially compensating Boissevain & the Amsterdam people for their efforts in promoting his wishes—justifies censure from you and us. I do not think we can blame him for arranging with Barings for the £3,000,000 Stg. issue of 5%'s: it was my impression at the time that you would not desire to take the business on the same terms. The recent issue of £4,000,000 Stg. there is no doubt you could have made successfully, but I judge this would have been improper, & in violation of a positive understanding had when the former issue was made.

I say all this to lessen your estimate of his shortcomings. You must remember that, except Mr. Smith, Stephen had no support in Montreal from parties in interest, but has stood alone & borne the brunt of the battle during all these years.[60]

Charles Rose and Grenfell, though critical of Stephen, finally held Bliss responsible for the loss of the 1885 business to the Barings. To meet their accusations that he had been remiss, perhaps deliberately, in keeping them adequately informed, he agreed that a junior partner in New York, R. J. Cross, would join the C. P. directorate and journey monthly to Montreal to attend every meeting. Soon after, in 1887, Morton acquiesced to a seat on the board to preserve the now amicable relations between the New York financiers and Stephen. That same year they made use of their Canadian connections to sustain William D. Washburn and the "Soo."

Once again, as in 1882, banker involvement facilitated the creation of cross-border links tying the traffic of the U.S. and Canada. Their intervention to set up secret negotiations between Stephen and Washburn resulted in a perpetual traffic agreement with the "Soo" that Stephen judged "his greatest service to the maintenance of the power and independence of the national highway."[61]

In the decades following the Civil War, William Washburn belonged to a small group of Minneapolis millers who moved to overcome crucial marketing and transportation impediments to large-scale operations. Like many Western businessmen, Washburn's goals outstripped his managerial abilities and capital supplies, forcing him to turn to New York for aid. In 1879, as president of the Minneapolis & St. Louis, he had appealed in desperate need of funds to Morton, Bliss & Company. The banking firm had put up both equity and loan capital for expansion, but as a final solution had negotiated consolidation with the Rock Island. Washburn had been forced out of the management, and relieved of running this line, he promptly turned his attention to another rail project in 1883.

A decade earlier his brother Israel, then governor of Maine, had urged the Minneapolis Board of Trade to consider a direct rail route for the Twin Cities to the East via Sault Ste. Marie, Ontario. The proposal to open rich Wisconsin and Michigan territory, naturally tributary to Minneapolis, had been ridiculed in 1873 as the "North Pole Railway."[62]

By the early 1880s Minneapolis had emerged as the nation's milling center for flour exports. The trend to large-scale

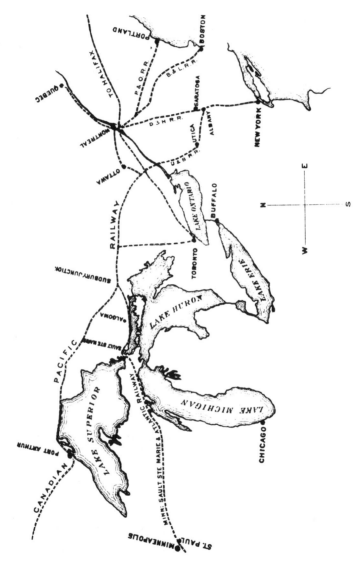

*The Minneapolis, Sault Ste. Marie & Atlantic Railway, 1887.
General Research and Humanities Division, The New York Public
Library, Astor, Lenox and Tilden Foundations.*

production in the late 1870s impelled millers such as Washburn and Charles Pillsbury to introduce aggressive merchandising techniques and to reconsider the plan to reach Eastern and overseas markets for processed products. Their control of an all-rail route to the tidewater via Canada would free Minneapolis from the dominance of rail rates set in Chicago by roads hostile to the millers' interests.

With Washburn as president, the millers organized the Minneapolis, Sault Ste. Marie & Atlantic in 1883. The stock of the "Soo" and its direction was in the hands of the major milling companies of the city. Building began in 1884, but before long Washburn again sought funds from Morton, Bliss & Company. Considering the condition of the money markets, the bankers thought it useless throughout 1885 to float a loan. Neither their firm nor any other was successfully merchandising American railroad bonds abroad. However, another alternative existed for funding a Great Lakes gateway to Canada: the Bank of Montreal advanced Washburn $750,000 for further eastward building.[63]

The loan signaled Stephen's interest in the project and alerted the bankers to a possible combination, once the road was completed. In April 1887 Morton, Bliss & Company became official Transfer Agent for the road and offered $5 million "Soo" first-mortgage, five-percent, forty-year gold bonds, issued at the rate of $20,000 per mile on completed and fully equipped road. Of the 450 miles from Minneapolis to the Sault, 150 miles had already been built. The remaining 300 miles covered by the issue would be finished by the end of the year. The issue seemed particularly attractive since the C.P. and the Duluth, South Shore & Atlantic had agreed to build a bridge across the St. Mary's river at the Sault to be used by all three lines.[64]

The major Minneapolis flour companies, whose capacity totalled 28,000 barrels a day, believed the all-rail route to the tidewater, independent of Chicago and unaffected by the Interstate Commerce Act, would capture the bulk of the flour product of the Northwest. With the completion of the "Soo," the bridge, and the Algoma branch of the C. P., there would be a 1,090-mile through route connecting Minneapolis to Montreal. The only alternative would be the 1,380-mile route via Chicago and New York.[65]

As for Stephen, his aspirations with regard to the "Soo" were still somewhat undefined in the spring of 1887. Both Stephen and Smith continued eager to tap the traffic of the Western states and the antagonism they felt toward James J. Hill of the Great Northern may have encouraged them to seek another connection between the Twin Cities and the western lines of the C. P. When Hill resigned from the C. P. board in 1883, the possibilities for cooperation had sharply deteriorated. Clearly if the "Soo" built northwest into the Manitoba wheat fields and from there to the Pacific, as it was rumored, the transcontinental would be in direct competition with Hill's Great Northern. However, in 1886 Stephen had assured Hill that he had no notion of any such plans when the Bank of Montreal advanced Washburn monies. Those monies were earmarked only for an eastern route from the Twin Cities, certainly not for a western line or for a parallel road to compete with the Manitoba line from Minneapolis.[66]

In April when Morton, Bliss & Company announced subscriptions for the "Soo" issue, a simultaneous announcement was made in London by Morton, Rose & Company. Both firms began receiving buyers at the publicly offered price of ninety-two and a half. Yet hardly had a month passed when Bliss complained to Stephen that the issue had already proved a disappointment. Would he come to their aid? The bankers offered to put up a considerable amount to tide Washburn over, but would Stephen and Smith "come to his rescue" and provide the balance? If the Bank of Montreal would make the loan, or if they could come up with some other plan for a short-term advance, the bankers would enable the C. P. to lease the "Soo."[67]

In refusing the leasing proposal, Stephen made it abundantly clear that he desired "virtual control" before any funds would be forthcoming. The bankers' decision to continue to aid Washburn thus reflected their knowledge that negotiations for a merger would continue with the C. P., which would bolster their stocks and bonds. When Washburn appeared in New York in December, depressed and fearful that the "Soo" was on the verge of failure, they quite literally, as Bliss said, could not "afford to let Mr. Washburne fail." Failure would have a depressing influence not only in the New York money market, but to a wide extent in the Northwest. On the other hand, a C. P. alliance would send security prices spiraling.[68]

The bankers had two immediate goals; first, to raise funds to finish construction, and secondly, to transfer control to the C. P. According to Washburn's estimates, the amount needed to finish the "Soo" came to $800,000. To begin with, the bankers discounted Washburn's notes coming due to the extent of

$150,000, payable in six months. As collateral, they took all of Washburn's preferred and common "Soo" stock and as a commission received 500 shares. To raise additional funds, they settled on a stock syndicate. Shareholders would either provide their proportion of stock, at cost, to the syndicate or pay an equivalent cash assessment. The cost of the stock paid in averaged twelve and a half and the syndicate bought it for twenty-five, for resales.[69]

Early in 1888 the bankers arranged for secret meetings between Washburn and Stephen. By February, Stephen had conferred with Macdonald on a "Soo" plan that would pass Parliament. Washburn went to Montreal since Stephen was so anxious to settle on terms he wanted him on the scene.

On January 7, 1888, the first C. P. through train from Montreal arrived in Sault Ste. Marie with Sir Donald Smith on board. He was met by Washburn to celebrate the occasion and discuss the establishment of regular through service from Minneapolis to the seaboard.[70] As a final triumph before retiring from the presidency of the C. P. in August 1888, Stephen pointed with great satisfaction to the new through connection.[71] That same month a debate mounted in the U. S. Congress over the tie-in between American political figures and Canadian railroad affiliations. Senator Gorman called for an investigation of the possibility of Canadian control of U. S. railroads. Questioning whether Canadian companies were enjoying special privileges, he read with a flourish the names of the directors of the C. P., which included L. P. Morton, the vice-presidential nominee of the Republican Party, and William E. Scott, representative from Pennsylvania. It was subsequently revealed that Calvin S. Brice, chairman of the Democratic Executive Committee, held two of his nine railroad offices in Canadian roads extending their business in the U. S. Would these gentlemen personally profit from Cleveland's proposed free-trade policy? In the House John Lind of Minnesota and Thomas Bayne of Pennsylvania charged Scott with supporting reduced tariffs harmful to New England railways because he would profit from the diversion of business to the C. P.[72] The tariff measure failed, but by 1888 the "Soo" had become a valuable feeder for the C. P. Minnesota flour was shipped by the Sault Ste. Marie and taken from there by the C. P. to points near New England where it was transferred again to the Canada Atlantic, the Vermont & Central, or Grand Trunk and taken to New England for export or American consumption. By 1890 the

C. P., using the "Soo" and the Duluth, South Shore & Atlantic, had gained access to the traffic of the Twin Cities, a route to Lake Superior, and an alternative route from Winnipeg via the "Soo" to its lines in Ontario Province. In another two decades it had become the crucial east-west link on the south side of the Great Lakes, once feared by Hill.[73]

During the Congressional debates of 1888 Morton refused to comment on the fact that he had been a director of the C. P. The press pointed out that immediately after his nomination for vice-president he had resigned from the board. According to the published disclaimers, he had never attended a meeting or exercised any of his functions as a director. He had been chosen merely to fill the place temporarily until an election was held and a Canadian director chosen.[74] Nothing, of course, could have been further from the truth. Morton, his partners in London and in New York had been and were to be intimately involved in the decisions affecting financing and direction of the C. P. and its affiliates on both sides of the border, at least until the death of George Bliss in 1896 and the dissolution of Morton, Bliss & Company in 1897.

Epilogue

To the account of conservative investment bankers who in the 1890s took control to rationalize an overexpanded industry and place railroads on a viable financial basis, we should add the very active and inclusive role of reputable financiers in fostering the dramatic growth of the 1870s and 1880s. During that era, when long-term credits were relied on for continuing construction, investment bankers literally underwrote railway extensions. By purchasing bonds in vast quantities directly from railroad corporations they guaranteed immediate funds, while relieving the corporation of the risks and delays of merchandising. In addition, the special services they offered the public, by attracting outside investors, also facilitated the flow of funds. But financial intermediaries of this period were considerably more than mobilizers of other people's money or the spokesmen for a creditor clientele, and it is the twofold nature of their role as capital suppliers that has been emphasized here. Beckoned by the railroad contagion of the early 1870s, they became involved in direct financing and planning of construction both south and west. High interest rates on appreciating securities, particularly when obtained at discount as commissions, bonuses, and through construction-company arrangements, induced private bankers to become substantial stockholders in projects designed to create interregional links to far-flung urban markets and overseas outlets. In response to the optimism of the postwar boom and counting on government guarantees and aid, they supplied venture funds and subscribed to newly issued stock of both new and established companies envisioning new connections, and in both cases purchased long-term credits for their own accounts. Indeed, until the development stage drew to an end in the late 1880s they continued to supply venture, equity, and bonded capital.

Certainly the outstanding characteristic of the railroad business of Morton, Bliss & Company—even when constrained by the caution of the more active senior partner, George Bliss—is that the firm encouraged the network's expansion. From 1869 onwards, these bankers assumed responsibility for long-range, extensive projects. The days of local lines serving local needs were over and in the early 1870s investors reacted eagerly to grandiose designs for road promising increased traffic returns. Since such large-scale enterprise offered multiple uses for funds and as many possibilities for profit, the bankers continued throughout the 1880s to direct and finance interregional strategies.

Whatever the monies derived from bond sales, from short-term advances, from trustee and related financial services, their primary motive for participating in construction of through lines, or for that matter for sponsoring system-building by through-traffic alliances, was their desire to increase returns on their own share holdings as well as the securities of their clients. Whether in financing building for the Milwaukee & St. Paul, for the Katy, for the New Orleans, Mobile & Texas, or for the truly developmental Canadian Pacific, they linked profit expectations to stock appreciation. In urging east-west ties for the Indianapolis, Cincinnati & Lafayette, in pressing for a connection with the Chesapeake & Ohio, and in working for an even larger system which encompassed the Kentucky Central and a traffic interchange with the East Tennessee & Virginia, the bankers looked to potential market returns on capital. Similarly, they advocated merger and combination in the mid-1870s to bolster depreciated securities of defaulted, weak, or smaller properties.

The premise that bankers, acting as protectors of their creditor clientele, checked railway growth and competition is hardly applicable to the firm's operations during the 1870s and 1880s. Though they were at moments restrained, the overall pattern of their activities can perhaps be better characterized as speculative and expansionary. They advocated new construction, combination, and system-building as alternative profit-making strategies, prompted in each case by the firm's investment map and conditions within the industry.

The depression of the mid-1870s did serve to emphasize the question of safety, both for their own and their clients' investments. But while the downturn modified for a time their attitude toward investment possibilities, so that thereafter they were more wary in making large, long-range, direct outlays, with the upturn of the early 1880s the firm once again committed funds to new construction. At the same time, the problems posed by capital deficiencies, by default, by receivership, foreclosure, and reorganization, had served to alter the nature of prior relationships. In seeking restoration, creditors increasingly turned to investment bankers to negotiate sales or leases, or arrange for refinancing and reorganization. As heads of Bondholders Committees, bankers purchased railroad properties and undertook their operation—sometimes until disposal to a larger company could be concluded, or in order to retain permanent control. Not only bondholders, but railroad executives too turned to financiers for aid during this period of severe monetary contraction. Even sound, long-established companies such as the Illinois Central became vulnerable to banker pressure. Rather than turning bankers away from the dangers of railroad alliances, the depression enlarged the sphere of their influence and schooled them in the techniques of corporate financial management.

In moments of crisis, Morton, Bliss & Company were in fact the sole support for railroad properties. Their advances kept the Gilman, Clinton & Springfield operating until it was taken over by the Illinois Central. The Minneapolis & St. Louis would have failed in 1881 if not for the monies they provided. And their aid was crucial in sustaining the Canadian Pacific in 1884 and 1885. However, as a matter of policy the firm desired to keep open all possible capital sources. They welcomed alliances with other bankers which enabled them to share and limit liabilities. Their preference for group banker participation is reflected in all their major affiliations—the Milwaukee & St. Paul; the Katy; the Indianapolis, Cincinnati & Lafayette; the New Orleans, Mobile & Texas; the Illinois Central; the Union Pacific; and the Canadian Pacific.

Although data is lacking on just how much capital this firm supplied to the industry, there is ample evidence, as we have seen, of their influence on railroad policy. When bankers' names appeared in bond advertisements, it was not as window dressing to create confidence in railroad securities. They had considerably more power as a result of their extensive contacts, their access to information, their role in mobilizing the capital markets, and owing to their own holdings than was publicly known. Their influence was indeed augmented by the behind-the-scenes arrangements and private determination of policy, outside the jurisdiction of the board, which characterized their close relations with railroad executives, and especially those with the more notorious speculators of the period. Such highly personalized relationships would not, however, survive once the bureaucratic structure matured and decision-making became increasingly separated from implementation.

In the mid-1890s, the period when banker control was publicly acknowledged, Morton, Bliss & Company was in the process of dissolution. Their significant contributions had been during the pioneer stage of railroad building. At the onset of the depression of 1893 and what has come to be known as Morganization, George Bliss was seventy-seven years old and ill. Levi Morton, who had just completed his term as vice-president of the U. S. and had been bypassed for renomination, directed his energies to reordering his political career. At Bliss's death in 1896, negotiations began for the New York firm's reorganization as the Morton Trust Company. As of October 1, 1899, Morton, who was seventy-five, became nominal chairman of a board of directors which included James Alexander, president of the Equitable Life Insurance Society; George F. Baker, president of the First National Bank; Frederick Cromwell, treasurer of the Mutual Life Insurance Company; Henry M. Flagler, vice-president of Standard Oil; Joseph C. Hendrix, president of the National Union Bank; Joseph Laroque of Shipman, Laroque & Company; W. G. Oakman, president of Guaranty Trust Company; and William C. Whitney and A. Wolff of Kuhn, Loeb & Company. The formation of this financial corporation, like its merger subsequently with Morgan's Guaranty Trust Company, paralleled the movement toward consolidation and specialization in the industrial sector that was to mark the new era.

Appendix:
Railroad-Banker Affiliations, 1873

Railroad Affiliation	Mileage*	Function	Investment Banking Firm
Albany & Susquehana	198	J. P. Morgan Director	Drexel, Morgan & Co.
Atlantic & Pacific	913	Joseph Seligman Director	J. & W. Seligman & Co.
Brunswick & Albany	184 (242)	Henry Clews Director	Henry Clews & Co.
Burlington, Cedar Rapids & Minnesota	466	Henry Clews Director	Henry Clews & Co.
Cairo & Vincennes	167	Joseph Drexel Director	Drexel, Morgan & Co.
Cedar Falls & Minnesota (leased to Dubuque & Sioux City, subleased to Illinois Central)	75	John S. Kennedy Director	J. S. Kennedy & Co.
Charlotte, Columbia & Augusta	207	Morris K. Jesup	M. K. Jesup & Co.
Chesapeake & Ohio	315 (428)	Fisk & Hatch Fiscal Agent Transfer Agent	Fisk & Hatch
Cincinnati, Hamilton & Dayton	98	Winslow, Lanier & Co. Fiscal Agent	Winslow, Lanier & Co.
Cincinnati & Indiana (leased to Indianapolis, Cincinnati & Lafayette)	20	John Kennedy Director	J. S. Kennedy & Co.
		Thomas Perkins Director	Perkins, Head & Co.
Cincinnati & Martinsville (leased to Indianapolis, Cincinnati & Lafayette)	39	George Bliss Director	Morton, Bliss & Co.

Cleveland, Columbus, Cincinnati & Indianapolis	549	John J. Cisco Director	John J. Cisco & Son
		William B. Duncan Director	Duncan, Sherman & Co.
Cleveland & Pittsburgh (leased to Pennsylvania)	310	Charles Lanier Director	Winslow, Lanier & Co.
Delaware, Lackawanna & Western	908	George Bliss Director	Morton, Bliss & Co.
Dubuque & Sioux City	158	Morris K. Jesup Director	M. K. Jesup & Co.
		J. P. Morgan Director	Drexel, Morgan & Co.
Dubuque & Southwestern	58	M. K. Jesup & Co. Fiscal Agent	M. K. Jesup & Co.
Erie	1544	John J. Cisco Director	John J. Cisco & Son
		William B.Duncan Director	Duncan, Sherman & Co.
Evansville, Terre Haute & Chicago	62	Winslow, Lanier & Co. Fiscal Agent	Winslow, Lanier & Co.
Harlem Extension	122	William B. Duncan	Duncan, Sherman & Co,
Illinois Central	1264	George Bliss Director	Morton, Bliss & Co.
		Louis Von Hoffman Director	Louis Von Hoffman & Co.
		J. P. Morgan Director	Drexel, Morgan & Co.
Indianapolis, Cincinnati & Lafayette	237	George Bliss Director	Morton, Bliss & Co.
		John Kennedy Director	J. S. Kennedy & Co.
		Thomas Perkins Director	Perkins, Head & Co.
International	180 (550)	John Kennedy Director	J. S. Kennedy & Co.
Joliet & Chicago (leased to Chicago & Alton)	38	M. K. Jesup & Co. Transfer Agent	M. K. Jesup & Co.
Lackawanna & Bloomsburg	118	George Bliss Director	Morton, Bliss & Co.
Louisiana & Missouri River, (leased to Chicago & Alton)	109 (266)	M. K. Jesup & Co. Transfer Agent	M. K. Jesup & Co.
Louisville, New Albany & Chicago	306	Frederick Schuchardt Director	Frederick Schuchardt & Son
		G. L. Schuyler Director	Jones & Schuyler

Memphis & Charleston	315	Winslow, Lanier & Co. Transfer Agent	Winslow, Lanier & Co.
Milwaukee & St. Paul	1738	Levi P. Morton Director	Morton, Bliss & Co.
Missouri, Kansas & Texas	675	Levi Morton Director	Morton, Bliss & Co.
		J. P. Morgan Director	Drexel, Morgan & Co.
Mobile & Ohio	565	William Duncan Director	Duncan, Sherman & Co.
Morris & Essex (leased to D. L. & W.)	228	George Bliss Director	Morton, Bliss & Co.
New Orleans, Mobile & Texas	233	George Bliss Director	Morton, Bliss & Co.
		Joseph Seligman Director	J. & W. Seligman & Co.
		Louis Von Hoffman Director	Louis Von Hoffman & Co.
New York, Boston & Montreal	175 (350)	Joseph Seligman Director	J. & W. Seligman & Co.
New York Central	1628	Duncan, Sherman & Co. Transfer Agent	Duncan, Sherman & Co.
Northeastern (S.C.)	110	Morris K. Jesup Director	M. K. Jesup & Co.
Northern Pacific	559 (2000)	Jay Cooke & Co. Fiscal Agent	Jay Cooke & Co.
Ohio & Mississippi	423	Frederick Shuchardt Director	Frederick Schuchardt & Son
Omaha & Northwestern	40 (180)	August Kountz Director	Kountz Brothers
Oswego & Syracuse (leased to D. L. & W.)	81	George Bliss Director	Morton, Bliss & Co.
Philadelphia, Wilmington & Baltimore	113	Kidder, Peabody & Co. Transfer Agent	Kidder, Peabody & Co.
Pittsburgh, Fort Wayne & Chicago	423	J. F. D. Lanier Director	Winslow, Lanier & Co.
Syracuse & Binghamton (leased to D. L. & W.)	98	George Bliss Director	Morton Bliss & Co.
Union Pacific	1032	George Bowdoin Director	Morton, Bliss & Co.

*Includes total mileage owned and operated. Figures in parenthesis are for projected mileage as listed in Poor's *Manual,* 1873-1874. While the affiliation of Fisk & Hatch to the Central Pacific and that of Drexel, Morgan to the Pennsylvania are usually dated in the early 1870s, they are not included since no specific affiliations are listed in Poor's.

Source: Poor's *Manual of the Railroads of the United States 1873-74.*

Notes

INTRODUCTION TO PART I

1. Carter Goodrich, ed., *Canals and American Economic Development* (New York, 1961), pp. 172-73 ff.

2. Fritz Redlich, *The Molding of American Banking: Men and Ideas* (New York, 1968), 2: 60-84. For a particularly valuable study of canal financing and the role of this banking house, see Nathan Miller, *Enterprise of a Free People* (Ithaca, N.Y., 1962), pp. 77-111 ff. The various activities of private bankers and their potential contribution in the early period is argued by Richard Sylla, "Forgotten Men of Money: Private Bankers in Early U. S. History," *Journal of Economic History*, 36 (March 1976): 173-88. The origin of investment banking is reviewed by Vincent Carosso, *Investment Banking in America: A History* (Cambridge, 1970), pp. 1-13.

3. Further evidence of the investment activities of private bankers in the canal era is presented by Harry N. Scheiber, *Ohio Canal Era: A Case Study of Government and the Economy, 1820-1861* (Athens, Ohio, 1969), pp. 38-39, 46-50, 373-78.

4. Ibid., p. 39. For a discussion of New York City mutual savings banks and their developmental role in financing transportation projects before the Civil War, see Alan L. Olmstead, *New York Savings Banks in the Ante-bellum Years, 1819-1861 (Chapel Hill, N.C., 1976), pp. 80 ff.*

5. Albert Fishlow, *American Railroads and the Transformation of the Antebellum Economy* (Cambridge, 1965), pp. 165 ff.

6. Frederick A. Cleveland and Fred W. Powell, *Railroad Finance* (New York, 1912), pp. 30-33, 50-64.

7. Alfred D. Chandler, Jr., *The Railroads: The Nation's First Big Business* (New York, 1965), pp. 9ff. See also Alfred D. Chandler, Jr., "Patterns of American Railroad Finance, 1830-1850," *Business History Review* 28 (September 1954): 248-63.

8. Calculated from data in U. S. Bureau of the Census, *Historical Statistics of the United States, Colonial Times to 1970, Bicentennial Edition* (Washington, D. C., 1975), 2: 734.

9. *American Railroad Journal*, July 3, 1852, reprinted in Chandler, *The Railroads*, pp. 60-64.

10. Ibid., p. 62.

11. Carosso, *Investment Banking in America*, p. 13.

12. J. F. D. Lanier, *Sketch of the Life of J. F. D. Lanier* (New York, 1870), pp. 19-29.

13. Henry V. Poor, *Manual of the Railroads of the United States*, 1868-69, p. 30.

14. "Names of Parties Subscribing to Stock," Union Pacific Railroad Company,

September, 1863; *Report of the Organization and Proceedings of the Union Pacific Railroad Company* (New York, 1864).

15. Alfred D. Chandler, Jr., *Henry Varnum Poor, Business Editor, Analyst, and Reformer* (Cambridge, 1956), pp. 73-107, 158-80.

16. William Moorhead to Jay Cooke, October 11, 1869, quoted in Ellis P. Oberholtzer, *Jay Cooke, Financier of the Civil War* (Philadelphia, 1907), p. 149, also pp. 189-96; Henrietta Larson, *Jay Cooke, Private Banker* (Cambridge, 1936), p. 361.

17. Dolores Greenberg, "Yankee Financiers and the Establishment of Trans-Atlantic Partnerships: A Re-examination," *Business History* 16 (January 1974): 17-35.

CHAPTER 1

1. Stephen Birmingham, *Our Crowd: The Great Jewish Families of New York* (New York, 1967), p. 87.

2. Robert P. Sharkey, *Money, Class, and Party; An Economic Study of Civil War and Reconstruction* (Baltimore, Md., 1967), p. 221.

3. Cyrus Adler, *Jacob Schiff: His Life and Letters* (Garden City, 1929), vol. 1; Birmingham, *Our Crowd*, pp. 58-168; Vincent Carosso, *Investment Banking in America: A History* (Cambridge, 1970), pp. 18-20; Henry Clews, *Fifty Years in Wall Street* (New York, 1915), pp. 7, 584; Edwin J. Perkins, *Financing Anglo-American Trade: The House of Brown, 1800-1880* (Cambridge, Mass., 1975), pp. 1-59; Barry E. Supple, "A Business Elite: German-Jewish Financiers in Nineteenth Century New York," *Business History Review* 31 (Summer 1957): 157-76; Linton Wells, "The House of Seligman," 3 vols., 1931 (unpublished MSS., New-York Historical Society).

4. Reverend D. O. Morton to L. P. Morton, Hanover, New Hampshire, August 19, 1844, Morton Manuscripts, New York Public Library.

5. D. O. Morton, Jr., to L. P. Morton, Enfield, April 28, 1842, Morton MSS. See also the family-approved biography, Robert McElroy, *Levi Parsons Morton: Banker, Diplomat, and Statesman* (New York, 1930). In contemporary accounts, Morton's career was presented as an exemplar of the poor boy who, unaided, climbed from the very bottom to the top of the ladder: *Contemporary American Biography* (New York, 1892), pp. 61-63; *Fads and Fancies of Representative Americans*, no. 43, p. 110; Henry D. Northrup, *The Lives of Harrison and Morton* (Philadelphia, 1888). The biographical profiles in such nineteenth-century sources were frequently provided by the subject. Morton paid $175 for that placed in the *National Cyclopedia of American Biography*.

6. D. O. Morton, Jr., to L. P. Morton, Enfield, April 28, 1842, Morton MSS.

7. John D. Hillis, "Life and Public Services of Levi Parsons Morton," p. 64, Morton MSS.

8. L. P. Morton to D. Morton, Boston, January 28, 1849, January 5, 1850, Morton MSS.; Edward Chase Kirkland, *Men, Cities, and Transportation* (Cambridge, Mass., 1948), 2: 454-56.

9. Margaret Myers, *The New York Money Market* (New York, 1931), p. 63; Perkins, *Financing Anglo-American Trade,* pp. 115-46; *Banker's Magazine* (New York), July 1866, May 1868.

10. Mary Morton to D. Morton, May 11, 1852, Morton MSS.

11. George S. Boutwell to L. P. Morton, November [?], 1903; Morton to Boutwell, November 10, 1903, Morton MSS.; George Boutwell, *Reminiscences of Sixty Years in Public Affairs* (New York, 1902), 2: 187; Edmund Stedman, "Biographical Notes," Morton MSS.

12. Herbert Satterlee, *J. Pierpont Morgan: An Intimate Portrait* (New York, 1939), pp. 58-59.

13. Elizabeth C. K. Hobson, *Recollections of a Happy Life* (New York, 1916), p. 34.

14. Commercial failures in 1861 totaled 6,993 compared to 4,932 in 1857 (*Bankers' Magazine* [New York], February 1867).

15. Fritz Redlich, *The Molding of American Banking and Ideas* (New York, 1968), 2: 60-73; Alfred D. Chandler, *Henry Varnum Poor* (Cambridge, Mass., 1956), p. 94.

16. *Bankers' Magazine* (New York), January 1864; *Commercial and Financial Chronicle,* July 29, October 7, 1865; *Merchants and Bankers' Almanac,* 1865.

17. Myers, *New York Money Market,* p. 71n.

18. For a discussion of the fluctuations in the gold premium, see Davis R. Dewey, *Financial History of the United States* (New York, 1934), pp. 294-97. The suspension of specie payments and the effect on the price of gold as a commodity is discussed by Albert S. Bolles, *The Financial History of the United States from 1861 to 1885* (New York, 1894), pp. 130-58. Foreign-exchange dealings are described by Charles F. Dunbar, *The Theory and History of Banking* (New York, 1917), pp. 103-31. Their management by an international banking house is treated by Edwin J. Perkins, "Managing a Dollar-Sterling Exchange Account: Brown, Shipley and Co. in the 1850's," *Business History* 16 (January 1974): 48-64. See also Perkins, *Financing Anglo-American Trade,* pp. 199-209; Myers, *New York Money Market,* pp. 36-37; Ellis P. Oberholtzer, *Jay Cooke, Financier of the Civil War* (Philadelphia, 1907), pp. 369-70.

19. Leland Jenks, *The Migration of British Capital to 1875* (London, 1927), pp. 233-62; *Bankers' Magazine* (London), 1863-1866; the Société Génerale de Crédit Mobilier was created as a joint stock form in 1852 by the government of Napoleon III. It was particularly important in promoting investment in railways and public works and served, Rondo Cameron explains, as the prototype for the "mixed banks" that emerged on the Continent later in the century (Rondo Cameron, et al., *Banking in the Early Stages of Industrialization* [New York, 1967], pp. 108, 115, 162, 316).

20. *Bankers' Magazine* (London), February 1863.

21. Walter Bagehot, *Lombard Street,* in *Works of Walter Bagehot,* ed. Forrest Morgan (Hartford, Conn., 1889), 5: 138.

22. Jenks, *Migration of British Capital,* pp. 267-93. For a reappraisal of the dating and circumstances, see Dolores Greenberg, "Yankee Financiers and the Establishment of Trans-Atlantic Partnerships: A Re-examination," *Business History,* 16 (January 1974): 17-35. For the London opening of Brown, Shipley and Co., see Perkins, *Financing Anglo-American Trade,* pp. 61-65.

23. Jay Cooke had been adamant in his refusal to negotiate a loan abroad, but the success of the Confederate Cotton Loan introduced in London in 1864 by Schroeder & Co. on behalf of Erlanger & Co., Paris, induced Chase to bargain with the Barings (*Bankers' Magazine* [London], February 1864; Oberholtzer, *Jay Cooke,* pp. 285-89, 525-27).

24. Press clipping, January 24, 1870, Morton MSS.; Carl Sandburg, *Abraham Lincoln, The War Years* (New York, 1939), pp. 517-18.

25. Quoted in McElroy, *Levi Parsons Morton,* p. 50; Henry Hall, *America's Successful Men of Affairs* (New York, 1895), 1: 94.

26. *Commercial and Financial Chronicle,* July 1866; Jenks, *Migration of British Capital,* p. 268; Myers, *New York Money Market,* p. 289; Oberholtzer, *Jay Cooke,* pp. 513-17.

27. Clipping, Morton MSS.

28. Burns went to Paris in 1869, where, until 1878, he served as the managing director of the Paris branch of the London Banking Association and as a director of the United States Mortgage Company in Europe. According to a contemporary account, he did not join the London firm until 1878, but, according to Satterlee, Burns joined his father-in-law's firm immediately after the marriage. Both may be correct since Junius Morgan had established a Paris office in 1869 (Clipping, Morton MSS.; Satterlee, *J. Pierpont Morgan*, 119; Charles P. Kindleberger, "Origins of Direct Investment in France," *Business History Review* 48 [Autumn 1974]: 387).

29. George Bliss to L. P. Morton, January 31, February 2, 1878; Bliss to Charles D. Rose, London, November 9, December 12, 1878; Bliss MSS., New-York Historical Society; Clyde William Phelps, *The Foreign Expansion of American Banks: American Branch Banking Abroad* (New York, 1927), pp. 3-14.

30. Merrill Denison, *Canada's First Bank: A History of The Bank of Montreal* (Toronto, 1967), 2: 155-58, 172; Morden H. Long, "Sir John Rose and the informal beginnings of the Canadian High Commissionership," *Canadian Historical Review* 12 (March 1931): 25-42; Joseph Pope (ed.), *Correspondence of Sir John Macdonald* (New York, 1921).

31. Quoted in Henrietta Larson, *Jay Cooke, Private Banker* (Cambridge, 1936), p. 319.

32. *Dictionary of American Biography*, p. 373; Hall, *America's Successful Men*, 1: 93; *Washington Capital*, March 2, 1884; "Personal Memorandum of Levi P. Morton," Morton MSS.; McElroy, *Levi Parsons Morton*, pp. 47-52. This George Bliss should not be confused with the lawyer who was a central figure in the Star Route frauds.

33. Metropolitan Railway Company, "Articles of Association" (New York, 1864). Chittenden and Phelps were also among the subscribers, and Chittenden, like Bliss, would join the management of the Delaware, Lackawanna & Western. For discussion of the response of capitalists involved in Western railroads to urban rail prospects, see Eugene J. McMechen, "The Rapid Transit Struggle in New York, 1864-1879" (unpublished Master's thesis, Hunter College, New York, 1975).

34. Clippings, Morton MSS.

35. *New York World*, November 20, 1874; *Commercial and Financial Chronicle*, September 2, 1865.

36. *Merchants and Bankers' Almanac*, 1867; Hall, *America's Successful Men*, 1: 105; Satterlee, *J. Pierpont Morgan*, p. 110; Bliss to Morton, November 8, December [?], 1883, Bliss MSS.

37. Thomas Cochran, *Railroad Leaders, 1845-1890* (New York, 1953), pp. 46-47. Fish frequently relied on Bliss for advice in the 1880s, when he was Illinois vice-president. See Bliss MSS., especially for 1884.

38. Walter Burns to Morton, February 14, 1896; Morton Trust Co., "Notice," July 1 1899; New York News Bureau, "Notice," June 28, 1899; Morton MSS.

39. Clipping, January 24, 1871, Morton MSS.

40. For Rose's role and the intervention of Morton with Secretary Fish and President Grant, see Morton MSS., 1870-1872; Macdonald letterbooks, 1870-1872, Public Archives of Canada; *Journal of Commerce*, April 26, 1872; *London Times*, May 8, 1872; *New York Evening Post*, August 14, 1872.

41. *London Times*, June 28, 1873; *New York Times*, September 9, 1873; McElroy, *Levi Parsons Morton*, pp. 57-69.

42. After the treaty had passed the Senate, Horace Porter, Grant's Secretary, expressed their informal gratitude: "I do not know any who deserves success more than you in regard to the treaty and you now have it. . .What you have done has been fully appreciated here." Porter to Morton, May 26, 1872, Morton MSS. When Morton in turn thanked the Drexels and George Childs, Childs replied: "We received your kind notes and feel that you give us entirely too much credit in the matter of the Treaty. I know that more is due to you than to

anyone else, and if it had not been for the efforts of Sir John Rose and yourself I feel assured that the Treaty would have proved a failure. I have a letter from the Executive Mansion this morning announcing our complete victory. Porter did good service. Drexel sends regards" (Childs to Morton, May 27, 1872, Morton MSS). The following year Morton, Rose & Co. replaced Clews, Habicht & Co. as the government's agents.

43. *New York Tribune*, April 28, 1876; Boutwell, *Reminiscences*, 2: 187; McElroy, *Levi Parsons Morton*, pp. 57-69.

44. *New York Commercial Advertiser*, January 18, 1873.

45. *Evening Post*, October 23, 1873.

CHAPTER 2

1. Alfred D. Chandler, Jr., ed., *The Railroads* (New York, 1965), pp. 43-88; Thomas C. Cochran, *Railroad Leaders, 1845-1890* (Cambridge, Mass., 1953), pp. 31-35, 62-78, 98-102; Julius Grodinsky, *Transcontinental Railway Strategy, 1869-1893* (Philadelphia, 1962), p. 13, passim; Fritz Redlich, *The Molding of American Banking* (New York, 1968), 2: 348-64; John Stover, *The Railroads of the South, 1865-1900: A Study in Finance and Control* (Chapel Hill, N.C., 1955), pp. 122-54, passim.

2. Henrietta M. Larson, *Jay Cooke, Private Banker* (Cambridge, Mass., 1936), pp. 244 ff.

3. Quoted in Stephen Birmingham, *Our Crowd: The Great Jewish Families of New York* (New York, 1967), p. 130.

4. Arthur M. Johnson and Barry E. Supple, *Boston Capitalists and Western Railroads*, (Cambridge, Mass., 1967), p. 210. Fogel's figures show that by the summer of 1872 the sum raised by the sale of various issues came to $63.5 million (Robert W. Fogel, *The Union Pacific Railroad* [Baltimore, 1960], p. 72; Redlich, *American Banking*, 2: 362).

5. Harris Fahnestock, quoted in Larson, *Cooke*, p. 276.

6. *The Nation*, August 15, 1872; *Commercial and Financial Chronicle*, March 9, 1872; Henry V. Poor, *Manual of the Railroads of the United States*, 1868-69, pp. 26-32; 1869-70, pp. xlvii-xlix; 1870-71, pp. xl-xliii; 1875-76, pp. 1a ff. (hereafter referred to as "Poor's *Manual*").

7. *Railroad Gazette*, July 23, 1870.

8. *Commercial and Financial Chronicle*, May 27, 1871.

9. For total investment and bonded-debt estimates for 1866, see Stover, *The Railroads of the South*, p. 37. For investment data and miles of railroad built annually thereafter, see United States Bureau of the Census, *Historical Statistics of the United States, Colonial Times to 1970* (Washington, 1975), 2: 732-34. Increases in railroad capitalization are presented by Rendigs Fels, "American Business Cycles, 1865-79," *American Economic Review* 41 (June 1951): 326. For estimates of constant-dollar gross and net investment, by decades, see Albert Fishlow, "Productivity and Technological Change in the Railroad Sector, 1840-1910," *Output, Employment and Productivity in the United States after 1800* (New York, 1966), pp. 589-613.

10. Julius Grodinsky, *Transcontinental Railway Strategy, 1869-1893: A Study of Businessmen* (Philadelphia, 1962), p. 40.

11. *Railroad Gazette*, August 13, 1870.

12. The *London Times* series in the summer of 1870 warning of fraud and mismanagement in American railroads had not had the desired effect. See *Commercial and Financial Chronicle*, December 21, 1872.

13. Dorothy Adler, *British Investment in American Railways*, ed. Muriel Hidy (Charlottesville, Va., 1970), pp. 75-77; David M. Ellis, "The Homestead Clause in Railroad Land Grants," in David M. Ellis, ed., *The Frontier in American Development* (Ithaca, N.Y., 1969), pp. 47-73; J. F. D. Lanier, *Sketch of the Life of J. F. D. Lanier* (New York, 1870), p. 51.

14. Adler, *British Investment*, pp. 86-89; Margaret G. Myers, *The New York Money Market* (New York, 1931), pp. 289-90.

15. *Commercial and Financial Chronicle*, May 31, November 1, 1873; January 10, 1874.

16. Adler, *British Investment*, p. xii.

17. *Commercial and Financial Chronicle*, May 10, 1873.

18. The statistical data for imported capital are inadequate. The Census lists foreign investments only for 1869 based on Myers's figures, which are newspaper estimates (U.S. Bureau of the Census, *Historical Statistics*, 2: 869; Myers, *New York Money Market*, pp. 289-290); Fels's figures for 1876 on net capital imports include governments (Fels, "American Business Cycles," p. 326). See also Adler, *British Investment*, pp. 86-89.

19. Carter Goodrich, *Government Promotion of American Canals and Railroads, 1800-1890* (New York, 1960), pp. 270-71.

20. Lloyd Mercer, "Taxpayers or Investors: Who Paid For the Land Grant Railroads?" *Business History Review* 46 (Autumn 1972): 287; Lloyd Mercer, "Building Ahead of Demand: Some Evidence for the Land Grant Railroads," *Journal of Economic History* 34 (June 1974): 492-500.

21. For his railroad positions, see the annual issues of Poor's *Manual*, and for notices of coupon payments, the *Commercial and Financial Chronicle*.

22. Jesup was also selling rails to the California Pacific, of which he became a director (Collis P. Huntington to Leland Stanford, New York, December 24, 1870, January 30, 1871, Huntington Papers, Mariners' Museum, Newport News, Va.).

23. Thomas C. Cochran and William Miller, *Railroad Leaders, 1845-1890: The Business Mind in Action* (Cambridge, Mass., 1953), pp. 69, 103, 116, 454, 465-66.

24. Herbert Satterlee, *J. Pierpont Morgan* (New York, 1934), p. 130; Poor's *Manual*, 1870-71, p. 252; 1871-72, pp. 448, 526.

25. Stover, *The Railroads of the South*, pp. 104-21. Jesup became a director, as did financier Adrien Iselin, of Wilson's E.T.V. & G. in 1874 (Poor's *Manual*, 1875-76, p. 342).

26. *D.A.B.*; Poor's *Manual*. Kennedy's partners were Henry Baker and John S. Barnes. Kennedy also allied with John Cisco and William E. Dodge in Texas railroads (James P. Baughman, *Charles Morgan and the Development of Southern Transportation* [Nashville, Tenn., 1968], pp. 201-2).

27. See chapters 4, 8; also Albro Martin, *James J. Hill and the Opening of the Northwest* (New York, 1976).

28. See chapter 10.

29. Chandler, *Henry Varnum Poor*, p. 105; annual listings in Poor's *Manual; Railroad Gazette*, January 3, 1871.

30. Lanier, *Sketch of the Life of J. F. D. Lanier*; Redlich, *American Banking*, 2: 354-55; annual listings in Poor's *Manual*; Stover, *The Railroads of the South*, pp. 102, 116.

31. John Stover, *American Railroads* (Chicago, 1961), p. 82. The advertisements of Henry Clews, for example, like some of the other railroad banking specialists, noted that "special attention" would be given to "negotiation of securities of New Railroads" (Poor's *Manual*, 1867-70, bankers' advertisements). See Cochran, *Railroad Leaders*, p. 213, for a differing view.

32. H. Craig Miner, *The St. Louis-San Francisco Transcontinental Railroad* (Lawrence, Kans., 1972), pp. 81 ff.; *Railroad Gazette*, May 6, 1871, July 30, 1872, July 19, 1873. For Seligman's role in the New Orleans, Mobile & Texas and the Katy, see chapters, 3, 5.

33. Miner, *The St. Louis-San Francisco*, p. 81.

34. Birmingham, *Our Crowd*, p. 138 (italics mine).

35. Cochran, *Railroad Leaders*, pp. 31-35, 62-78, 98-102.

36. Harris Fahnestock to Jay Cooke, June 8, 1872, quoted in Larson, *Jay Cooke,* p. 381.

37. See Appendix.

38. When Morton joined the U.P. management in March 1871, it included the soon-to-be-notorious Oakes Ames, his associate in the Milwaukee & St. Paul, the Katy, and the New Orleans, Mobile & Texas.

39. *Commercial and Financial Chronicle*, March 11, 1873; *New York World*, March 12, 1873. When the *Chronicle* in 1874 complained of the brevity of the annual statement of this important company, Morton, Bliss & Co., financial agent, prepared a supplementary land department report (*Commercial and Financial Chronicle*, March 4, May 2, 1874).

40. Redlich, *The Molding of American Banking*, 2: 360-77.

41. Chandler, *The Railroads,* pp. 43-88.

CHAPTER 3

1. Thomas C. Cochran and William Miller, *Railroad Leaders, 1845-1890: The Business Mind in Action* (Cambridge, Mass., 1953), pp. 35, 70.

2. Bliss to Charles Rose, London, November 19, 1878, Bliss MSS.

3. Bliss to C. Rose, London, December 12, 1878, London, Bliss MSS.

4. Ibid.

5. Bliss to Morton, January 31, February 2, 1878, Bliss MSS.

6. *Documents Relating to the Organization of the Milwaukee and St. Paul Railway Company* (New York, 1863), p. 8; Carl Snyder, *American Railways as Investments* (New York, 1907), p. 213; S. F. Van Oss, *American Railroads as Investments* (New York, 1893), p. 463.

7. Henry V. Poor, *Manual of the Railroads of the United States,* 1868-69, p. 370; 1869-70, p. 428 (hereafter referred to as "Poor's *Manual*").

8. *Fifth Annual Report of the Milwaukee and St. Paul Railway Company*, 1868 (Milwaukee, 1869).

9. Poor's *Manual*, 1870-71, p. 465; 1871-72, p. 500. John W. Cary, *The Organization and History of the Chicago, Milwaukee & St. Paul Railway Company* (Milwaukee, 1890). As Cary, the general counsel of the company, prepared the manuscript to reveal to the managers how and when property was acquired, it is less a history than a carefully selective record. For a study, partial to Mitchell, see August Derleth, *The Milwaukee Road: Its First Hundred Years* (New York, 1948).

10. Poor's *Manual*, 1870-71, p. 500; *Railroad Gazette*, June 5, 1875.

11. Cary, *Organization and History of the Chicago, Milwaukee & St. Paul*, pp. 176 ff.; *Railroad Gazette*, April 23, 1870; Poor's *Manual*, 1871-72, p. 417.

12. Cary, ibid.

13. Robert Fogel, *The Union Pacific Railroad, A Case In Premature Enterprise* (Baltimore, Md., 1960); Carl Degler, *The Age of the Economic Revolution, 1876-1900*

(Glenview, Ill., 1967), p. 23. The new focus can be seen also in Edward C. Kirkland, *Charles Francis Adams, Jr., 1835-1915, The Patrician At Bay* (Cambridge, Mass., 1965), p. 81. Not all historians have been quite so sympathetic; for a more critical judgment of construction company finance, see Carter Goodrich, *Government Promotion of American Canals and Railroads, 1800-1890* (New York, 1960), pp. 186-204. The classic account is William Z. Ripley, *Railroads: Finance and Organization* (New York, 1927), pp. 10-52.

14. Bliss to Morton, September 23, 1876; Bliss to S. Chittenden, Washington, D.C.,
15. Ibid., pp. 184-188; *Commercial and Financial Chronicle,* March 2, 1872. The press inaccurately reported that the purchase had been made from the St. Paul & Chicago rather than the construction company.
16. The price of the issue with the July coupon was ninety three (*Commercial and Financial Chronicle,* May 11, 1872; Harry Pierce, "Foreign Investments in American Enterprise," in David T. Gilchrist and W. David Lewis, eds., *Economic Change in the Civil War Era* [Greenville, S.C., 1965], p. 53).
17. The price of the issue was ninety-five (*Commercial and Financial Chronicle,* December 7, 1872).
18. Cary, *Organization and History of the Chicago, Milwaukee & St. Paul,* p. 140; *Commercial and Financial Chronicle,* January 20, 1872.
19. *Railroad Gazette,* May 18, 1872; *Commercial and Financial Chronicle,* May 18, 1872.
20. Poor's *Manual,* 1868-69, p. 370; 1869-70, pp. 6, 428; 1870-71, p. 465; August Derleth, *The Milwaukee Road: Its First Hundred Years* (New York, 1948), p. 94.
21. Poor's *Manual,* 1871-72, p. 242; 1872-73, p. 173.
22. *Commercial and Financial Chronicle,* March 22, 1873. Here again financiers relied on the construction company, and two were formed to obtain rights-of-way. Russell Sage was president of the Chicago & Milwaukee Construction Company for the stretch from Milwaukee to the Wisconsin state line, while another company was officially formed for financing and building the track in Illinois. By 1873 Sage had obtained the rights to the whole line, and the M. & St. P. then purchased it for $2.5 million in bonds and $2 million common stock. Also $2.5 million scrip preferred stock was attached to the bonds issued to the construction company. The scrip had no value but authorized the bondholders to vote. See the letter to the president of the Stock Exchange, December 27, 1872, in the *Commercial and Financial Chronicle,* January 4, 1873; Cary, *Organization and History of the Chicago, Milwaukee & St. Paul,* pp. 142 ff.
23. Cary, *Organization and History of the Chicago,* Milwaukee & St. Paul, p. 205; *Commercial and Financial Chronicle,* February 7, 1874; *Eleventh Annual Report of the Chicago, Milwaukee and St. Paul Railway Co.,* 1874.
24. *Commercial and Financial Chronicle,* March 7, 14, 1874.
25. Derleth, *The Milwaukee Road,* p. 111. For an excellent account of Mitchell's political activities, see George Miller, *Railroads and the Granger Laws* (Madison, Wisc., 1971), pp. 150-60.
26. Quoted in Derleth, *The Milwaukee Road,* p. 111.
27. Cary, *Organization and History of the Chicago, Milwaukee & St. Paul,* p. 205; *Railroad Gazette,* May 8, 29, June 19, 1875.
28. Poor's *Manual,* 1875-76, p. lvi.
29. *Railroad Gazette,* May 21, June 11, December 3, 1870; *Commercial and Financial Chronicle,* August 13, November 12, December 10, 1870. The Chattanooga railroad had been backed by New Yorkers and Bostonians since its incorporation in 1867, when the original group consisted of Oakes Ames, James A. Raynor, Henry J. Gardner, and Peter Butler (James P. Baughman, *Charles Morgan and The Development of Southern Transportation* [Nashville, Tenn., 1968], pp. 156 ff.).
30. The railroad from Mobile to New Orleans was 140 miles, that projected from New

Orleans to the Texas line at the Sabine River would be 227 miles, and the portion projected from the Sabine to Houston, 108 miles. The bankers joined the directorate officially in the March 1871 election (Poor's *Manual*, 1871-72, p. 533).

31. *Railroad Gazette*, March 11, 1871; *Commercial and Financial Chronicle*, July 1, 1871; Poor's *Manual*, 1871-72, p. 533.

32. *Railroad Gazette*, April 29, 1871; *Commercial and Financial Chronicle*, May 27, 1871.

33. *Railroad Gazette*, June 3, 1871; *Commercial and Financial Chronicle*, October 19, 1872.

34. *Commercial and Financial Chronicle*, October 19, 1872.

35. *Railroad Gazette*, October 19, 1872; Carter Goodrich, *Government Promotion of American Canals and Railroads, 1800-1890* (New York, 1960), p. 221. The conflict followed a brief accommodation period (Baughman, *Charles Morgan*, pp. 169-70).

36. *Railroad Gazette*, October 5, 1872. The state bonds were in payment for stock issues.

37. Ibid.

38. Letter to the *New Orleans Picayune*, October 5, 1872, quoted in *Railroad Gazette*, October 19, 1872; *Commercial and Financial Chronicle*, November 2, 1872.

39. *Commercial and Financial Chronicle*, May 3, 17, June 21, September 20, December 20, 1873. "The parties who constructed the line from Mobile to New Orleans, and secured the line from the Sabine to Houston, furnished all the means necessary for the construction, equipment and operation of these two divisions" (Poor's *Manual*, 1874-75, p. 700).

40. Von Hoffman's firm also participated in financing C. P. Huntington's Southern Pacific, and in September of 1873 Huntington owed the bankers $1 million gold for which they held $1,460,000 Southern Pacific bonds as collateral (Huntington to Mark Hopkins, New York, September 22, 23, October 1, 13, 17, 1873; January 19, April 17, 1874, Huntington Papers).

41. Miner notes that the Seligmans had an overview of their early investments and thought of them specifically as a "consortium" (H. Craig Miner, *The St. Louis-San Francisco Transcontinental Railroad* [Lawrence, Kans., 1972], p. 81).

42. V. V. Masterson, *The Katy Railroad and the Last Frontier* (Norman, 1952), p. 20.

43. Ibid.

44. Poor's *Manual*, 1870-71, p. 468; 1871-72, p. 159; Masterson, *The Katy*, p. 61.

45. Masterson, *The Katy*, p. 30. See also pp. 19 ff.; *Railroad Gazette*, June 25, 1870.

46. *Railroad Gazette*, May 28, 1870.

47. Ibid., June 25, May 21, 1870.

48. Masterson, *The Katy*, pp. 93-120.

49. Ibid., pp. 200-204; *Commercial and Financial Chronicle*, July 5, 1873.

50. Masterson, *The Katy*, p. 204.

51. Ibid., p. 202.

52. Ibid., p. 211.

53. Bliss to J. Rose, London, January ?, 1878, Bliss MSS.

54. Julius Grodinsky, *Jay Gould: His Business Career* (Philadelphia, 1957), pp. 234-37.

55. Bliss to J. Rose, London, December 5, 1879, Bliss MSS.

56. Poor's *Manual*, 1868-69, p. 94.

57. Illinois Central, *Centennial Report, The Financial Story of Our First Hundred Years, 1851-1951* (Chicago, 1951), p. 24.

58. Cochran, *Railroad Leaders*, p. 46.

59. William K. Ackerman, *Historical Sketch of the Illinois Central Railroad* (Chicago, 1890), pp. 112-14.

60. *Commercial and Financial Chronicle*, March 7, 1874; *Centennial Report*, p. 25; Poor's *Manual*, 1874-75, p. 175; John Stover, *Railroads of the South, 1865-1900* (Chapel Hill, N.C. 1955), pp. 155 ff.

61. *Commercial and Financial Chronicle*, February 28, 1874.

62. Ibid., February 21, March 7, 1874.

63. S. F. Van Oss, *American Railroads as Investments* (New York, 1893), p. 728.

64. Julius Grodinsky, *Transcontinental Railway Strategy, 1869-1893: A Study of Businessmen* (Philadelphia, 1962), p. 10; Stover, *Railroads of the South*, p. 55.

INTRODUCTION TO PART II

1. Henry V. Poor, *Manual of the Railroads of the United States*, 1875-76, p. 1a (hereafter referred to as "Poor's *Manual*"). For data on mileage, see U. S. Bureau of the Census, *Historical Statistics of the United States, Colonial Times to 1970* (Washington, D.C., 1975), 2: 732.

2. Poor's *Manual,* 1875-76, pp. 1a-lvii.

3. *Report of the President to the Directors of the Indianapolis, Cincinnati & Lafayette R. R. Company, for the Year Ending June 30, 1874,* p. 13.

4. *Commercial and Financial Chronicle*, January 10, 1874; Poor's *Manual*, 1875-76, p. liv.

5. Rendigs Fels, *American Business Cycles: 1865-1897* (Chapel Hill, N.C., 1959), p. 111; Fels, "American Business Cycles, 1865-79," *American Economic Review* 41 (June 1951): 347 ff.

6. *Commercial and Financial Chronicle*, May 31, November 1, 1873; January 10, February 21, 28, March 7, 1874; Collis P. Huntington to Leland Stanford, New York, May 9, 1874, Huntington Papers. See U. S. Bureau of the Census, *Historical Statistics of the United States*, 2: 869, for data on total foreign investment.

7. *Commercial and Financial Chronicle*, February 21, 1874; Huntington to Stanford, New York, February 24, 1874, Huntington Papers.

8. *Commercial and Financial Chronicle*, February 7, 1874; John W. Cary, *The Organization and History of The Chicago, Milwaukee & St. Paul Railway Company*, p. 205. The *Railroad Gazette* June 13, 1874, also reported that new first-mortgage issues were for sale at six and seven percent for such Eastern roads as the Old Colony, the Fitchbury, the Nashua & Rochester, the Washington City and Point Lookout Company. For the Pennsylvania issue, see Poor's *Manual*, 1874-75, p. 455.

9. *Railroad Gazette*, November 13, 1875.

10. Poor's *Manual*, 1874-75, p. 455.

11. *Railroad Gazette*, June 26, 1875.

12. Henry H. Swain, *Economic Aspects of Railroad Receiverships* (New York, 1898), pp. 70-71.

13. *Railroad Gazette*, June 26, 1875.

14. Swain, *Economic Aspects of Railroad Receiverships*, pp. 70-71; *Commercial and Financial Chronicle*, January 22, 1876.

15. *Railroad Gazette*, June 23, 1876. For a fascinating discussion of Granger legislation dealing with the "alarmed capital argument" set within the context of expanding industrial capitalism, see George H. Miller, *Railroads and the Granger Laws* (Madison, Wisc., 1971), pp. 161-94.

16. Bliss to J. Rose, Washington, D.C., May 25, 1876; Bliss to Morton, Newport, May 27,

1876; Bliss to G. S. Bowdoin, London, May 10, 1876, Bliss MSS.

17. Bliss to Morton, Newport, August 4, 1876, Bliss MSS.

18. Bliss to Isaac Anderson, New Haven, September 15, 1876, Bliss MSS.

19. Swain, *Economic Aspects of Railroad Receiverships*, pp. 70-71; Bliss to J. Rose, London, September 28, November 17, 28, 1876; Bliss to M. E. Ingalls, Cincinnati, September 7, 1876; Bliss to P. D. Grenfell, December 6, 1876, Bliss MSS.

20. Fels, *American Business Cycles*, p. 111.

21. Bliss to Grenfell, London, September 18, 1877.

22. Fels, *American Business Cycles,* p. 111; *Railroad Gazette,* August 2, 1878.

CHAPTER 4

1. Bliss to M. E. Ingalls, November 6, 1880, Bliss MSS.

2. See chapter 3.

3. George S. Cottman, *Centennial History and Handbook of Indiana* (Indianapolis, Ind., 1915), pp. 127-30; Cincinnati Commission of Railroads and Telegraphs, *Annual Report of the Commissioner of Railroads and Telegraphs, 1870,* 1: 592-94.

4. *Railroad Gazette*, October 29, 1870; *Commercial and Financial Chronicle*, November 5, 1870.

5. Henry H. Swain, *Economic Aspects of Railroad Receiverships* (New York, 1898), pp. 68, 84-87.

6. *Railroad Gazette*, November 12, 1870. The Pennsylvania did own 300 I.C. & L. bonds acquired at seventy-five percent of par. H. W. Schotter, *The Growth and Development of the Pennsylvania Railroad Company* (Philadelphia, 1927), p. 89.

7. For a discussion of other major receiverships of the 1870s, see Albro Martin, "Railroads and the Equity Receivership: An Essay on Institutional Change," *Journal of Economic History* 34 (September 1974): 685-709.

8. *District Court of the United States for the District of Indiana in the Matter of the Indianapolis, Cincinnati and Lafayette Railroad on Petition of Joel F. Richardson et al, and the City of Laurenceburg Adjudication of Bankruptcy Pleadings and Evidence,* 1871, pp. 330-36.

9. *Commercial and Financial Chronicle*, November 5, 1870.

10. Swain, *Economic Aspects of Railroad Receiverships*, pp. 53-58.

11. *Railroad Gazette*, November 12, 1870.

12. Bliss to Perkins, Boston, February 5, 1877, Bliss MSS.

13. *Railroad Gazette*, December 31, 1870; March 11, 1871.

14. Ibid., March 11, 1871.

15. Ibid., April 1, 1871; October 19, 1872.

16. Quoted in *Railroad Gazette*, December 31, 1870. After the Civil War, Cincinnati needed new railway connections to regain her commercial prosperity, as the traffic of the Ohio Valley had shifted to St. Louis, Cleveland, and Chicago (Charles Ambler, *A History of Transportation in the Ohio Valley* [Glendale, Calif., 1932]).

17. *The Directors' Report to the Stockholders of the Indianapolis, Cincinnati and Lafayette Railroad Company, August 1873*, p. 8.

18. Ibid., p. 5. See also "Report to Stockholders, 1871," reprinted in the *Commercial and Financial Chronicle*, December 16, 1871; *Railroad Gazette*, July 29, November 18, 1871.

19. Coupon payments were to be deferred up to ten years (*Report to the Stockholders,* 1873, pp. 6 ff.; *Commercial and Financial Chronicle*, February 15, June 14, 1873; *Railroad Gazette*, May 22, 1873).

20. *Report to the Stockholders*, 1873, p. 7.

21. *Commercial and Financial Chronicle*, November 22, 1872.

22. The Illinois connection, like that with the B. & O., brought to fruition their early plans announced at the stockholders' meeting in January 1871 (*Commercial and Financial Chronicle*, January 28, February 11, 1871; *Railroad Gazette*, February 4, 1871).

23. *Report of the President to the Directors of the Indianapolis, Cincinnati and Lafayette R. R. Company, for the Year Ending June 30, 1874*, pp. 9, 13.

24. Ibid.

25. *Commercial and Financial Chronicle*, April 18, 1874. Kennedy became vice-president in 1874.

26. *Report of the President to the Directors of the I. C. & L.*, 1874, p. 9.

27. *Annual Report of the Indianapolis Board of Trade, January 1874*.

28. *Commercial and Financial Chronicle*, April 18, 1874.

29. *Report of the President and Directors of the Indianapolis, Cincinnati & Lafayette Railroad Company for the Year Ending June 30, 1875*, pp. 8 ff. For fiscal 1874-1875, Poor's accused the officers of "failing to furnish any report though repeatedly applied to" (Poor's *Manual*, 1874-75, p. 705).

30. *Report of the President and Directors of the Indianapolis, Cincinnati & Lafayette Railroad for the Year Ending June 30, 1876*, pp. 3 ff.

31. Ibid. An agreement was also renegotiated for the B. & O., to continue annual purchases of $50,000 of 1869 bonds at eighty-five to add to their holdings of $174,000 (Poor's *Manual*, 1875-76, p. 296).

32. Bliss to Morton, September 9, 1876, Bliss MSS.

33. Bliss to Morton, September 23, 1876, Bliss MSS.

34. Bliss to Chittenden, Washington, D.C., December 10, 1877, Bliss MSS. J. S. Kennedy was involved in the settlement reached (*Railroad Gazette*, March 15, 1878).

35. Bliss to Morton, Washington, D.C., January 1, 1877, Bliss MSS.

36. *Railroad Gazette*, March 15, 1878. The monied institutions were having difficulty employing funds; the problem for them was an excess of funds and the shortage of acceptable collateral (Bliss to J. Rose, London, February 2, 1877; Bliss to R. W. Luce, Hyde Park Bank, Pennsylvania, June 5, 1877, Bliss MSS).

37. Bliss to Ingalls, Cincinnati, September 7, 1876, Bliss MSS.

38. Bliss to Thomas H. Perkins, Boston, March 7, 1877, Bliss MSS.

39. Bliss to Ingalls, Cincinnati, March 29, 1880, Bliss MSS.

40. *Aschcroft's Railway Directory for 1868* (New York, 1868); Henry V. Poor, *Manual of the Railroads of the United States*, annual issues, 1869 ff.

41. Bliss to Ingalls, Cincinnati, July 5, August 21, 1876; Bliss to E. F. Osborn, Cincinnati, August 3, 1876; Bliss to Ingalls, December 30, 1878; Bliss to Osborn, February 2, 1879, Bliss MSS.

42. Bliss to Ingalls, December 30, 1878; Bliss to William A. Booth, Secretary, New York, October 4, 1877, Bliss MSS.

43. *Report of the Receiver of the Indianapolis, Cincinnati & Lafayette Railroad Company for the Five Months Ending December 31, 1876*.

44. *Report of the Indianapolis, Cincinnati & Lafayette Railroad Company, for the Year Ending June 30, 1877, by M. E. Ingalls, Receiver*, p. 3.

45. Bliss to Perkins, Boston, January 1, 5, 1877, June [?], 1878, Bliss MSS.

46. Bliss to Perkins, Boston, November 12, 1878, Bliss MSS.

47. Bliss to Ingalls, Cincinnati, November 18, 22, 1878, Bliss MSS.

48. Bliss to Ingalls, Cincinnati, December 16, 1878; May 26, 1879; Bliss to Perkins, Boston, July 8, 10, 1879, Bliss MSS.

49. Bliss to Ingalls, July 7, 10, November 22, December 16, 1878; May 23, July 8, 10, 1879, Bliss MSS. George Bliss, Jr., accompanied Ingalls on a western trip in the summer of 1878 while the elder Bliss worked on the reorganization plan.

50. Bliss to Ingalls, Cincinnati, February 10, 1879. For the problems of reorganization, see also Bliss to Ingalls, February 25, 28, March 4, April 4, June 18, October 11, 29, November 14, 18, 1879, Bliss MSS.

51. For the reorganization plan, see *Railroad Gazette*, July 25, September 19, 1879.

52. *Railroad Gazette*, December 31, 1879.

53. Bliss to C. D. Head and T. H. Perkins, December 5, 1879, Bliss MSS.

54. Bliss to Perkins, December 11, 1879, Bliss MSS.

55. Bliss to William Goddard, Providence, December 6, 1879, Bliss MSS.

56. Bliss to Perkins, Boston, January 13, 1880. In January 1880 he sent the head of the Purchasing Committee $26,022.50, one-half his subscription for bonds deposited with the committee. He bought $9,000 worth of Funded Debt Bonds and continued purchases of as much as he could get (Bliss to Ingalls, January 8, 1880; Bliss to A. E. Burnside, January 24, 1880). See also March 6, 29, April 4, 9, 20, 27, May 5, 1880, Bliss, MSS.

57. Bliss to Ingalls, Cincinnati, February 24, March 29, 1880; Bliss to Charles Booth, New York, November 16, 1880, Bliss MSS.

58. Bliss to Ingalls, Cincinnati, April 1, 5, 1880, Bliss MSS.

59. Bliss to Reverend John R. Keep, Hartford, March, 23, 1880; Bliss to Noah Porter, New Haven, March 31, 1880. "If it is bought I will consider it under your and my jt. control, and we can use it in enlisting the interest of Huntington" (Bliss to Ingalls, March 2, 1880). See also March 6, 29, April 4, 9, 20, 27, May 5, 1880, Bliss MSS.

60. C. P. Huntington to Bliss, New York, March 31, 1880, Bliss MSS.

61. Bliss to Noah Porter, New Haven, March 31, 1880, Bliss MSS.

62. Bliss to Ingalls, Cincinnati, July 23, 1880, Bliss, MSS.

63. Bliss to Ingalls, Cincinnati, April 16, 1880, Bliss MSS.

64. Bliss to Reverend J. R. Keep, Hartford, April 8, 1880, Bliss MSS.

65. Bliss to Ingalls, Cincinnati, April 23, May 5, 1880, Bliss MSS.

66. Bliss to Ingalls, Cincinnati, April 5, 23, May 5, June 3, 1880, Bliss MSS.

67. Bliss to Ingalls, Cincinnati, June 12, 28, July 7, 1880, Bliss MSS.

68. Bliss to Ingalls, Cincinnati, July 31, 1880; Bliss to C. P. Huntington, November 3, 1880, Bliss MSS.

69. Bliss to Ingalls, Cincinnati, September 8, 1880. See also July 16, 23, August 27, 1880, Bliss MSS.

70. Bliss to Ingalls, July 16, 1880; Bliss to Wilbur Day, January 22, 1881, Bliss MSS.

71. Bliss to Ingalls, November 6, 1880, Bliss MSS.

72. Bliss to Joseph Fay, Boston, January 30, 1880, Bliss MSS.

CHAPTER 5

1. *Railroad Gazette*, February 17, August 10, 1872; *Commercial and Financial Chronicle*, May 27, 1871.

2. See chapter 3 for discussion of this line in the early 1870s.

3. Maury Klein and Kozo Yamamura, "The Growth Strategies of Southern Railroads, 1865-1893," *Business History Review* 41 (Winter 1967): pp. 358-77.

4. *Railroad Gazette*, May 21, 1870.

5. Ibid.

6. *Railroad Gazette*, October 5, 1872; Carter Goodrich, *Government Promotion of American Canals and Railroads* (New York, 1960), p. 221; James P. Baughman, *Charles Morgan and the Development of Southern Transportation* (Nashville, Tenn., 1968), p. 171.

7. Bliss to J. Fay, Woodshole, May 29, 1878, Bliss MSS. Not a year later, the *Washington Gazette* called for a congressional investigation of Morton and his banking firm for negotiations dating back to 1872 with South Carolina's financial agent, H. H. Kimpton, for merchandising $720,000 of "illegally issued" state bonds and $423,000 of state-guaranteed bonds. The alleged nature of the transaction prompted an attack on the banking firm for "bribery, open and flagrant," of the governor, the state controller, and members of the Supreme Court. Morton, moreover, was personally accused of buying the vote of Louisiana and of being the "holder of money deposited for that purpose" (*Washington Gazette*, March 23, 27, 1879).

8. Charles Fairman, *Reconstruction and Reunion, 1864-88*, Part One, in *The Oliver Wendell Holmes Devise: History of the Supreme Court of the United States*, ed. Paul A. Freund, vol. 6 (New York, 1971), chapter 17.

9. *Commercial and Financial Chronicle*, May 3, 17, June 21, September 20, December 20, 1873; Henry V. Poor, *Manual of the Railroads of the United States,* 1875-76, p. 700; Baughman, *Charles Morgan*, pp. 170-71.

10. *Railroad Gazette*, June 9, 1876.

11. Ibid.; Baughman, *Charles Morgan*, pp. 169-70, 174-200.

12. *Railroad Gazette*, February 2, 1877, April 9, 1878.

13. *Railroad Gazette*, May 3, 10, 1878.

14. Bliss to Morton, Paris, May 27, 1878, Bliss MSS.

15. *Railroad Gazette,* June 17, 1878; Baughman, *Charles Morgan*, p. 219.

16. Bliss to Morton, Paris, May 20, 1878, Bliss MSS. The H. McComb that headed the group was not the McComb involved in the Illinois' southern connection and with Morgan in the Gulf, Western Texas & Pacific.

17. Ibid.

18. Ibid.

19. Bliss to Morton, June 6, 1879, Bliss MSS. Charles Whitney represented Morgan.

20. Joseph Seligman headed the Purchasing Committee. Morgan's terms were as follows: "Resolved: that the members of this committee accept for themselves, and will recommend to the bondholders represented by them the acceptance of the terms named, say; $300,000 payable as follows: $50,000 in 1 year from the date at which the title passes, $50,000 in 2 years from the date at which the title passes, $50,000 in 3 years from the date at which the title passes, $50,000 in 4 years from the date at which the title passes, $100,000 in 5 years from the date at which the title passes, it being understood that as soon as the counsel of the committee and the counsel of the Purchaser can examine the title, the transfer shall be made in proper legal form, from the Trustee of the Bondholders to the Purchasers; and the above named payments to be made by Debenture bonds of the Morgan's Louisiana & Texas RRd. bearing even date with the transfer of the title and interest at the rate of six per cent with semi-annual coupons attached; said bonds principle and interest payable at some bank in New York, to be issued in such sums as will enable the Committee to conveniently settle with the Bondholders, and to be endorsed or otherwise guaranteed by Mr. Charles A. Whitney" (Bliss to James A. Raynor, New York, June 12, 1879; Bliss to Oliver Ames, Northeastern, June 27, 1879, Bliss MSS).

21. *Railroad Gazette*, October 7, 1879.

22. Ibid., October 1, 1879; Maury Klein, *History of the Louisville & Nashville Railroad* (New York, 1972), pp. 139, 158.

23. Bliss to Oliver Ames, Boston, December 18, 1879; January 5, 1880, Bliss MSS.

24. Bliss to Oliver Ames, Boston, January 5, 1880; Bliss to James Raynor, Trustee, New Orleans, November 21, 1879. For the protracted difficulties, see Bliss to John Tucker, Selma, February 20, 1880; Bliss to Thomas Hunt, New Orleans, February 5, 1880; Bliss to Morton, February 2, 1880; Bliss to G. W. Harris, February 10, 1880; Bliss to John E. Parsons, February 2, 1880, Bliss MSS.

25. Bliss to Oliver Ames, January 13, 1880, Bliss MSS.

26. Bliss to Morton, August 11, 1879, Bliss MSS.

27. *Railroad Gazette*, March 12, 19, April 30, 1880.

28. Bliss to Hon. E. C. Billings, New Orleans, April 17, 1880; Bliss to Oliver Ames, Boston, April 19, 1880, Bliss MSS.

29. *Railroad Gazette*, March 19, April 30, 1880.

30. Ibid., October 1, 1880; Bliss to Oliver Ames, December 4, 1880, Bliss MSS.

31. Bliss to Morton, June 24, 1880, Bliss MSS. L. & N. first mortgage gold 6's were offered by the firm in limited amount (*New York World*, June 17, 1880). John J. Cisco was also selling L. & N. 6's secured by the New Orleans-Mobile railroad (*New York World*, June 26, 1880).

32. Bliss to Judge E. C. Billings, New Orleans, May 12, 1880; Bliss to Oliver Ames, April 8, 1880, Bliss MSS.

33. Bliss to Hon. John A. Campbell, New Orleans, January 31, June 6, September 29, October 26, 28, 1880, Bliss MSS.

34. Bliss to Morton, July 31, 1880, Bliss MSS.

35. Bliss to Frank Ames, Canton, Mass., January [?], 1881, Bliss MSS.

36. Julius Grodinsky, *Transcontinental Railway Strategy, 1869-1893* (Philadelphia, 1962), pp. 164 ff.

37. *Railroad Gazette*, January 28, February 25, March 3, October 20, 1876; Baughman, *Charles Morgan*, pp. 195, 218-19.

38. Bliss to Morton, Newport, June 8, 1881, Bliss MSS.

39. Bliss to Morton, Newport, June 8, 10, 1880, Bliss MSS.

40. Ibid.

41. Bliss to Morton, Rhode Island, June 10, 1881, Bliss MSS.

42. Arthur M. Johnson and Barry E. Supple, *Boston Capitalists and Western Railroads* (Cambridge, Mass., 1967).

43. To solve the problem of high tides washing the roadbed into the Gulf of Mexico at points where it was just above sea level, the management had it anchored, making it one of the very few such roadbeds in the United States. Klein, *History of the Louisville and Nashville Railroad*, p. 158.

44. Thomas C. Cochran and William Miller, *The Age of Enterprise*, rev. ed. (New York, 1961), pp. 163-64. See also Robert D. Marcus, *Grand Old Party: Political Structure in the Gilded Age, 1880-1896* (New York, 1971), pp. 135-38.

45. The American disdain for institutions has been treated in various studies. Its effect on both slavery and abolitionism is the theme of Stanley M. Elkins, *Slavery, A Problem in American Institutional And Intellectual Life* (New York, 1963). For manifestations of anti-institutionalism and its effects on the ideology of the early nineteenth century, see John William Ward, *Andrew Jackson, Symbol for an Age* (New York, 1970). Wallace D. Farnham, in a study of the government's neglect in meeting its responsibility to the Union Pacific Railroad, also emphasizes that the prevailing concepts of government demanded

privilege without restraints—that is, a government that did not in fact govern ("The Weakened Spring of Government: A Study in Nineteenth-Century American History," *American Historical Review* 68 [April 1963]: 662-80).

46. Bliss to Morton, December 31, 1880, Bliss MSS.

47. Bliss to Emily Billings, New Orleans, December 20, 1880, Bliss MSS.

48. Bliss to Emily Billings, New Orleans, December 31, 1880. The same day he wrote Morton, enclosing a letter from Judge Woods to Billings, "meant only for your eye and discretion" (Bliss to Morton, December 31, 1880, Bliss MSS).

49. Bliss to Morton, January 3, 1881, Bliss MSS.

50. Bliss to Emily Billings, New Orleans, January 5, 1881, Bliss MSS.

51. Ibid.

52. Bliss to Morton, January 22, 1881, Bliss MSS.

53. Bliss to Emily Billings, New Orleans, January 29, 1881, Bliss MSS.

54. Bliss to Morton, January 25, 1881, Bliss MSS.

55. Bliss to Morton, January 22, 1881, Bliss MSS.

56. Bliss to Emily Billings, New Orleans, January 22, 29, 1881, Bliss MSS.

57. Bliss to Dr. Noah Porter, New Haven, January 31, 1881. Bliss also wrote to Emily to reassure her that the reports would not affect the confirmation. "You referred to Senator Conkling. Let me tell you that he is a true man, of the strictest honor and can be relied upon to do all in his power in favor of Judge Billings. He will not only vote for him but will do all he is able to promote confirmation.

"The reports to which you refer, Mr. Morton's attention was called to before he left Washington and he spoke to Senator Conkling about them, who told him that he had better go to the Attorney General's office and see if there had been any presentation of them there formally or if there was any record of them there. Mr. Morton called at once and upon betting Senator Conkling there was nothing there he said: 'I don't think then they will have any weight or are of any importance as affecting the confirmation.' I have more feared, since discussing the matter with Mr. Morton last evening, that the President—in view of the efforts made—may withdraw the nomination—but I trust this will not be done" (Bliss to Emily Billings, New Orleans, January 31, 1881, Bliss MSS).

58. Bliss to Emily Billings, New Orleans, February 4, 1881. "The Louisville Nashville combination is a strong one. It reaches the residents of a great number of states; but all my direct information has been that it would not be successful" (Bliss to Emily Billings, February 2, 1881, Bliss MSS).

59. Bliss to Emily Billings, New Orleans, February 4, 1881; Bliss to Hon. E. C. Billings, Washington, D.C., February 8, 1881, Bliss MSS.

60. *D.A.B.*; Marcus, *Grand Old Party*, pp. 23-26; *New York World*, January 21, 1881.

61. Bliss to Emily Billings, February 4, 1881, Bliss MSS.

62. Wm. E. Curtis to Morton, July 20, 1880, Morton MSS.; *New York Sun*, May 16, 1904; Robert McElroy, *Levi Parsons Morton* (New York, 1930), pp. 105-107, 119-30.

63. *New York Graphic*, October 29, 1880; *New York World*, January 21, 1881; Marcus, *Grand Old Party*, pp. 45-48.

64. Bliss to Hon. E. C. Billings, Washington, D.C., February 15, 1881, Bliss MSS.

65. Bliss to Morton, telegram, March 5, 1881, Bliss MSS.

66. Bliss to Emily Billings, April 13, 1881, Bliss MSS.

67. Bliss to Hon. Wm. W. Phelps, March 1, 1881, Bliss MSS.

68. Bliss to Morton, September 6, 1881, Bliss MSS.

69. M. E. Ingalls to L. P. Morton, May 14, 1891, Morton MSS.

CHAPTER 6

1. According to the Cooke-Morgan chronology still invoked, Cooke's misalliance with the Northern Pacific and the difficulties of Fisk & Hatch and Henry Clews & Company marked the demise of institutionalized banker significance until the 1880s. See, for example, Elisha P. Douglass, *The Coming of Age of American Business* (Chapel Hill, N.C., 1971), pp. 298-302; Ross M. Robertson, *History of the American Economy* (New York, 1973), pp. 426-27.

2. Albro Martin, "Railroads and Equity Receivership," *Journal of Economic History* 34 (September 1974): 688; H. H. Swain, *Economic Aspects of Railroad Receiverships* (New York, 1898), pp. 55-57.

3. *Railroad Gazette,* August, 6, 13, September 17, 23, December 17, 1870; February 25, March 11, April 1, September 23, November 25, 1871.

4. Ibid., September 23, 1871.

5. *Commercial and Financial Chronicle,* July 12, 1873; Swain, *Economic Aspects of Railroad Receiverships,* p. 93. Henry V. Poor, *Manual of the Railroads of the United States,* 1873-74, p. 168, reported on the basis of information provided by the company that the cost had been $4 million.

6. *Commercial and Financial Chronicle,* December 20, 1873.

7. *Railroad Gazette,* January 10, March 28, April 4, 1874; *Commercial and Financial Chronicle,* March 14, 21, 1874.

8. *Railroad Gazette,* April 4, 1874.

9. Ibid., June 13, 1874. Carnegie, who also took some of the bonds, had had prior dealings with Morton, Bliss & Co. The firm held a joint account for him and Pullman in Union Pacific stock in 1871, when the bankers were Transfer Agents for the road (Joseph Frazier Wall, *Andrew Carnegie* [New York, 1970], pp. 288-89).

10. *Railroad Gazette,* August 15, October 3, 24, November 28, December 19, 1874. The I. C. crossed the road at Gilman and at Clinton.

11. George Bliss was a member of the I.C. Board at the same time that Morton, Rose & Co., besides distributing I.C. securities in London, handled coupon payments and security transfers.

12. *Railroad Gazette,* January 2, 1875.

13. E. M. Prince, the master of chancery, to S. H. Melvin, quoted in *Railroad Gazette,* ibid.

14. Ibid., June 26, July 27, August 28, 1875.

15. Swain, *Economic Aspects of Railroad Receiverships,* pp. 53-58; *Railroad Gazette,* September 4, 11, 18, October 2, 1875.

16. *Railroad Gazette,* November 6, 1875; February 25, March 10, 17, April 7, 14, 21, May 19, 1876.

17. Bliss to Morton, Newport, June 16, 1876, Bliss MSS. Bondholders wishing to join in the purchase were instructed to deposit their securities with the New York firm.

18. Bliss to Morton, Rose & Co., London, January 1, 1876, Bliss MSS. Morton only served for two months, but he and Seyton were both elected to the I.C. board in July 1875 (*Railroad Gazette,* July 17, August 28, September 4, 1875).

19. Bliss to John Douglas, Chicago, June 7, 1876; Bliss to Morton, Newport, June 15, 1876, Bliss MSS.

20. Quoted from the *German-American Economist,* in *Railroad Gazette,* October 23, 1875. The English Association of American Bond and Shareholders was eventually organized in 1884 in an attempt to gain protection. The form was similar to that already used in Holland (Frederick A. Cleveland and Fred W. Powell, *Railroad Promotion and Capitalization in the United States* [New York, 1909], p. 100).

21. John Stover, *The Railroads of the South, 1865-1900* (Chapel Hill, N.C., 1955). His

chapter "A Story of Receiverships" reviews the actions of such creditors as those of the Mobile & Montgomery, the Elizabeth & Paducah, and the Atlantic, Mississippi & Ohio.

22. Bliss to Morton, Newport, June 15, 1876, Bliss MSS. Out of $2 million first-mortgage bonds, $1,961,000 were represented in purchase (*Railroad Gazette*, June 23, 1876). For use of the voting trust to protect bondholders, see Cleveland and Powell, *Railroad Promotion*, pp. 100-101.

23. *Report of the Illinois Railroad and Warehouse Commission, June 1876*, p. 170; Bliss to Morton, Newport, July 6, 1876, Bliss MSS.

24. Bliss to Morton, Newport, June 16, 1876; Bliss to Douglas, Chicago, July 17, 1876, Bliss MSS.

25. Bliss to Morton, Newport, July 17, 1876, Bliss MSS.

26. Ibid.

27. Bliss to Douglas, Chicago, July 17, 1876, Bliss MSS.

28. Bliss to J. Rose, London, July 19, 1876; Bliss to Morton, Newport, July 29, 1876, Bliss MSS.

29. Bliss to Charles Seyton, Springfield, September 7, 9, 22, 25, November 2, 1876, Bliss MSS.

30. *Railroad Gazette*, September 1, 1876. A retraction was published September 15, 1876.

31. Bliss to Seyton, Springfield, September 9, 1876, Bliss MSS.

32. Bliss to Seyton, Springfield, September 25, 27, November 2, 14, 1876, Bliss MSS.

33. Bliss to Seyton, September 27, 1876; Bliss to Morton, Washington, D.C., October 6, 1876, Bliss MSS.

34. Bliss to Seyton, London, November 2, 14, 1876, Bliss MSS.

35. William K. Ackerman, *Historical Sketch of the Illinois Central Railroad* (Chicago, 1890), pp. 105 ff; Bliss to P. D. Grenfell, London, December 6, 1876; Bliss to Wm. Firth, Bradford, England, April 24, 1877, Bliss MSS.

36. *Report of the Delegates, Selected By the Joint Committee Appointed At A Meeting Of British Shareholders Of the Illinois Central Railroad Company, Held in London, On The 26th January 1877, And by the Administration Office for American Railroad Securities In Amsterdam, April 1877*, pp. 4-7.

37. Bliss to J. Rose, London, November 17, 1876, Bliss MSS.

38. Bliss to Grenfell, London, January 27, 1877, Bliss MSS.; Harry Pierce, "Foreign Investments in American Enterprise," in *Economic Change in the Civil War*, eds. David T. Gilchrist and W. David Lewis (Greenville, S.C., 1965).

39. Bliss to Hugh Gilman, London, February 14, 1877, Bliss MSS.

40. Bliss to Morton, Newport, August 4, 1876, Bliss MSS.

41. Bliss to J. Rose (private), London, March 13, 1877, Bliss MSS.

42. Bliss to J. Rose, London, November 17, 28, 1876, Bliss MSS.

43. Bliss to Grenfell, London, December 6, 1876; Bliss to Col. H. McComb, New York, December 9, 1876. See also Bliss to McComb, December 15, and the note sent later that day before the I.C. board met at one o'clock asking McComb to sign approval of their agreement.

44. For a detailed account of the negotiations, but one which does not identify the banker's role, see Stover, *Railroads of the South*, pp. 178-79. See also Bliss to L. V. F. Randolph, treasurer, I.C., Chicago, December 18, 20, 1876; Bliss to D. M. Bates, New York, December 20, 1876, Bliss MSS. Bliss knew McComb, who had furnished Charles Dana of the *Sun* with the list of those receiving Crédit Mobilier stock and also with the letter of Oakes Ames stating that the shares were placed "where they would do the most good." McComb, a member of the ring, apparently felt cheated (D. S. Muzzey, *James G. Blaine* [New York, 1934], p. 66). Morton, Bliss & Co. was transfer agent for the U.P. at the time.

45. Ackerman, *Historical Sketch of the Illinois Central*, pp. 106-8.

46. Carter Goodrich, *Government Promotion of American Canals and Railroads* (New

York, 1960), pp. 201, 291.

47. Bliss to J. Rose, London, February 16, 1877, Bliss MSS.

48. Bliss to J. Rose, London, July 19, 1876; Bliss to Morton, Newport, July 29, 1876, Bliss MSS.

49. Bliss to J. Rose, February 16, 1877; Bliss to Grenfell, London, January 1, March 3, 4, 13, 1877, Bliss MSS.

50. Bliss to J. Rose, London, February 16, March 13, 1877, Bliss MSS.

51. Bliss to Capt. Galton, Chicago, April 7, 1877; Bliss to Oyens, Chicago, April 7, 1877, Bliss MSS.

52. *Report of the Delegates*, pp. 24, 8.

53. Thomas C. Cochran, *Railroad Leaders, 1845-1890* (Cambridge, Mass., 1953), p. 317.

54. *Report of the Delegates*, p. 12.

55. S. F. Van Oss, *American Railroads as Investments* (New York, 1893), pp. 723-35.

56. *Centennial Report, The Financial Story of Our First Hundred Years, 1851-1951* (Chicago, 1951), p. 12.

57. Ibid., p. 24.

58. Bliss to Morton, Newport, June 25, 1877; Bliss to Seyton, Springfield, June 4, 1877; Bliss to Charles Rose, London, September 7, 1877, Bliss MSS.

59. Bliss to Morton, London, December 22, 1877, Bliss MSS.

60. Bliss to Seyton, Springfield, December 12, 13, 14, 1877, Bliss MSS.

61. Bliss to Seyton, Chicago, December 14, 1877, Bliss MSS.

62. Bliss to Seyton, Chicago, December 18, 19, 1877; Bliss to Morton, Rose & Co., London, December 18, 1877; Bliss to R. Biddle Roberts and R. E. Williams, Chicago, December 22, 1877, Bliss MSS.

63. Bliss to Morton, Rose & Co., London, January 18, 1878, Bliss MSS.

64. Bliss to Morton, London, April 16, 1878, Bliss MSS.

65. Bliss to R. Biddle Roberts, Chicago, November 5, 10, 1879, May 5, 1880, July 19, 1881, Bliss MSS.

66. Bliss to Seyton, London, March [?], 1881 (italics mine), Bliss MSS.

67. Bliss to Morton, Rose & Co., London, November 11, 1881. Douglas's efforts were also remembered: "Mr. Douglas rendered very important assistance to the Gilman Bondholders, and you have always felt, as well as myself, that he was entitled to fair compensation. The amount named by you is small remuneration, and Mr. Oyens approves, as do I, of its being paid to him." Bliss to Seyton, Springfield, May 14, 1877, Bliss MSS.

68. *Railroad Gazette*, 1876.

69. *Remarks of E. T. Jeffery Before the Board of Railroad and Warehouse Commissioners of the State of Illinois, Springfield, September 2, 1887* (Chicago, 1887), pp. 9-19.

70. Stover, *Railroads of the South*, pp. 124 ff.

71. Ibid., pp. 136-37.

72. Cochran, *Railroad Leaders*, pp. 32, 70-73. Since Seyton was representing Dutch and English bondholders of this road, Bliss hoped his firm could be brought in on favorable terms (Bliss to Seyton, London, November 22, December 30, 1878, Bliss MSS).

INTRODUCTION TO PART III

1. Bliss to Henry Dunham, January 6, 1879; Bliss to T. H. Perkins, Boston, January 14, 1879, Bliss MSS.

2. Alfred Chandler, Jr. *The Railroads, The Nation's First Big Business* (New York,

1965), pp. 14-15; H. H. Swain, *Economic Aspects of Railroad Receiverships* (New York, 1898), pp. 70-71.

3. Quoted in Chandler, *The Railroads*, p. 89.

4. Vincent P. Carosso, *Investment Banking in America* (Cambridge, Mass., 1970), pp. 50-78.

5. Chandler, *The Railroads*, p. 13.

6. *Commercial and Financial Chronicle: Investors' Supplement*, May 28, 1887. For average rail bond yields, see U.S. Bureau of the Census, *Historical Statistics of the United States, Colonial Times to 1970* (Washington, D.C., 1975), 2: 1003.

7. Ibid.

8. Ibid.

9. *Commercial and Financial Chronicle*, January 8, February 5, March 26, July 2, September 3, 1887.

CHAPTER 7

1. Bliss to J. Rose (private), London, March 13, 1877, Bliss MSS.

2. George Boutwell, *Reminiscences of Sixty Years in Public Affairs* (New York, 1902), 2: 187; Robert McElroy, *Levi Parsons Morton* (New York, 1930), chapters 2, 3. Morton, Bliss & Co. had been party to the 1876 contract for the four-and-a-half-percent loan representing the whole of the twenty-five-percent American interest. The Rothschilds and their party, including Morton, Rose & Co., took seventy-five percent for Europe. Morton's fund-raising activities for the Republicans are discussed in Robert D. Marcus, *Grand Old Party* (New York 1971), pp. 47-58, 95, 97. See also *Commercial Advertiser*, January 18, 1873.

3. Bliss to J. Rose (private), London, March 13, 1877, Bliss MSS.; John Sherman, *Recollections of Forty Years in the House, Senate and Cabinet* (Chicago, 1895), 2: 637-48; *World*, April 12, 1878; Sherman to Morton, November 12, 1878, Morton MSS.

4. Vincent P. Carosso, *Investment Banking in America* (Cambridge, Mass., 1970), p. 22.

5. Bliss to Charles Rose, London, January 12, 1877; Bliss to A. Blum, Paris, February 14, 1877; Bliss to Grenfell, London, September [?], 1877; Bliss to Morton, London, April 16, 1878; Bliss to Messrs. Tuft & Judson, St. Louis, June 20, 1878; Bliss to Seyton, London, December 30, 1878, Bliss MSS.

6. Bliss to T. H. Perkins, Boston, January 14, 1879; Bliss to Henry Dunham, January 6, 1879, Bliss MSS.

7. Bliss to C. Rose, London, January 12, 1877, Bliss MSS.

8. Bliss to Morton, London, November 21, December 29, 1877, Bliss MSS.

9. *Railroad Gazette*, August 2, 1878.

10. Ibid.

11. Bliss to Morton, November 21, 1877, Bliss MSS.

12. *New York World*, January 1, July 1, October 1, 1878.

13. Bliss to Morton, Paris, June 1, 1878, Bliss MSS.

14. Bliss to Morton, September, 23, 1876; Bliss to S. Chittenden, Washington, D.C., December 10, 1877, Bliss MSS.

15. Bliss to Morton, January 4, 26, 1878, Bliss MSS. For regulation of the exchange, see Robert Sobel, *The Big Board* (New York, 1965), pp. 85-86.

16. Bliss to Morton, January 31, 1878, Bliss MSS.

17. Bliss to Morton, February 12, 1878, Bliss MSS.

18. Bliss to Morton, February 19, 1878, Bliss MSS.

19. Bliss to Morton, London, March 12, April 16, July 9, 1878, Bliss MSS.

20. Bliss to Morton, London, March 12, April 16, 1878, Bliss MSS.

21. Bliss to the Hon. W. E. Dodge, New York, May 4, 8, 1878. A parcel of bonds had been sold to the D. L. & W. at a particularly low price—a fact Bliss believed was "desirable not to have known" (Bliss to Morton, London, April 5, 1878, Bliss MSS).

22. Bliss to Morton, Paris, June 1, July 9, 1878, Bliss MSS.; *New York World*, July 1, 1878.

23. *New York World*, October 1, 1878; Bliss to Morton, July 9, 1878; Bliss to Alex Williams, April 29, 1879; Bliss to Messrs. R. Durfee & Sons, Illinois, May 6, 1879, Bliss MSS.

24. Morton, Rose & Co. already had a share interest in this road. Bliss to J. Rose, London, September 9, 1876, February 16, 1877; Bliss to Morton, July 19, 1877, Bliss MSS.

25. Bliss to Morton, London, January 31, February 2, March 29, 1878; Bliss to T. H. Perkins, Boston, June 10, 1878, Bliss MSS.

26. Bliss to Morton, London, April 5, 1878, Bliss MSS.

27. Bliss to Morton, Paris, June 1, 1878, Bliss MSS.

28. Bliss to Morton, June 28, July 9, August 13, 1878; April 26, 1879, Bliss MSS.; *New York World*, July 2, 1878.

29. Bliss to C. Rose, London, July 30, 1878; Bliss to Grenfell, London, August 2, 14, 1878; Bliss to T. H. Perkins, Boston, September 3, 1878, Bliss MSS.

30. *Railroad Gazette*, August 2, 1878.

31. Bliss to Morton, December 18, 1877, January 1, June 6, 1878, Bliss MSS.

32. See chapter 4.

33. *New York World*, January 2, 1878.

34. Bliss to Wilbur Day, New Haven, January 22, 1881, Bliss MSS.

35. Bliss to Morton, Paris, May 27, 1878, Bliss MSS.

36. Bliss to Morton, April 16, 1878; Bliss to John Gilman, Baltimore, March 17, 21, 1879; Bliss to R. Shattuck, New York, March 17, 1879. Bliss MSS.

37. T. W. Acheson, "Changing Social Origins of the Canadian Industrial Elite," *Business History Review* 47 (Summer 1973): 189-217.

38. Heather Gilbert, *Awakening Continent: The Life of Lord Mount Stephen* (Aberdeen, 1965), pp. 8-13.

39. Merrill Denison, *Canada's First Bank: A History of The Bank of Montreal* (Toronto, 1967), 2: 172, 183-85.

40. Gilbert, *Awakening Continent*, pp. 23, 38.

41. Ibid.

42. *Farley v. Hill et al.*, United States Circuit Court, District of Minnesota, September 13, 1889, *The Federal Reporter* (St. Paul), 34: 517.

43. See chapter 10.

44. *Dubuque Herald*, September 15, 1889, quoted in Jesse Kelso Farley, Jr., *Twelve Generations of Farleys* (Evanston, Ill., 1943), Appendix, pp. 26 ff.; United States Circuit Court, District of Minnesota, *John S. Kennedy & Co. v. the Northern Pacific Railroad Co., the St. Paul & Pacific Railroad Co., the First Division and Others to Show Cause.* See also Bill of Complaint, 1873.

45. *Railroad Gazette*, October 29, 1870, November 12, 1870; *Commercial and Financial Chronicle*, November 5, 1870.

46. Though it is doubtful if Farley, as he later claimed in a series of court cases, originated the scheme, nonetheless, he was not a disinterested party, nor did the bankers expect him to be: "We think it will pay you to take an interest with Kittson and Hill, and we are glad to hear that they have offered it to you" (Kennedy to Farley, February 25, 1878, *Farley v. Kittson*, Appeal from the Circuit Court of the United States, *United States Reports* [New

York, 1887], 120: 311). After the Kennedy suit of 1873 two companies were formed, separately bonded and reporting separately to the Minnesota Railroad Commission. Farley was appointed, at Kennedy's insistence, receiver for the St. Paul & Pacific Railway Co. in 1873, and he remained receiver until 1879. In 1875 an arrangement was made between the stockholders and bondholders of the St. Paul & Pacific First Division Company for a directorate to be constituted in the interests of the bondholders. Farley took possession, in the interests of the bondholders, on March 13, 1876, and then in October Kennedy, as trustee, assumed formal possession, while Farley became general manager of this company. See Henry V. Poor, *Manual of the Railroads of the United States*, 1878-79—hereafter referred to as Poor's *Manual; The Federal Reporter* (1889), 39:515; Minnesota Railroad and Warehouse Commission, *Biennial Report*, 1873-1878.

47. Minnesota Railroad and Warehouse Commission, "Report for year ending June 30, 1876," Minnesota Railroad and Warehouse Commission, *Biennial Report*, 1875/76. For an accountant's estimate of the Dutch capital and the probable delivery price of the bonds, see the testimony of Conway Hillman in *John S. Kennedy and Henry Dimock v. the Great Northern Railway Co.*, United States Circuit Court, District of Minnesota (1909), 3: 1769 ff.

48. J. Farley to the Hon. John J. Randall, December 23, 1875, Minnesota Railroad and Warehouse Commission, *Biennial Report,* 1874/75, pp. 209-10.

49. William R. Marshall to Gov. John S. Pillsbury, Minnesota Railroad and Warehouse Commission, *Biennial Report*, 1875/76, pp. 1-2.

50. J. Farley to William Marshall, December 22, 1876, ibid., p. 137.

51. Quoted in J. G. Pyle, *The Life of James J. Hill* (New York, 1917), p. 215.

52. Gilbert, *Awakening Continent*, p. 41, quoted from testimony in the case of *Jesse P. Farley v. N. W. Kittson et. al.*, United States Circuit Court, District of Minnesota, in Equity, Ent. 131. C. Ch.

53. Quoted in Gilbert, *Awakening Continent*, pp. 42-43. Albro Martin relies on Stephen's later testimony and accepts his claim that John Rose turned Stephen down in December 1877. However, Morton was in London into the spring of 1878 and was in constant touch with Bliss about the ongoing negotiations and especially the terms Stephen offered in March. By then John Rose had left the London firm. See Albro Martin, *James J. Hill and the Opening of the Northwest* (New York, 1976), pp. 143-44, 239-40.

54. Bliss to J. Rose, London, January 1, 1878, Bliss MSS.

55. Bliss to Stephen, Montreal, January 19, 1878, Bliss MSS.

56. Bliss to Morton, Rose & Co., London, January 21, 1878, Bliss MSS.

57. Bliss to Gen. E. F. Winslow, Cedar Rapids, January 17, 26, 31, 1878, Bliss MSS.

58. Bliss to Morton, Rose & Co., London, January 21, 1878, Bliss MSS.

59. Bliss to Morton, January 26, 1878, Bliss MSS.

60. Pyle, *James Hill,* pp. 226-32.

61. Bliss to Stephen, Montreal, March 19, 1878; Bliss to Morton, March 22, 1878, Bliss MSS.

62. Quoted in Pyle, *James Hill*, p. 213.

63. Ibid., p. 214.

64. Bliss to Morton, London, March 22, 1878, Bliss MSS.

65. Ibid. See also Bliss to Morton, April 20, 1878, Bliss MSS.

66. Gilbert, *Awakening Continent*, p. 44.

67. Bliss to Morton, Paris, May 27, 1878, Bliss MSS.

68. Gilbert, *Awakening Continent*, pp. 44-49.

69. Bliss to Morton, June 26, 1878, Bliss MSS.

70. Quoted in Gilbert, *Awakening Continent*, pp. 49-52.

71. Bliss to C. Rose, London, September 17, 1879, Bliss MSS.

72. Poor's *Manual*, 1880-1900; St. Paul, Minneapolis & Manitoba Railway Company, *Annual Reports*, 1880-1900.

73. Minnesota Railroad and Warehouse Commission, *Biennial Report*, 1877, p. 101; Poor's *Manual*, 1878-79.

74. *Farley v. Kittson, United States Reports*, 1887, 120: 304-11; *Farley v. Hill, Federal Reporter*, 1889, 39: 516.

75. Heather Gilbert, "The Unaccountable Fifth: Solution of a Great Northern Enigma," *Minnesota History* 44 (Spring 1971): 175-77.

76. Bliss to C. Rose, London, September 17, 1879, Bliss MSS.

CHAPTER 8

1. Bliss to Charles Rose, London, May 2, 1879, Bliss MSS.

2. Alexander D. Noyes, *Forty Years of American Finance* (New York, 1909), pp. 55-61; Bliss to Josiah M. Fiske, c/o M. R. & Co., July 11, 1879, Bliss MSS.

3. Bliss to J. Rose, London, December 5, 1879, Bliss MSS.; Rendigs Fels, "American Business Cycles, 1865-1879," *American Economic Review* 41 (June 1951): 345 ff.

4. Bliss to W. F. Day, May 9, 1879; Bliss to J. Rose, London, December 5, 1879, Bliss MSS.

5. Bliss to C. Rose, London, May 2, 1879, Bliss MSS.

6. The following excerpts are illustrative: "Newell called, says the traffic of Lake Shore is large, so far as volume of freight is concerned, prices, of course, very low; but confidentially, he expressed the opinion that the net earnings of the month would not be less than ¼ percent on the share capital. This is cutting it pretty fine, and I do not see that such a result can cause an advance in the stock. I expect to see Newell again before he leaves town" (Bliss to Morton, Newport, R. I., May 24, 1876). "I bought 500 shares W. U. 'Jt. A/C' with Orton at 64½ upon a note received from him addressed to you. He thinks Gould is anxious to buy, and says A&P is going to the d——ogs!. . .I went round to see French. He told me that 'the old man' [Vanderbilt] had covered his Lake Shore but remained short on Erie" (Bliss to Morton, Newport, May 25, 1876). "All the evidence that can be gathered indicates a strong desire to purchase Western Union on the part of both G. [Gould] and K. [Keene]; the evidence to the contrary comes solely from Silover & Beldon—Garrison says Silover owes a million now that he can't pay and is going through the Bankrupt Ct. Should we base business upon the statement of representatives of such men when our own judgment and the testimony from so many quarters strengthens the belief that the statements are not correct?" (Bliss to Morton, Washington, D. C., January 1, 1877). "Saw Barlow. . . .His belief road will be brought to a sale at end of 60 days. . . .Barlow may desire some bonds on joint account at proper time—He prefers to wait until something more definite regarding attempt to hinder and delay" (Bliss to Morton, London, January 31, 1878). "He [Sage] feels strong on N. West and St. Paul, common and preferred—Should he feel tempted to sell out he would feel differently tomorrow—his judgment uniformly approves the course which is for his own interest, whatever his position may be" (Bliss to Morton, July 9, 1878, Bliss MSS).

7. Bliss to E. D. Worcester, New York, November 15, 1878, Bliss MSS.

8. Henry Clews, *Fifty Years in Wall Street* (New York, 1915), p. 517.

9. Bliss to Morton, January 30, 1880, Bliss MSS.

10. Robert Sobel, *The Big Board* (New York, 1965), p. 108; Fritz Redlich, *The Molding of American Banking* (New York, 1968), 2: 383.

11. Clews, *Fifty Years*, p. 516.

12. Bliss to Morton, December 6, 8, 1879, January 28, 1880; Bliss to H. J. Sartwell, January 29, 1880, Bliss MSS.

13. Bliss to Morton, March 2, April 10, 1880, Bliss MSS.

14. Ibid. In June 1880, when the syndicate closed, Morton, Bliss & Co. received $186,000; $31,000 was for the London firm (Bliss to Morton, June 10, 1880, Bliss MSS).

15. Bliss to Morton, January 13, 1880, Bliss MSS.

16. Bliss to Morton, January 12, 1880, Bliss MSS.

17. Bliss to Morton, January 14, 1880, Bliss MSS.

18. Bliss to Morton, January 13, 1880, Bliss MSS.

19. Bliss to Morton, January 14, 15, 1880, Bliss MSS.

20. Bliss to Morton, January 29, 1880, Bliss MSS.

21. Bliss to Morton, February 25, 1880; Bliss to Grenfell, London, February 28, 1880, Bliss MSS.

22. Bliss to Wilbur Day, May 8, 1879; Bliss to C. Rose, May 2, 1879, Bliss MSS.

23. Eugene J. McMechen, "The Rapid Transit Struggle in New York, 1864-1879" (Master's thesis, Hunter College, 1975); subscription list, New York Elevated Railroad Co., December 5, 1877, Cyrus Field Papers, New York Public Library.

24. Bliss to Morton, November 29, 1879, Bliss MSS.

25. Bliss to Morton, December 2, 1879. When the decision was made to delay the Metropolitans, Drexel, Morgan and Winslow, Lanier took an entire parcel of C. B. & Q. bonds from Forbes instead (Bliss to Morton, December 6, 1879, Bliss MSS).

26. Bliss to Morton, February 2, 6, 1880, Bliss MSS.

27. Bliss to Morton, February 9, 1880, Bliss MSS.

28. The reconstituted Morton syndicate included W. R. Garrison of the Manhattan Elevated and Missouri Pacific for $2 million; T. B. Musgrave, $1.5 million; the American Exchange Bank, $500,000 (Bliss to W. R. Garrison, February 7, 1880; Bliss to Morton, February 10, 1880, Bliss MSS). For Garrison's involvement in New York's railroad building, see McMechen, "The Rapid Transit Struggle in New York."

29. Bliss to Morton, February 10, 1880, Bliss MSS.

30. Bliss to Morton, February 11, 1880, Bliss MSS.

31. Ibid.

32. Bliss to Morton, April 4, 1879, Bliss MSS.

33. Ibid.

34. Bliss to Morton, April 2, 1879, Bliss MSS.

35. Ibid.

36. Bliss to Morton, Washington, D.C., April 7, 1879; Bliss to Grenfell, London, May 17, 1879, Bliss MSS.

37. Bliss to Grenfell, London, May 17, 1879; Bliss to Alex Williams, Boston, April 29, May 1, 1879, Bliss MSS.

38. Bliss to Morton, January 26, February 2, 1880; Bliss to Grenfell, London, January 27, 1880, Bliss MSS. The bonds were advertised for public sale in January (*New York World*, January 15, 1880).

39. Bliss to Morton, May 5, 1880, Bliss MSS.

40. Bliss to Morton, May 14, 1879, Bliss MSS.

41. Bliss to Morton, April 8, 10, 13, 1880, Bliss MSS.

42. Bliss to Morton, April 21, 1880, Bliss MSS.

43. Bliss to Morton, May 4, 1880; Morton, Rose & Co. cable to Bliss, May 4, 1880; Bliss to Morton, May 8, 1880, Bliss MSS.

44. Bliss to Morton, December 11, 1880, Bliss MSS. The antagonism of Western farmers to the money interest was frequently directed against Jewish bankers (Irwin Unger, *The*

Greenback Era: A Social and Political History of American Finance [Princeton, N.J.: 1964], pp. 210-12). Within the banking community working relations were relatively easy and unmarred by inherited upper-class elite attitudes that prompted men such as Brooks and Henry Adams to fasten on the Jewish banker, charging that his parasitical mania for gold threatened Western civilization (Frederick Copler Jaher, "The Brahmins in the Age of Industrial Capitalism," in *The Age of Industrialism in America,* ed. Frederick Copler Jaher [New York, 1968], pp. 196-97).

45. The agreement of the Atchison and the St. Louis & Frisco to build jointly to the Pacific would be financed in part by subscriptions Seligman offered Bliss in April 1880. According to the terms, the Atchison took half the issue; as syndicate manager, Seligman took whatever was not subscribed for by the shareholders as well as a specified $300,000. Kidder, Peabody, bankers for the Atchison, took $300,000; Winslow, Lanier, $200,000; Morton, Bliss, $200,000; and John Stewart was offered $300,000 (Bliss to Morton, April 21, 1880, Bliss MSS. See also Julius Grodinsky, *Transcontinental Railway Strategy, 1869-1893* [Philadelphia, 1962], pp. 165-69; Julius Grodinsky, *Jay Gould,* [Philadelphia, 1957], pp. 380 ff.; H. Craig Miner, *The St. Louis-San Francisco Transcontinental Railroad,* [Lawrence, Kans., 1972], pp. 130-31; Robert Riegel, *The Story of the Western Railroads* [New York, 1926], pp. 189-91).

46. Carosso, *Investment Banking,* pp. 51-78, outlines the process from origination through retailing.

47. Bliss to Morton, May 7, 1880; Bliss to Grenfell, London, May 20, 1880, Bliss MSS.

48. *Railroad Gazette,* July 9, 1880.

49. The issue was backed by a Columbia government subsidy of $225,000 a year (a first lien on the property), which was transferred to the bankers under a trust arrangement. A sinking fund of $45,000 a year had been created to retire a portion of the bonds within ten years, with the remainder to be retired in thirty (Bliss to C. Rose, London, October 22, 1880; Bliss to Grenfell, London, October 23, 27, 28, 1880; Bliss to Alex Williams, December 3, 1880; Bliss to Morton, December 11, 1880; Biss to T. W. Park, December 8, 1880, Bliss MSS.; *New York World,* December 25, 1880).

50. *Railroad Gazette,* July 9, 1880.

51. Bliss to Morton, March 2, 1880, Bliss MSS.

52. Bliss to Morton, February 3, 1880, Bliss MSS.

53. Bliss to Morton, February 5, 9, March 8, 10, 11, 13, 1880; Bliss to J. B. Trevor, February 5, 1880, Bliss MSS.

54. Bliss to Morton, May 24, 1880, Bliss MSS.

55. Bliss to Chittenden, February 1, 1879, Bliss MSS.; Roscoe Conkling to Morton, August 1, 29, 1880, Morton, MSS.

56. Bliss to J. Rose (private), London, March 13, 1877, Bliss MSS.

57. Bliss had accepted a directorship in September 1877 of this strategic road that cut across eastern Iowa from the southern to the northern border south of Minnesota. The firm had taken a contract for bonds (which it did not expect to sell immediately) and Morton, Rose & Co. would handle coupon payments in London (Bliss to Fred Taylor, president, September 26, October 11, November 20, 1877; Bliss to Morton, November 21, December 18, 1877; Bliss to Grenfell, London, August 21, 1879; Bliss to Morton, August 21, 1879, Bliss MSS.).

58. Bliss to Morton, September 17, 1879; Bliss to Grenfell, London, May 17, August 21, 1879, Bliss MSS.

59. *New York World,* January 1, 1881.

60. Bliss to Head & Perkins, Boston, January 28, 1880, Bliss MSS.

61. Bliss to Morton, May 24, June 14, 1879, Bliss MSS.; Robert McElroy, *Levi Parsons Morton; Banker, Diplomat and Statesmen* (New York, 1930).

62. Bliss to Morton, May 24, June 14, 1879, Bliss MSS. For the early history of the Minneapolis & St. Louis and its control until 1873 by bankers associated with Jay Cooke, see Frank P. Donovan, Jr., *Mileposts on the Prairie: The Story of the Minneapolis & St. Louis Railway* (New York, 1950), pp. 36-37. Bliss had planned the earlier D. M. & Ft. D. reorganization of 1874 (see *Commercial and Financial Chronicle,* February 4, 1874). He remained on as a director and his banking firm acted as fiscal agent. For the reorganization of 1879, see *New York World,* July 1, 1879.

63. Lance Davis, "Capital Immobilities and Finance Capitalism: A Study of Economic Evolution in the United States, 1820-1920," *Explorations in Entrepreneurial History,* second series, 1 (Fall 1963), pp. 88-105.

64. Biss to Morton, May 24, June 14, 1879; February 5, 9, 1880; Bliss to W. D. Washburne, December 23, 1879, Bliss MSS. The bankers' spelling of "Washburne" differs from the standardized versions in the literature. The text here omits the "e," except in direct quotations.

65. Bliss to Washburne, January 5, 1880, Bliss MSS.

66. Bliss to Washburne, December 23, 1879, January 5, 1880, Bliss MSS.

67. Bliss to Washburne, January 12, 1880, Bliss MSS.

68. Bliss to Morton, January 8, 1880, Bliss MSS.

69. Bliss to Abner Kingman, January 18, 1880; Bliss to Morton, February 3, 5, 6, 9, 14, 1880, Bliss MSS.

70. Bliss to Morton (personal), January 7, 1881, Bliss MSS.

71. Ibid.

72. Bliss to Morton, March 14, 28, 1881, Bliss MSS.

73. Alfred D. Chandler, Jr., *The Railroads: The Nation's First Big Business* (New York, 1965), pp. 97-125.

74. Bliss to Morton, May 2, 1882, Bliss MSS.

75. Bliss to Morton, January 20, February 14, 1882, Bliss MSS.

76. Bliss to Morton, May 2, 1882, Bliss MSS.

77. The same year the Minnesota railroad commissioner noted that "the process of consolidating numerous lines of road into grand systems of railway is a striking fact in the history of the year reported" (Minnesota Railroad and Warehouse Commission, *Biennial Report,* June 30, 1881).

78. Bliss to Morton, December 5, 1881, January 11, 1882, Bliss MSS.

79. Bliss to Morton, May 2, 1882, Bliss MSS; Isaac Atwater, *History of the City of Minneapolis, Minnesota* (New York, 1893), p. 335.

80. Morton to J. M. Bailey, U. S. Consul, Hamburg, April 19, 1884, Morton MSS.: Bliss to P. D. Grenfell, July 1, 1884, Bliss MSS.

81. Bliss to J. Rose, London, January [?], 1881, Bliss MSS.

82. Bliss to Ingalls, March 8, 1882, Bliss MSS.

83. Bliss to Ingalls, February 2, March 13, 1882, Bliss MSS.

CHAPTER 9

1. Vincent P. Carosso, *Investment Banking in America* (Cambridge, Mass., 1970), pp. 38 ff.; John Stover, *Railroads of the South, 1865-1900* (Chapel Hill, N.C., 1955), p. 55. Overestimations of Morgan as an innovator are legion as a result of the disregard of the activities of other bankers. See, for example, Jonathan Hughes, "J. Pierpont Morgan, the Investment Banker as Statesman," in *The Vital Few, American Progress and Its*

Protagonists, ed. Jonathan Hughes (Boston, 1966).

2. See chapter 4 for banker operation of the Big Four's predecessor, the Indianapolis, Cincinnati & Lafayette. From the time of the reorganization and the renaming of the road, the Cincinnati, Indianapolis, St. Louis & Chicago Railroad, Bliss and Ingalls consistently referred to it as the Big Four. Similarly, the press in describing the C. & O. reorganization and the later merger of the two companies identified Ingalls as the president of the Big Four. This road should not be confused with the Cleveland, Cincinnati, Chicago & St. Louis, also referred to as the "Big Four."

3. Bliss to Wilbur Day, New Haven, January 22, 1881, Bliss MSS.

4. Bliss to Albert Keep, April 12, 1880; Bliss to Ingalls, Cincinnati, May 4, July 7, 1880; September 6, 1881; Bliss to T. Perkins, Boston, September 17, 1881, Bliss MSS.

5. Bliss to Ingalls, November 24, 1880; Bliss to T. Perkins, December 7, 1880, Bliss MSS.

6. Ibid.

7. Ibid.; *New York World,* November 11, 1881.

8. Joseph H. Schumpeter, "The Creative Response in Economic History," *Journal of Economic History* 3 (May 1948).

9. Bliss to Ingalls, December 18, 1880, Bliss MSS.

10. Ibid.

11. Bliss to Ingalls, December 23, 1880, Bliss MSS. The Big Four did not, after all, take control of the I. D. & S.

12. Bliss to Ingalls, March 28, 1880, Bliss MSS.

13. Bliss to Ingalls, April 11, 1882, Bliss MSS.

14. Thomas C. Cochran, *Railroad Leaders, 1845-1890: The Business Mind in Action* (Cambridge, Mass., 1953), p. 78.

15. Bliss to Ingalls, May 20, 1881, Bliss MSS.

16. Bliss to Ingalls, November 9, 1881, Bliss MSS.

17. Bliss to Ingalls, November 21, 1881, Bliss MSS.

18. Bliss to Ingalls, December 15, 1881; Bliss to E. F. Osborn, treasurer, C.I.St.L.&C., January 19, April 23, June 6, 10, July 19, 1881, Bliss MSS. When Bliss made a purchase of shares, or of Vernon & Greensburg bonds, he deposited the sum to the credit of the railroad at the American Exchange Bank, which continued after the reorganization as their bank of deposit. For a glowing account of the company, see *The Directors' Report to the Stockholders, of the Indianapolis, Cincinnati & Lafayette Railroad Company, 1881.* See also *Report to the Stockholders, 1882.*

19. Bliss to Ingalls, December 15, 17, 1881; Bliss to Ingalls, February 2, 1882; Bliss to Joseph Fay, Boston, January 30, 1882, Bliss MSS.

20. Bliss to Ingalls, June 13, 1881; Bliss to Messrs. Geo. W. Ballou & Co., Sept. 18, 1888, *Bliss MSS.*

21. Bliss to Ingalls, February 17, 1881. Bliss purchased 4,920 preferred shares at par; 39, 919 common at sixty for $2,359,140; the total figure including commissions and interest came to $2.8 million. Presumably, this figure represented holdings for Huntington, since Bliss took only 1,110 preferred shares for himself. This statement was of the amount due to Ballou, from whom the shares were purchsed, and does not show how much was actually paid. B. S. Cunningham of the Citizens National Bank of Cincinnati was also induced to take a share (Bliss to Cunningham, October 21, 1881; Bliss to Ingalls, October 21, 1881; Bliss to B. S. Cunningham, October 28, 1881; Bliss to Ingalls, November 3, 1881). By November, Huntington held a majority of the shares (Bliss to Ingalls, November 5, 1881). Bliss told Ingalls that he had only 1/6 of the whole and his holdings should not be overestimated by Ingalls (Bliss to Ingalls, March 13, 1882, Bliss MSS.).

22. *Railroad Gazette,* December 31, 1880. Bliss's arguments can be found in Bliss to Ingalls, January 19, March 28, June 13, 1881, Bliss MSS.

23. Bliss to Ingalls, March 1, 13, 1882, Bliss MSS.

24. Bliss to Ingalls, April 11, 1881, April 17, May 22, 31, June 1, 2, 17, 1882, Bliss MSS.; Carosso, *Investment Banking*, p. 26.

25. Bliss to Ingalls, April 17, 1882, Bliss MSS.

26. Bliss to Ingalls, March 13, 1882, Bliss MSS.

27. *Report to the Stockholders, June 30, 1882.*

28. Bliss to Morton, January 15, 1882, Bliss MSS.

29. Bliss to Ingalls, June 25, 1883, Bliss MSS.

30. Bliss to Ingalls, September 29, 1883, Bliss MSS.

31. Bliss to Cunningham, Cincinnati, October 25, November 7, November 24, 1883; Bliss to Ingalls, November 10, 15, 1883, Bliss MSS.

32. Bliss to Cunningham, December 19, 1883, Bliss MSS.

33. Bliss to Cunningham, December 22, 27, 1883, Bliss MSS.

34. Bliss to Huntington, April 30, 1884; Ingalls to Elliot H. Pendelton, February 27, 1884; Bliss to Ingalls, February 28, 1884, Bliss MSS.

35. Julius Grodinsky, *Transcontinental Railway Strategy, 1869-1893: A Study of Businessmen* (Philadelphia, 1962), p. 163.

36. Bliss to Cunningham, December 19, 1883, Bliss MSS.

37. *Report to the Stockholders, 1884.*

38. He wrote Ingalls at the beginning of January: "I have made inquiries enough to enable me to say that the money cannot be procurred as proposed by you.

"I have seen Mr. Huntington this afternoon and he says he has no money. At the same time he is not, nor am I willing that the Company should suffer.

"I will try to see Mr. Huntington again within two or three days and he may feel a little differently, and if so we may each help you to a limited extent.

"I am yet owing a part of the East money I put into the Kentucky Central, & now I expect soon to have to put in more. By the way: what is the prospect? Are the Shareholders coming into the arrangement?" (Bliss to Ingalls, January 30, 1884. See also Bliss to Ingalls, January 31, February 4, 1884; Bliss to M. E. Osborn, February 11, 1884, Bliss MSS.).

39. "In reply to that part of your letter. . .in which you express a desire to make a long 'big four' loan in this City, I am forced to say that I do not think such a loan can be made, and meet it. . . .Our experience is that of everybody and of all the Lines that I know anything about and today I believe there are few lines that have not a. . .troublesome floating debt" (Bliss to Ingalls, February 28, 1884. See also Bliss to Ingalls, February 21, 1884; Bliss to T. Perkins, March 16, 18, May 26, 1884, Bliss MSS.).

40. Bliss to Morton, Rome, May 16, 1884, Bliss MSS.

41. Henry Clews, *Fifty Years in Wall Street* (New York, 1915), p. 520.

42. Bliss to Theodore Bliss, May 12, 1884, Bliss MSS.

43. Bliss to Ingalls, May 31, 1884; Bliss to Morton, Berlin, June 20, 1884. See also Bliss to Ingalls, July 23, September 24, 1884, Bliss MSS.

44. Bliss to Ingalls, March 2, 1885, Bliss MSS.

45. *Report to the Stockholders, 1885.*

46. Bliss to Ingalls, March 12, 1886, Bliss MSS.

47. Bliss to Ingalls, April 12, 15, 1886, Bliss MSS.

48. Bliss to Ingalls, May 8, 1886, Bliss MSS.

49. Bliss to Ingalls, May 19, 1886, Bliss MSS.

50. Bliss to Ingalls, June 17, 1886, Bliss MSS.; *Report to the Stockholders, 1886.*

51. *Commercial and Financial Chronicle*, October 1, 1881.

52. *Report to the Stockholders, 1887.* See *Commercial and Financial Chronicle*, February 26, October 1, 1887, for discussion of the newly issued stock.

53. Bliss to Ingalls, October 8, 1887, Bliss MSS.

54. Bliss to C. D. Head & T. H. Perkins, Boston, October 13, 1887, Bliss MSS.

55. Bliss to Morton, Cannes, January 7, 1888, Bliss MSS.

56. Bliss to Alex Williams, Boston, April 25, 1887, Bliss MSS.

57. Bliss to Ingalls, June 16, 1886, Bliss MSS.

58. Bliss to M. Treat, Northampton, January 7, 1887; Bliss to E. Gates, treasurer, New York, February 24, 1886. Bliss, Huntington and Eliot Pendleton acted as the Reorganization Committee. In coming into the agreement, stockholders who had paid the ten-percent assessment of 1884 now paid only two percent; others paid fourteen percent. Bliss headed the Bondholders Committee, which bought the road for $1.3 million in April 1887. The K. C. was sold to the L. & N. in 1890 after extensive work and persuasion by Bliss. See 1887-1890, Bliss MSS.

59. *Commercial and Financial Chronicle*, October 15, 29, 1888.

60. Bliss to Morton, London, February 24, 1888, Bliss MSS.

61. *Commercial and Financial Chronicle*, February 4, 1888; February 11, March 3, 31, 1888.

62. Ibid. Their share of $500,000 was cut to $425,000, and of this they gave Senator Conkling $75,000.

63. Bliss to Wilbur Day, New Haven, November 26, 1888; Bliss to [?], November 27, 1888, Bliss MSS.

64. Bliss to Ingalls, January 7, 1889, Bliss MSS.

65. Bliss to Ingalls, September 11, October 28, 1889; Bliss to Abram Hewett, New York, October 2, 7, 1889; and letters throughout 1889, 1890, and into 1892, Bliss MSS. W. N. Page was the president of Ganley Mountain Coal Co., and the account was handled by Morton, Bliss & Co.

66. Bliss to R. Adriance, September 11, 1889; Bliss to Ingalls, September 11, 1889; Bliss to Mrs. W. H. Fogg, December 19, 1889, Bliss MSS.

67. For example, see Carosso, *Investment Banking*, pp. 38 ff.

68. Bliss to Ingalls, February 18, 1890; Bliss to Hamilton M. K. Twombly, May 3, 1890; Bliss to Abram Hewett, May [?], 1890, Bliss MSS.

CHAPTER 10

1. According to Cochran, Drexel, Morgan & Company and Winslow, Lanier & Company became the "guiding force" in the Northern Pacific from the time of the 1880 bond syndicate (Thomas C. Cochran, *Railroad Leaders, 1845-1890* [Cambridge, Mass., 1953], pp. 48-51).

2. Pierre Berton, *The Impossible Railway: The Building of the Canadian Pacific* (New York, 1972); John Murray Gibbon, *History of the Canadian Pacific* (New York, 1937); Heather Gilbert, *Awakening Continent: the Life of Lord Mount Stephen* (Aberdeen, 1965); O. D. Skelton, *The Railway Builders* (Toronto, 1916).

3. Hugh G. J. Aitken, et al., *The American Economic Impact on Canada* (Durham, N. C., 1959); Michael Bliss, "Canadianizing American Business: The Roots of the Branch Plant," in *Close the 49th Parallel,* ed. Ian Lumsden (Toronto, 1970); Kari Levitt, *Silent Surrender: The Multinational Firm in Canada* (Toronto, 1970); Allan Smith's "Introduction" to the reissue of Samuel E. Moffett, *The Americanization of Canada* (Toronto, 1972); Stephen Scheinberg, "Invitation to Empire: Tariffs and American Economic Expansion in Canada," *Business History Review* 47 (Summer 1973).

4. Morden H. Long, "Sir John Rose and the Informal Beginnings of the Canadian High *Commissionership,"* *Canadian Historical Review* 12 (March 1931), pp. 33-34. The treaty also confirmed bonding privileges which allowed goods to pass under seal across the borders without delay to facilitate trade greatly. For details, see William J. Wilgus, *The Railway Interrelations of the United States and Canada* (New Haven, Conn., 1937), pp. 157-58.

5. Macdonald to J. Rose, November 30, 1871, April 17, October 18, 1872, February 13, 1873, Macdonald letterbooks, Public Archives of Canada.

6. John Murray Gibbon, *Steel of Empire, The Romantic History of the Canadian Pacific* (New York, 1935); Macdonald had little notion of conflict of interest ethics, or subordinated such concerns to his political aims. He saw nothing objectionable in frequently sending business to Morton, Rose & Company, placing them in competition with the Dominion's financial agents, when it solidified his political alliances or furthered favored railway construction. In 1871 when the Intercolonial Railway Commissioners used the name of Morton, Rose in their advertisements and made all payments for railway iron through the firm, it aroused quite a stir. An inquiry was ordered in Parliament to investigate Rose's relations to the government. Macdonald reassured him, "I need scarcely say to you that personally I value your services in Canada very much, and the disinterested spirit in which you act for us." The inquiry led nowhere (Macdonald to Rose, May 11, 1871; March 16, 19, 1870, Macdonald letterbooks).

7. J. Rose to Macdonald, August 7, 1879, in John Macdonald, *Correspondence of Sir John Macdonald*, ed. Joseph Pope (New York, 1921).

8. Bliss to C. Rose, London, July 30, 1878, September 17, October 31, 1879; Bliss to J. Rose, December 5, 1879; Bliss to Morton, November 14, December 13, 1879, Bliss MSS.

9. Macdonald to Goldwin Smith, July 7, 1880, in Macdonald, *Correspondence of Sir John Macdonald*.

10. Stephen to Macdonald, July 9, 1880, quoted in Gilbert, *Awakening Continent*, p. 63.

11. Bliss to Morton, April 4, 1880, Bliss MSS.

12. Bliss to Grenfell, London, August 10, 27, 1880, Bliss MSS.

13. See chapter 7 for a discussion of the firms' investment guidelines.

14. Bliss to C. Rose, September 30, 1880, Bliss MSS.

15. Bliss to J. Rose, September 29, 1880, Bliss MSS.

16. Bliss to Grenfell, telegram, Niagara, November 8, 1880, Bliss MSS. The Stephens group could have kept the original clause of the charter, stating that transfers would be subject to the provisions of the bylaws, as they were a majority; instead, they chose to insert a clause restricting transfers, eliminating the possible shifts that might occur.

17. Bliss to C. Rose, October 14, 22, 1880; Bliss to Grenfell, October 23, 28, 29, 1880, Bliss MSS.

18. *New York World*, November 3, 1880; *New York Commercial Advertiser*, December 7, 1880. A copy of the C.P.R. contract can be found in Gilbert, *Awakening Continent*, pp. 262-71.

19. Stephen and those whom Bliss identified as his associates had control of two-thirds of the five million capital that was to be issued. According to Bliss, this group consisted of seven parties, each to get nine and a half percent; Smith, Hill, Kennedy, Northcote, Angus and McIntyre were probably in Stephen's group. Morton, Bliss, and Morton, Rose and the French banking house took, I believe, the other third. Morton, Bliss & Co. secretly gave part of their interest to Billings, of the Northern Pacific, knowing that Kennedy would be greatly opposed to letting Billings have an interest (Bliss to Grenfell, October 25, 1880, Bliss MSS). According to Gibbon, the share list was as follows: Donald Smith 5,000, George Stephen 5,000, J. J. Hill 5,000, Duncan McIntyre 5,000, Morton, Rose & Co. 7,410, J. S. Kennedy & Co., 4,500 (Gibbon, *History of the Canadian Pacific*, p. 210). However, two

days after the bill passed, Kennedy telegraphed Bliss for a subscription for "the 18,140 shares Canadian Pacific stocks as per [their] list and by draft on. . .[Morton, Bliss] for $544,200 paid for the 30% called thereon" (Bliss to Morton, February 17, 1881, Bliss MSS).

20. See Skelton, *Railway Builders*, pp. 139 ff.; Gibbon, *History of the Canadian Pacific*, pp. 200 ff.; Gilbert, *Awakening Continent*, pp. 69-83; Wilgus, *Railway Interrelations*, p. 134.

21. See also, for discussions of C.P. policy, Bliss to Grenfell, March 22, 1881; Bliss to C. Rose, April 12, 1881, Bliss MSS.

22. Bliss to C. Rose, April 12, 1881; Bliss to Grenfell, April 19, 1881; Bliss to Morton, May 25, 1881; Bliss to Edmund B. Osler, May 25, 1881, Bliss MSS.

23. Bliss to Stephen, Montreal, June 3, 1881; Bliss to Morton, June 11, August 26, 1881, Bliss MSS.

24. Quoted in Gilbert, *Awakening Continent*, p. 84. See also discussion and review of the press reaction in Gibbon, *History of the Canadian Pacific*, p. 224.

25. J. S. Kennedy and the Bank of Montreal took the bonds at ninety-two and a half plus interest, payable at different periods, extending over ten months, and they were, moreover, given an option for one year for $5 million more at 95, and a further option for eighteen months after that for another $5 million at ninety-seven and a half. One-half percent interest was allowed for the undertaking, which included their services in selling as well (Bliss to Morton, France, August 26, 1881, Bliss MSS).

26. Skelton, *Railway Builders*, p. 141.

27. Bliss to Grenfell, September 21, 1881; Bliss to J. Rose, May 19, 1882, Bliss MSS.; J. Rose to Stephen, October 20, 1882, in Macdonald, *Correspondence of Sir John Macdonald*.

28. Bliss to J. Rose, June 5, 1882, Bliss MSS. For a discussion of the distinctive features of the land grant and its administration, see James B. Hedges, *The Federal Railway Land Subsidy Policy of Canada* (Cambridge, Mass., 1934). The five million acres were not in fact bought by the company—only two million were. For a discussion of press reaction and the delay in allocating the land grand, see Gilbert, *Awakening Continent*, pp. 103-10. For Rose's role in encouraging emigration, see especially Macdonald to Rose, November 3, 1883, Macdonald letterbooks; and for criticism of the allotment to speculators, see Macdonald to Rose, January 4, 1883, in Macdonald, *Correspondence of Sir John Macdonald*.

29. Bliss to J. Rose, May 19, 1882, Bliss MSS.

30. Bliss to Stephen, Montreal, June 14, 1882, Bliss MSS.

31. They took an interest in this road to secure the value of the interest they already had in the Credit Valley. See Bliss to E. B. Osler, c/o George Stephen, Montreal, December 28, 1881; Bliss to Stephen, January 5, 1882; Bliss to Grenfell, January 11, May 5, 1882; Bliss to Stephen, May 11, 1882, Bliss MSS.

32. Wilgus, *Railway Interrelations*, pp. 86, 108, 167.

33. Bliss to Stephen, May 11, 1882; Bliss to Commodore Vanderbilt, Grand Central Depot, May 1, 1882, Bliss MSS.

34. Gilbert, *Awakening Continent*, pp. 114-15.

35. Bliss to Morton, September 18, 1883, Bliss MSS.

36. Bliss to Morton, September 16, 26, 1883, Bliss MSS.

37. Ibid. By October, the stock market in the States was down considerably, and general business prospects were poor. Drexel and Winslow, Lanier were very concerned about the N. P.: "Just now, those who heavily invested in stocks under the control of Villard are suffering most severely. The parties in interest are trying to devise some scheme to provide for the floating-debt of the Northern Pacific" (Bliss to Morton, Paris, October 5, 1883;

Bliss to Morton, Paris, October 26, 1883, Bliss MSS).

38. Gilbert, *Awakening Continent*, p. 158.

39. Ibid.

40. Skelton, *Railway Builders*, p. 156.

41. Bliss to C. Rose, October 26, 1883; Bliss to Morton (personal and private), November 5, 1883, Bliss MSS.

42. Bliss to C. Rose, October 26, 1883, Bliss MSS.

43. Bliss to Grenfell, November 16, 1883, Bliss MSS.

44. Ibid. See also Bliss to Grenfell, December 4, 1883, Bliss MSS.

45. Ibid.

46. Bliss to Morton, December 5, 1883, Bliss MSS.

47. Ibid.

48. Bliss to Stephen, December 12, 1883, Bliss MSS.

49. Bliss to Morton, Paris, January 10, 15, 1884, Bliss MSS.

50. Bliss to Grenfell, February 5, 1884. See also Bliss to E. B. Osler, Toronto, March 24, 1884, Bliss MSS.; Stephen to J. Rose, January 5, 1884, in Macdonald, *Correspondence of Sir John Macdonald*.

51. Quoted in Gilbert, *Awakening Continent*, p. 155.

52. Bliss to Morton, April 26, 1884, Bliss MSS.; Stephen to J. Rose, January 5, 1884, in Macdonald, *Correspondence of Sir John Macdonald*; Skelton, *Railway Builders*, pp. 150-51.

53. Bliss to Morton, April 26, July 1, 1884, Bliss MSS. See also Morton to Grenfell, June 12, 1884, Morton MSS.

54. Gilbert, *Awakening Continent*, p. 160.

55. Bliss to Morton, March 3, 1885; Bliss to Stephen, March 10, 1885, Bliss MSS.; Morton to Morton, Rose & Co., London, May 5, 1885, Morton MSS.

56. Bliss to Stephen, March 27, 1885, Bliss MSS.

57. Morton to C. D. Rose, April 14, 1885, Paris, Morton MSS.

58. Bliss to Stephen, April 4, 1885, Bliss MSS.

59. Bliss to Stephen, May 2, 5, 21, 1885, Bliss MSS.

60. Bliss to Grenfell, April 20, 1886, Bliss MSS.

61. Gilbert, *Awakening Continent*, p. 250. Gilbert makes no mention of Morton, Bliss & Company in these arrangements, and, indeed, their participation was to be kept secret.

62. Charles B. Kuhlman, *The Development of the Flour-Milling Industry in the United States* (Boston, 1929), pp. 151-54.

63. Morton to Washburne, January 21, 1885, Morton MSS; Bliss to Washburne, April 3, 1885, Bliss MSS.; Albro Martin, *James J. Hill and the Opening of the Northwest* (New York, 1976), pp. 288-89.

64. *Commercial and Financial Chronicle*, April 6, 1887. Prospectus for "Issue of $5,000,000 Minneapolis, Sault Ste. Marie & Atlantic Railway," April 1887. For the background of this company, formed in 1883, see Leslie Suprey, *Steam Trains of the Soo* (Mora, 1967).

65. Prospectus.

66. Martin, *James J. Hill, and the Opening of the Northwest* (New York, 1976), pp. 246, 288-89; Kuhlman, *The Development of the Flour-Milling Industry*, pp. 152-53.

67. Bliss to Stephen, Montreal, May 22, 1887; Bliss to Morton, February 3, 24, 1888; Bliss to J. S. Pillsbury, Minneapolis, February 2, 1888, Bliss MSS.; Gibbon, *History of the Canadian Pacific*, p. 338.

68. Bliss to Morton, Paris, December 2, 9, 1887, Bliss MSS.

69. Ibid. As a result of his debts to them, in 1895, Morton, Bliss & Company took a lien on Washburn's house.

70. *Commercial and Financial Chronicle*, January 7, 1888.

71. Gilbert, *Awakening Continent*, p. 250.

72. Press clippings, Morton MSS.; Charles S. Campbell, Jr., "American Tariff Interests and the Northeastern Fisheries, 1883-1888," *Canadian Historical Review* 45 (September 1964); 212-28.

73. Wilgus, *Railway Interrelations,* pp. 135, 143-44.

74. *New York World*, August 5, 1888; *Philadelphia Press*, August 7, 1888; press clippings, Morton MSS.

Bibliography

PRIMARY SOURCES

I. Manuscripts

New York. New-York Historical Society. August Belmont papers.

New York. New-York Historical Society. George Bliss papers.

Hoboken, New Jersey. Delaware, Lackawanna & Western Railroad Company. Delaware, Lackawanna & Western papers.

New York. New York Public Library. Cyrus Field papers.

Newport News, Virginia. Mariners' Museum and Library. Collis P. Huntington papers.

Ottawa. Public Archives of Canada. John Macdonald letterbooks.

New York. New York Public Library. Levi P. Morton papers.

New York. New-York Historical Society. Joseph Seligman papers.

New York. Seligman Archives, J. & W. Seligman & Co. J. & W. Seligman & Co. papers.

II. Contemporary Newspapers and Periodicals

Bankers' Magazine (London). 1857-80.

Bankers' Magazine (New York). 1857-90.

Commercial and Financial Chronicle. 1865-90.

Fads and Fancies of Representative Americans. 1889-90.

Harper's Weekly. 1874.

Journal of Commerce. 1872.

London Times. 1872-73.

The Nation. 1872-73.

New York Commercial Advertisers. 1873-80.

New York Daily Tribune. 1876-83.

New York Evening Post. 1872-74.

New York Herald. 1877-82.

New York Sun. 1904.

New York Times. 1865-85.

New York Tribune. 1876-80.

New York World. 1874-88.

Railroad Gazette. 1860-90.

Washington Gazette. 1879.

III. Documents, Proceedings, and Statistics

Ashcroft's Railway Directory for 1868. New York: John W. Amerman, 1868.

Cincinnati, Indianapolis, St. Louis & Chicago Railway. *Annual Reports, 1881-89.*

Cincinnati Commission of Railroads and Telegraphs. *Annual Report of the Commissioner of Railroads and Telegraphs*. Cincinnati, Ohio, 1870.

The Directors' Report to the Stockholders of the Indianapolis, Cincinnati & Lafayette Railroad Company. August 1873.

The Federal Reporter 34 (St. Paul, Minn., 1889).

Illinois Central Railroad Company. *Report of the Delegates, Selected by the Joint Committee Appointed at a Meeting of British Shareholders of the Illinois Central Railroad Company, Held in London, on the 26th January, 1877, and by the Administration Office for American Railroad Securities in Amsterdam, April, 1877.*

Indianapolis Board of Trade. *Annual Reports of the Indianapolis Board of Trade, 1874-79.*

Ingalls, M. E. *Report of the Receiver of the Indianapolis, Cincinnati & Lafayette Railroad Company, for the Five Months Ending December 31, 1876.*

———. *Report Of The Indianapolis, Cincinnati & Lafayette Railroad Company, for the Year Ending June 30, 1877, by M. E. Ingalls, Receiver.*

Jeffery, E. T. *Remarks of E. T. Jeffery before the Board of Railroad and Warehouse Commissioners of the State of Illinois, Springfield, September 2, 1887*. Chicago: Rand McNally & Company, 1887.

King's Railway Directory for 1869. New York: A. H. King, 1869.

Metropolitan Railway Company. "Articles of Association." New York, 1864.

Milwaukee & St. Paul Railway Company. *Documents Relating to the Organization of the Milwaukee and St. Paul Railway.* New York: W. C. Bryant, 1863.

———. *Fifth Annual Report,* 1868.

———. *Eleventh Annual Report,* 1874. [Corporation renamed The Chicago, Milwaukee & St. Paul Railway Company.]

Minneapolis & St. Louis Railway Company. *Annual Report,* 1879.

Minnesota Railroad and Warehouse Commission. *Biennial Report,* 1873-78. St. Paul, Minn.: Pioneer Press Co.

Poor, Henry V. *Manual of Railroads of the United States.* New York: H. V. and H. W. Poor.

Reports of the President to the Directors of the Indianapolis, Cincinnati & Lafayette Railroad Company. 1874-76.

St. Paul, Minneapolis & Manitoba Railway Company. *Annual Reports,* 1880-1900.

St. Paul & Pacific Railroad Company. *Agreement for Reorganization of the Main and Branch Lines of the First Division of the St. Paul & Pacific Railroad Company. August 13, 1875.* New York.

Union Pacific Railroad Company. "List of Parties Subscribing to Stock, September, 1863."

———. *Proceedings of the Commissioners of the Union Pacific Railroad and Telegraph Company, at their Convention, Chicago, Illinois, September 2, 1862.*

———. *Report of the Organization and Proceedings of the Union Pacific Railroad Company.* New York: W. G. Bryant & Co., 1864.

United States Circuit Court, District of Minnesota, *John S. Kennedy and Henry Dimock v. the Great Northern Railway Co. 3 vols.* 1909.

United States Circuit Court, District of Minnesota, *John S. Kennedy & Co. v. the Northern Pacific Railroad Co., the St. Paul & Pacific Railroad Co., the First Division and Others to Show Cause, 1873.*

U. S. Bureau of the Census. *Historical Statistics of the United States, Colonial Times to 1970, Bicentennial Edition.* Washington, D.C.: Government Printing Office, 1975.

———. *Long-Term Economic Growth, 1860-1965.* Washington, D.C.: Government Printing Office, 1966.

U. S. District Court. *District Court of the United States for the District of Indiana in the Matter of the Indianapolis, Cincinnati and Lafayette Railroad on Petition of Joel F. Richardson et al. And the City of Lawrenceburg, Adjudication of Bankruptcy Pleadings and Evidence, 1871.*

United States Reports, 120. New York, 1887.

IV. Autobiographies, Reminiscences, and Private Papers

Adams, Henry. *The Education of Henry Adams.* New York: Random House, 1931.

Blaine, James G. *Twenty Years of Congress.* Norwich, Conn., 1893.

Boutwell, George. *Reminiscences of Sixty Years in Public Affairs.* New York: McClure, Phillips & Company, 1902.

Carnegie, Andrew. *Autobiography of Andrew Carnegie.* New York: Houghton Mifflin Company, 1920.

Clews, Henry. *Fifty Years in Wall Street.* New York: Irving Publishing Company, 1915.

Dodge, Grenville M. *How We Built the Union Pacific.* [1910?]. March America Facsimile Series, no. 97. Ann Arbor, Mich.: University Microfilms Inc.

Farley, Jesse Kelso, Jr. *Twelve Generations of Farleys.* Evanston, Ill.: 1943.

Grant, Ulysses. *General Grant's Letters To a Friend, 1861-1880.* Boston: Crowell & Company, 1897.

Hillis, John D. "Life and Public Services of Levi Parsons Morton." Unpublished manuscript. New-York Historical Society, Morton Papers.

Hoar, George F. *Autobiography of Seventy Years.* New York: Charles Scribner's Sons, 1906.

In Memoriam: Jesse Seligman. New York: Philip Comen, 1894. [Printed for private circulation].

Lanier, J. F. D. *Sketch Of The Life of J. F. D. Lanier.* New York: Printed for family use only, 1870.

Levi Parsons Morton, A Biographical Sketch. New York: The Press Association, 1911.

McCulloch, Hugh. *Men and Measures of Half a Century.* New York: Charles Scribner's Sons, 1900.

Macdonald, John. *Memoirs of the Right Honorable Sir John Macdonald.* Edited by Joseph Pope. Ottawa, 1894.

———.*Correspondence of Sir John Macdonald.* New York: Doubleday, Page & Company, 1921.

"Memorial' The Old Guard of New York." July 6, 1920 [On the death of Levi P. Morton].

Morton, Levi. P. *Personal Memorandum of Levi P. Morton.* New York: Morton Trust Company, [1904?].

New York State Chamber of Commerce. "Memorial Minutes of the New York State Chamber of Commerce, June 3, 1920." [On the death of Levi P. Morton].

Noyes, Alexander Dana. *A Short Financial History Of The Government and People Of The United States Since The Civil War, 1865-1907.* New York: G. P. Putnam's Sons, 1909.

Schurz, Carl. *The Reminiscences of Carl Schurz.* New York: The McClure Company, 1908.

Sherman, John. *Recollections of Forty Years in the House, Senate, and Cabinet.* Chicago: The Weiner Company, 1895.

Wells, Linton. "The House of Seligman." 1931. Unpublished manuscript, New-York Historical Society, Seligman papers.

V. Maps

The Chicago, Milwaukee & St. Paul Railway. *Rand, McNally & Company Railway Guide, The Travelers' Handbook to all Railway and Steamboat Lines of North America.* Chicago, [September 1874]. P. 301.

The Cincinnati, Indianapolis, St. Louis & Chicago Railway. *Rand McNally Official Railway Guide.* Chicago: Rand McNally & Company, July 1886. P. 368.

The Illinois Central Railway. *Appleton's Railway and Steam Navigation Guide.* New York: D. Appleton & Co., May 1873. P. 204.

The Indianapolis, Cincinnati & Lafayette Railroad. *Rand, McNally & Company Railway Guide. The Travelers' Handbook to all Railway and Steamboat Lines of North America.* Chicago, [September 1874]. P. 179.

The Minneapolis, Sault Ste. Marie & Atlantic Railway. Morton, Bliss & Company. Prospectus for "Issue of $5,000,000 Minneapolis, Sault Ste. Marie & Atlantic Railway Bonds." New York, April 18, 1887.

The Missouri, Kansas & Texas Railway. *Appleton's Railway and Steam Navigation Guide.* New York: D. Appleton & Co., May 1873.

The New Orleans, Mobile & Texas Railway. *Appleton's Railway and Steam Navigation Guide.* New York: D. Appleton & Co., May 1873. P. 237.

The New Orleans, St. Louis & Chicago Railroad. *Rand, McNally & Company Railway Guide, The Travelers' Handbook to all Rail-*

way and Steamboat Lines of North America. Chicago, [September 1874]. P. 240.

The Rock Island and Albert Lea Routes. *Rand McNally Official Railway Guide.* Chicago: Rand McNally & Company, July 1886. P. 214.

The St. Paul & Pacific. State of Minnesota. *Grants of Land, etc. By Congress, and Charter of the St. Paul & Pacific and of the First Division of the St. Paul & Pacific Railroad Companies, General Railroad Laws of Minnesota and of the Territory of Dakota.* St. Paul, Minn.: Pioneer Press, 1879.

SECONDARY SOURCES

I. Books and Monographs

Ackerman, William K. *Historical Sketch of the Illinois Central Railroad.* Chicago, 1890.

―――. *History of the Illinois Central Railroad Company and Representative Employees.* Chicago: Railroad Historical Company, 1900.

Adams, Charles Francis, Jr. *Railroads: Their Origins and Problems.* New York: G. P. Putnam's Sons, 1878.

Adams, Charles Francis, Jr., and Adams, Henry. *Chapters of Erie.* Ithaca, N.Y.: Great Seal Books, 1956.

Adler, Cyrus. *Jacob Henry Schiff; A Biographic Sketch.* New York: The American Jewish Committee, 1921.

―――. *Jacob H. Schiff: His Life and Letters.* Garden City, N.Y.: Doubleday, Doran and Company, Inc., 1929.

Adler, Dorothy. *British Investment in American Railways.* Edited by Muriel Hidy. Charlottesville, Va.: University of Virginia, 1970.

Aitken, Hugh G. J., et al. *The American Economic Impact on Canada.* Durham, N.C.: Duke University Press, 1959.

Allen, Frederick L. *The Great Pierpont Morgan.* New York: Harper, 1934.

Ambler, Charles Henry. *A History of Transportation in the Ohio Valley.* Glendale, Calif.: The Arthur H. Clark Company, 1932.

Atwater, Isaac, ed. *History of Minneapolis, Minnesota.* New York: Munsell & Company, 1893.

Bagehot, Walter. *Lombard Street* in *Works of Walter Bagehot,* vol. 5.

Edited by Forrest Morgan. Hartford, Conn.: Travelers Insurance Company, 1889.

Barger, Harold. *The Management of Money: A Survey of American Experience.* Chicago: Rand McNally, 1964.

Barrett, Don C. *The Greenbacks and Resumption of Specie Payments, 1862-1879.* Cambridge, Mass.: Harvard University Press, 1931.

Baughman, James P. *Charles Morgan and the Development of Southern Transportation.* Nashville, Tenn.: Vanderbilt University Press, 1968.

Belcher, Wyatt Winton. *The Economic Rivalry Between St. Louis and Chicago, 1850-1880.* New York: Columbia University Press, 1947.

Benson, Lee. *Merchants, Farmers and Railroads: Railroad Regulation and New York Politics, 1850-1887.* Cambridge, Mass.: Harvard University Press, 1955.

Berton, Pierre. *The Impossible Railway; The Building of the Canadian Pacific.* New York: A. A. Knopf, 1972.

Bining, Arthur, and Cochran, Thomas C. *The Rise of American Life.* New York: Charles Scribner's, 1964.

Birmingham, Stephen. *Our Crowd, The Jewish Families of New York.* New York: Dell Publishing Company, 1967.

Bolles, Albert S. *The Financial History of the United States, From 1861 to 1885.* New York: D. Appleton and Company, 1894.

Briggs, Asa. *Victorian People.* London: Oldenhams Press, 1954.

Brown, Robert Craig. *Canada's National Policy, 1883-1900: A Study in Canadian-American Relations.* Princeton, N.J.: Princeton University Press, 1964.

Brown Brothers and Company. *Experiences of a Century, 1818-1918.* New York: privately printed, 1918.

Brownlee, W. Elliot. *Dynamics of Ascent: A History of the American Economy.* New York: Alfred A. Knopf, 1974.

Brownson, Howard Grey. *The History of the Illinois Central Railroad to 1870.* Urbana, Ill.: University of Illinois, 1915.

Cameron, Rondo, et al. *Banking in the Early Stages of Industrialization: A Study in Comparative Economic History.* New York: Oxford University Press, 1967.

Carosso, Vincent P. *Investment Banking in America: A History.* Cambridge, Mass.: Harvard University Press, 1970.

Cary, John W. *The Organization And History of The Chicago, Milwaukee & St. Paul Railway Company.* Milwaukee, Wisc.: Cramer, Aikens & Cramer, 1892.

Chandler, Alfred D., Jr. *Henry Varnum Poor, Business Editor, Analyst and Reformer.* Cambridge, Mass.: Harvard University Press, 1956.

———.*Strategy and Structure: Chapters in the History of American Industrial Enterprise.* Cambridge, Mass.: M.I.T. Press, 1962.

———. ed. *The Railroads: The Nation's First Big Business.* New York: Harcourt Brace and World, 1965.

———. *The Visible Hand: The Managerial Revolution in American Business.* Cambridge, Mass.: Harvard University Press, 1977.

Clark, Thomas D. *A Pioneer Southern Railroad: From New Orleans to Cairo.* Chapel Hill, N.C.: University of North Carolina Press, 1936.

Cleveland, Frederick A., and Powell, Fred. W. *Railroad Promotion and Capitalization in the United States.* New York: Longmans, 2909.

Cochran, Thomas C., and Miller, William. *The Age of Enterprise.* Rev. ed. New York: Harper and Brothers, 1961.

———. *Railroad Leaders, 1845-1890: The Business Mind in Action.* Cambridge, Mass.: Harvard University Press, 1953.

Contemporary American Biography. New York: Atlantic Publishing and Engraving Company, 1892.

Corey, Lewis. *The House of Morgan.* New York: G. H. Watt, 1930.

Corliss, Carlton J. *Main Line of Mid-America: The Story of the Illinois Central.* New York: Creative Age Press, 1950.

Cottman, George S. *Centennial History and Handbook of Indiana.* Indianapolis, Ind.: Max R. Hyman, 1915.

Curti, Merle. *The Growth of American Thought.* New York: Harper & Brothers, 1943.

Daggett, Stuart. *Railroad Reorganization.* New York: Houghton Mifflin & Company, 1908.

Daniels, Winthrop. *American Railroads: Four Phases of Their History.* Princeton, N.J.: Princeton University Press, 1932.

Davis, Lance E.; Hughes, Jonathan R. T.; and McDougall, Duncan M. *American Economic History: The Development of a National Economy.* New York: Richard D. Irwin, 1969.

Decker, Leslie E. *Railroads, Lands, and Politics: The Taxation of the Railroad Land Grants, 1864-1897.* Providence, R.I.: Brown University Press, 1964.

Degler, Carl. *The Age of the Economic Revolution, 1876-1900.* Glenview, Ill.: Scott, Foresman and Company, 1967.

Denison, Merrill. *Canada's First Bank: A History of the Bank of Montreal.* Toronto: McClelland & Stewart, Ltd., 1967.

Derleth, August. *The Milwaukee Road: Its First Hundred Years.* New York: Creative Age Press, 1948.

Dewey, Davis R. *Financial History of the United States.* New York: Longmans, Green and Company, 1936.

Diamond, Sigmund. *The Reputation of the American Businessman.* New York: Harper and Row, 1966.

Donovan, Frank, Jr. *Mileposts On the Prairie: The Story of the Minneapolis & St. Louis Railway.* New York: Simmons-Boardman Publishing Corporation, 1950.

Dunbar, Charles F. *The Theory and History of Banking.* New York: G. Putnam's Sons, 1917.

Easterbrook, W. T., and Aitken, Hugh G. J. *Canadian Economic History.* Toronto: Macmillan Company, 1963.

Edwards, George W. *Evolution of Finance Capitalism.* New York: Longmans, Green and Company, 1938.

Elkins, Stanley M. *Slavery: A Problem in American Institutional and Intellectual Life.* New York: Grosset & Dunlap, 1963.

Evans, Cerinda. *Collis Potter Huntington.* Newport News, Va.: Mariners' Museum, 1954.

Fairman, Charles. *Reconstruction and Reunion 1864-88. Part One.* In *The Oliver Wendell Holmes Devise: History of the Supreme Court of the United States,* edited by Paul A. Freund, vol. 6. New York: Macmillan Company, 1971.

Faulkner, Harold Underwood. *American Economic History.* New York: Harper and Row, 1960.

Fels, Rendigs. *American Business Cycles, 1865-1897.* Chapel Hill, N.C.: University of North Carolina Press, 1959.

Fite, Gilbert C., and Reese, Jim E. *An Economic History of the United States.* 3rd ed. Boston: Houghton Mifflin Company, 1973.

Fogel, Robert W. *Railroads and American Growth: Essays in Econometric History.* Baltimore, Md.: Johns Hopkins University Press, 1964.

———. *The Union Pacific Railroad, A Case In Premature Enterprise.* Baltimore, Md.: Johns Hopkins University Press, 1960.

Friedman, Milton, and Schwartz, Anna J. A. *Monetary History of the United States, 1867-1960.* Princeton, N.J.: Princeton University Press, 1963.

Gates, Paul W. *The Illinois Central Railroad and Its Colonization Work.* Cambridge, Mass.: Harvard University Press, 1934.

Gibbon, John Murray. *Steel of Empire, The Romantic History of the Canadian Pacific.* New York: Bobbs-Merrill Company, 1935.

Gilbert, Heather. *Awakening Continent, The Life of Lord Mount Stephen.* Aberdeen: Aberdeen University Press, 1965.

Glazebrook, George Parkin de T. *A History of Canadian External Relations.* Toronto: Oxford University Press, 1950.

Gluck, Alvin C., Jr. *Minnesota and the Manifest Destiny of the Canadian Northwest: A Study in Canadian-American Relations.* Toronto: University of Toronto Press, 1965.

Goodrich, Carter, ed. *Canals and American Economic Development.* New York: Columbia University Press, 1961.

————. *Government Promotion of American Canals and Railroads, 1800-1890.* New York: Columbia University Press, 1960.

Gras, N. S. B., and Larson, Henrietta, M. *Casebook in American Business History.* New York: Appleton-Century-Crofts Inc., 1939.

Grodinsky, Julius. *Jay Gould: His Business Career, 1867-1892.* Philadelphia: University of Pennsylvania Press, 1957.

————. *Transcontinental Railway Strategy, 1869-1893: A Study of Businessmen.* Philadelphia: University of Pennsylvania Press, 1962.

Hall, Henry. *America's Successful Men of Affairs.* New York: The New York Tribune, 1895.

Hedges, James B. *Henry Villard and the Railways of the Northwest.* New Haven, Conn.: Yale University Press, 1930.

————. *The Federal Railway Land Subsidy Policy of Canada.* Cambridge, Mass.: Harvard University Press, 1934.

Hidy, Ralph W. *The House of Baring in American Trade and Finance.* Cambridge, Mass.: Harvard University Press, 1949.

Hobson, Elizabeth C. K. *Recollections of a Happy Life.* New York, 1916.

Hofstadter, Richard. *The American Political Tradition.* New York: Vintage Books, 1958.

Hovey, Carl. *The Life Story of J. Pierpont Morgan: A Biography.* New York: Sturges and Walton Co., 1911.

Hudson, James F. *The Railway and the Republic.* New York: Harper & Brothers, 1886.

Hughes, Jonathan R. T. *The Vital Few: American Economic Progress and Its Protagonists.* Boston: Houghton Mifflin Company, 1966.

Hurst, James Willard. *The Legitimacy of the Business Corporation in the Law of the United States.* Charlottesville, Va.: University of Virginia, 1970.

Illinois Central Railroad Company. *Centennial Report, The Financial Story of Our First Hundred Years, 1851-1951.* Chicago, 1951.

Innes, Harold A. *A History of the Canadian Pacific Railway.* London: P. S. King & Sons, Ltd., 1923.

―――. *Essays in Canadian Economic History.* Edited by Mary Q. Innes. Toronto: University of Toronto Press, 1956.

Jenks, Leland. *The Migration of British Capital to 1875.* London: Thomas Nelson and Sons, Ltd., 1927.

Johnson, Allen, and Malone, Dumas, eds. *Dictionary of American Biography.* New York: Charles Scribner's Sons, 1928 ff.

Johnson, Arthur M., and Supple, Barry E. *Boston Capitalists and Western Railroads: A Study in the Nineteenth-Century Railroad Investment Process.* Cambridge, Mass.: Harvard University Press, 1967.

Johnson, E. A. J., and Krooss, Herman E. *The American Economy.* New York: Prentice-Hall, 1960.

Josephson, Matthew. *The Robber Barons.* New York: Harcourt Brace & Company, 1934.

Katz, Irving. *August Belmont: A Political Biography.* New York: Columbia University Press, 1968.

―――. "Investment Bankers in American Government and Politics: The Political Activities of William W. Corcoran, August Belmont, Sr., Levi P. Morton, and Henry Lee Higginson." Ph.D. dissertation, New York University, 1964.

Kirkland, Edward E. *A History of American Life.* New York: Appleton-Century-Crofts, 1969.

―――. *Charles Francis Adams, Jr., 1835-1915, The Patrician at Bay.* Cambridge, Mass.: Harvard University Press, 1965.

―――. *Industry Comes of Age: Business, Labor, and Public Policy, 1860-1897.* New York: Holt, Rinehart and Winston, 1961.

―――. *Men, Cities and Transportation.* Cambridge, Mass.: Harvard University Press, 1948.

Klein, Maury. *History of the Louisville and Nashville Railroad.* New York: Macmillan and Company, 1972.

Kolko, Gabriel. *Railroads and Regulation, 1877-1916.* Princeton, N.J.: Princeton University Press, 1965.

Krooss, Herman E., and Blyn, Martin. *A History of Financial Intermediaries.* New York: Random House, 1971.

Kuhlman, Charles B. *The Development of the Flour-Milling Industry in the United States.* Boston: Houghton Mifflin Company, 1929.

Lambie, Joseph T., and Clemence, Richard V. *Economic Change in America; Readings in the Economic History of the United States.* Harrisburg, Pa.: Stackpole Company, 1954.

Lanier, Henry Wysham. *A Century of Banking in New York, 1822-*

1922. New York: George H. Doran Company, 1922.

Larrabee, William. *The Railroad Question: A Historical and Practical Treatise on Railroads and Remedies for Their Abuses*. Chicago: The Schulte Publishing Company, 1893.

Larson, Henrietta M. *Guide to Business History*. Cambridge, Mass.: Harvard University Press, 1948.

————. *Jay Cooke, Private Banker*. Cambridge, Mass.: Harvard University Press, 1936.

Laughlin, J. Laurence. *The History of Bimetalism in the United States*. New York: D. Appleton and Company, 1897.

Lehman Brothers. *A Centennial: Lehman Brothers, 1850-1950*. New York: n.p., 1950.

Levitt, Kari. *Silent Surrender: The Multinational Corporation in Canada*. Toronto: Macmillan of Canada, 1970.

Lewis, Oscar. *The Big Four: The Story of Huntington, Stanford, Hopkins, and Crocker, and the Building of the Central Pacific*. New York: A. A. Knopf, 1938.

Livesay, Harold C. *Andrew Carnegie and the Rise of Big Business*. Boston: Little, Brown and Company, 1975.

McElroy, Robert. *Levi Parsons Morton: Banker, Diplomat, and Statesman*. New York: G. P. Putnam's Sons, 1930.

McMechen, Eugene J. "The Rapid Transit Struggle in New York, 1864-1879." Master's thesis, Hunter College, 1975.

Marcus, Robert D. *Grand Old Party, Political Structure in the Gilded Age, 1880-1896*. New York: Oxford University Press, 1971.

Martin, Albro. *Enterprise Denied: Origins of the Decline of American Railroads, 1897-1917*. New York: Columbia University Press, 1971.

————. *James J. Hill and the Opening of the Northwest*. New York: Oxford University Press, 1976.

Masterson, Vincent V. *The Katy Railroad and the Last Frontier*. Norman, Okla.: University of Oklahoma Press, 1952.

Miller, George H. *Railroads and the Granger Laws*. Madison: University of Wisconsin Press, 1971.

Miller, Nathan. *The Enterprise of a Free People: Aspects of Economic Development in New York State During the Canal Period, 1792-1838*. Ithaca: Cornell University Press, 1962.

Miller, William, ed. *Men in Business: Essays in the History of Entrepreneurship*. Cambridge, Mass.: Harvard University Press, 1952.

Miner, H. Craig. *The St. Louis-San Francisco Transcontinental Railroad*. Lawrence, Kans.: University of Kansas, 1972.

Moffett, Samuel E. *The Americanization of Canada*. Introduction by Allan Smith. Toronto: University of Toronto Press, 1972.

Moody, John. *Masters of Capital*. New Haven, Conn.: Yale University Press, 1922.

Muir, Ross L., and White, Carl J. *Over the Long Term: The Story of J. & W. Seligman & Company*. New York: J. & W. Seligman & Company, 1964.

Muzzey, David S. *James G. Blaine: A Political Idol of Other Days*. New York: Dodd, Mead & Company, 1934.

Myers, Margaret G. *The New York Money Market*. New York: Columbia University Press, 1931.

National Cyclopedia of American Biography. New York: James T. White and Company, 1892 ff.

North, Douglass C. *The Economic Growth of the United States, 1790-1860*. Englewood Cliffs, N.J.: Prentice-Hall, Inc. 1961.

Northrup, Henry D. *The Lives of Harrison and Morton*. Philadelphia: International Publishing Company, 1888.

Oberholtzer, Ellis Paxson. *Jay Cooke, Financier of the Civil War*. Philadelphia: George W. Jacobs & Company, 1907.

Olmstead, Alan J. *New York Savings Banks in the Ante-bellum Years, 1819-1861*. Chapel Hill, N.C.: University of North Carolina Press, 1976.

Perkins, Edwin J. *Financing Anglo-American Trade: The House of Brown 1800-1880*. Cambridge, Mass.: Harvard University Press, 1975.

Phelps, Clyde William. *The Foreign Expansion of American Banks: American Branch Banking Abroad*. New York: Ronald Press Company, 1927.

Pierce, Harry H. *Railroads of New York, A Study of Government Aid, 1826-1875*. Cambridge, Mass.: Harvard University Press, 1953.

Pyle, Joseph G. *The Life of James J. Hill*. New York: Doubleday, Page & Company, 1917.

Quiett, Glenn C. *They Built the West: An Epic of Rails and Cities*. New York: D. Appleton-Century Company, Inc., 1934.

Redlich, Fritz. *History of American Business Leaders: A Series of Studies*. Ann Arbor, Mich.: Edwards Brothers, 1940.

———. *The Molding of American Banking: Men and Ideas*. New York: Johnson Reprint Corporation, 1968.

Riegel, Robert. *The Story of the Western Railroads*. New York: Macmillan Company, 1926.

Ripley, William Z. *Railroads: Finance and Organization*. New York:

Longmans, Green and Company, 1927.

Robbins, Sidney M., and Terleckyj, Nestor E. *Money Metropolis: A Locational Study of Financial Activities in the New York Region.* Cambridge, Mass.: Harvard University Press, 1960.

Robertson, Ross M. *History of the American Economy.* 3rd ed. New York: Harcourt Brace and World, Inc., 1973.

Rosenberg, Nathan. *Technology and American Growth.* New York: Harper and Row, 1972.

Rostow, W. W. *The Stages of Economic Growth: A Non-Communist Manifesto.* Cambridge, Mass.: Harvard University Press, 1960.

Rothman, David J. *Politics and Power: The United States Senate, 1869-1901.* Cambridge, Mass.: Harvard University Press, 1966.

Sandburg, Carl. *Abraham Lincoln, The War Years.* New York: Harcourt Brace and Company, 1939.

Satterlee, Herbert. *J. Pierpont Morgan: An Intimate Portrait.* New York: Macmillan Company, 1939.

Scheiber, Harry N. *Ohio Canal Era: A Case Study of Government and the Economy, 1820-1861.* Athens, Ohio: Ohio University Press, 1969.

Schonberger, Howard B. *Transportation to the Seaboard: The "Communication Revolution" and American Foreign Policy, 1860-1900.* Westport, Conn.: Greenwood Publishing Corporation, 1971.

Schotter, H. W. *The Growth and Development of the Pennsylvania Railroad Company.* Philadelphia: Press of Allen, Lane & Scott, 1927.

Sharkey, Robert P. *Money, Class and Party; An Economic Study of Civil War and Reconstruction.* Baltimore, Md.: Johns Hopkins University Press, 1967.

Shott, John G. *The Railroad Monopoly, An Instrument of Banker Control of the American Economy.* Washington, D.C.: Public Affairs Institute, 1950.

Skelton, O. D. *The Railway Builders.* Toronto: Glasgow, Brook & Company, 1920.

Snyder, Carl. *American Railways as Investments.* New York: The Moody Corporation, 1907.

Sobel, Robert. *The Big Board: A History of the New York Stock Market.* New York: The Free Press, 1965.

Soule, George, and Carosso, Vincent P. *American Economic History.* New York: Dryden Press, 1957.

Stover, John. *American Railroads.* Chicago: University of Chicago Press, 1966.

————. *The Railroads of the South, 1865-1900: A Study in Finance and Control.* Chapel Hill, N.C.: The University of North Carolina Press, 1955.

Sunderland, Edwin S. *Abraham Lincoln and the Illinois Central, Main Line of Mid-America.* New York: n.p., 1955.

Suprey, Leslie. *Steam Trains of the Soo.* Mora: B & W Printers, 1962.

Swain, Henry H. *Economic Aspects of Railroad Receiverships.* New York: Economic Studies of the American Economic Association, 1898.

Taylor, George Rogers, and Neu, Irene D. *The American Railroad Network, 1861-1890.* Cambridge, Mass.: Harvard University Press, 1956.

Temin, Peter. *Iron and Steel in Nineteenth-Century America: An Economic Inquiry.* Cambridge, Mass.: M.I.T. Press, 1964.

Thompson, Norman, and Edgar, J. H. *Canadian Railway Development.* Toronto: Macmillan Company of Canada, 1933.

Trottman, Nelson. *History of the Union Pacific: A Financial and Economic Survey.* New York: Ronald Press, 1923.

Ulmer, Melville J. *Capital in Transportation, Communications, and Public Utilities: Its Formation and Financing.* Princeton, N.J.: Princeton University Press, 1960.

Unger, Irwin. *The Greenback Era: A Social and Political History of American Finance, 1865-1879.* Princeton, N.J.: Princeton University Press, 1964.

Van Oss, S. F. *American Railroads as Investments.* New York: G. P. Putnam's Sons, 1893.

————. *American Railroads and British Investors.* London: E. Wilson & Company, 1893.

Wall, Joseph Frazier. *Andrew Carnegie.* New York: Oxford University Press, 1970.

Ward, John William. *Andrew Jackson: Symbol for an Age.* New York: Oxford University Press, 1970.

Wells, David A. *Recent Economic Changes.* New York: D. Appleton and Company, 1895.

Wilgus, William J. *The Railway Interrelations of the United States and Canada.* New Haven, Conn.: Yale University Press, 1937.

Winkler, John. *Morgan the Magnificent.* New York: Vanguard Press, 1930.

Woodward, C. Vann, ed. *The Comparative Approach to American History.* New York: Basic Books, Inc., 1968.

————. *Reunion and Reaction.* Boston: Little, Brown & Company, 1951.

II. Essays and Articles

Abbot, Lyman. "The American Railroad." *Harper's 49* (June 1874).

Acheson, T. W. "Changing Social Origins of the Canadian Industrial Elite." *Business History Review 47* (Summer 1973).

Baughman, James P. "New Directions in American Economic and Business History." In *American History: Retrospect and Prospect*. Edited by George A. Billias and Gerald N. Grob. New York: The Free Press, 1971.

Bliss, Michael. "Canadianizing American Business: The Roots of the Branch Plant." In *Close the 49th Parallel*. Edited by Ian Lumsden. Toronto: University of Toronto Press, 1970.

Brown, Junius H. "The Rothschilds (The Knights of the Red Shield)." *Harper's* 18 (December 1873 to May 1874).

Campbell, Charles S., Jr. "American Tariff Interests and the Northeastern Fisheries, 1883-1888." *Canadian Historical Review 45* (September 1964).

Cawalti, John G. "From Rags to Respectability: Horatio Alger." In *The National Temper*. Edited by Lawrence W. Levine and Robert Middlekauft. New York: Harcourt Brace and World, 1968.

Chandler, Alfred D., Jr. "The Beginnings of 'Big Business' in American Industry." *Business History Review* 33 (Spring 1959).

―――. "Patterns of American Railroad Finance, 1830-50." *Business History Review* 28 (September 1954).

Cochran, Thomas C. "Did the Civil War Retard Industrialization?" *Mississippi Valley Historical Review* 48 (September, 1961).

―――. "The Entrepreneur in American Capital Formation." In *Capital Formation and Economic Growth*. National Bureau of Economic Research. Princeton, N.J.: Princeton University Press, 1955.

―――. "The Legend of the Robber Barons." *The Pennsylvania Magazine of History and Biography* 74 (July 1950).

Davis, Lance E. "Capital Immobilities and Finance Capitalism: A Study of Economic Evolution in the United States, 1820-1920." *Explorations in Entrepreneurial History*, second series, 1 (Fall 1963).

―――. "The New England Textile Mills and the Capital Markets: A Study of Industrial Borrowing, 1840-1860." *Journal of Economic History* 20 (March 1960).

―――. "The Investment Market, 1870-1914: The Evolution of a National Market." *Journal of Economic History* 25 (September 1965).

Destler, Chester McArthur. "Western Radicalism, 1865-1901: Concepts and Origins." *The Mississippi Valley Historical Review* 31 (December 1944).

Dudden, Arthur P. "Men Against Monopoly: The Prelude to Trust-Busting." *Journal of the History of Ideas* 18 (October 1957).

Easterbrook, W. T. "Long-Range Comparative Study: Some Historical Cases." *Journal of Economic History* 17 (December 1957).

Ellis, David M. "The Homestead Clause in Railroad Land Grants." In *The Frontier in American Development*. Edited by David M. Ellis. Ithaca, N.Y.: Cornell University Press, 1969.

Farnham, W. D. " 'The Weakened Spring of Government': A Study in Nineteenth Century American History." *American Historical Review* 68 (April 1963).

Fels, Rendigs. "American Business Cycles, 1865-79." *American Economic Review* 41 (June 1951).

Fishlow, Albert. "Productivity and Technological Change in the Railroad Sector, 1840-1910." In *Output, Employment and Productivity in the United States after 1800*. National Bureau of Economic Research, Conference on Research in Income and Wealth. New York: Columbia University Press, 1966.

Fogel, Robert W. "The New Economic History: Its Findings and Methods." *Economic History Review* 19 (December 1966).

Gilbert, Heather. "The Unaccountable Fifth: Solution of a Great Northern Enigma." *Minnesota History* 44 (Spring 1971).

Graham, Frank D. "International Trade under Depreciated Paper: The United States, 1862-1879." *Quarterly Journal of Economics* 36 (February 1922).

Greenberg, Dolores. "A Study of Capital Alliances: The St. Paul & Pacific." *Canadian Historical Review* 57 (March 1976).

———. "Yankee Financiers and the Establishment of Trans-Atlantic Partnerships: A Re-examination." *Business History* 16 (January 1974).

Jaher, Frederick Copler. "The Boston Brahmins in the Age of Industrial Capitalism." In *The Age of Industrialization in America*. Edited by F. C. Jaher. New York: The Free Press, 1969.

Kindleberger, Charles P. "Origins of Direct Investment in France." *Business History Review* 48 (Autumn 1974).

Klein, Maury, and Yamamura, Kozo. "The Growth Strategies of Southern Railroads, 1865-1893." *Business History Review* 41 (Winter 1967).

Lerner, Eugene M. "Investment Uncertainty during the Civil War: A Note on the McCormick Brothers." *Journal of Economic History* 16 (March 1956).

Long, Morden H. "Sir John Rose and the informal beginnings of the Canadian High Commissionership." *Canadian Historical Review* 12 (March 1931).

MacDougall, J. Lorne. "The Character of the Entrepreneur: The Case of George Stephen." In *Canadian Business History*. Edited by David S. Macmillan. Toronto: McClelland and Stewart, 1972.

Martin, Albro. "Railroads and the Equity Receivership: An Essay on Institutional Change." *Journal of Economic History* 34 (September 1974).

―――. "The Troubled Subject of Railroad Regulation in the 'Gilded Age'—A Reassessment." *Journal of American History* 61 (September 1974).

Mercer, Lloyd. "Building Ahead of Demand: Some Evidence for the Land Grant Railroads." *Journal of Economic History* 34 (June 1974).

―――. "Taxpayers or Investors: Who Paid for the Land Grant Railroads?" *Business History Review* 46 (Autumn 1972).

Navin, Thomas R., and Sears, Marian V. "The Rise of a Market for Industrial Securities, 1887-1902." *Business History Review* 29 (June 1955).

North, Douglass C. "Life Insurance and Investment Banking." *Journal of Economic History* 14 (Summer 1954).

Peck, Merton, J. "Transportation in the American Economy." In *American Economic History*. Edited by Seymour Harris. New York: McGraw-Hill Book Company, Inc., 1961.

Perkins, Edwin J. "Managing a Dollar-Sterling Exchange Account: Brown, Shipley and Co. in the 1850's." *Business History* 16 (January 1974).

Pierce, Harry. "Foreign Investments in American Enterprise." In *Economic Change in The Civil War Era*. Edited by David T. Gilchrist and W. David Lewis. Greenville, S.C.: Eleutherian Mills-Hagley Foundation, 1965.

Pontecorvo, Giulio. "Investment Banking and Security Speculation in the Late 1920's." *Business History Review* 32 (Summer 1958).

Salsbury, Stephen. "The Effect of the Civil War on American Industrial Development." In *The Economic Impact of the American Civil War*. Edited by Ralph Andreano. Cambridge, Mass.: Schenkman Publishing Company, Inc., 1962.

Scheinberg, Stephen. "Invitation to Empire: Tariffs and American Economic Expansion in Canada." *Business History Review* 47 (Summer 1973).

Schwartz, Anna Jacobson. "Gross Dividend and Interest Payments by Corporations in the Nineteenth Century." In *Trends in the*

American Economy in the Nineteenth Century. National Bureau of Economic Research, Conference on Research in Income and Wealth. Princeton, N.J.: Princeton University Press, 1960.

Simon, Matthew. "The United States Balance of Payments, 1861-1900." In *Trends in the American Economy in the Nineteenth Century.* National Bureau of Economic Research, Conference on Research in Income and Wealth. Princeton, N.J.: Princeton University Press, 1960.

Stevens, Harry. "Bank Enterprises in a Western Town, 1815-1822." *Business History Review* 29 (June 1955).

Supple, Barry E. "A Business Elite: German-Jewish Financiers in Nineteenth Century New York." *Business History Review* 31 (Summer 1957).

Sylla, Richard. "Federal Policy, Banking Market Structure, and Capital Mobilization in the United States, 1863-1913." *Journal of Economic History* 29 (December 1969).

―――."Forgotten Men of Money: Private Bankers in Early U. S. History." *Journal of Economic History* 36 (March 1976).

Warburton, Clark. "Variations in Economic Growth and Banking Developments in the United States from 1835 to 1885." *Journal of Economic History* 18 (September 1958).

Young, John H. "Comparative Economic Development: Canada and the United States." *American Economic Review* 45 (May 1955)..

Youngson, A. J. "The Opening up of New Territories." In *Cambridge Economic History*, vol. 6, part 1. Cambridge, Mass.: Cambridge University Press, 1965.

Index